920 Kennedy

D1338868

KICK

Also by Paula Byrne

Jane Austen and the Theatre
Perdita: The Life of Mary Robinson
Mad World: Evelyn Waugh and the Secrets of Brideshead
The Real Jane Austen: A Life in Small Things
Belle: The True Story of Dido Belle

As co-editor

Stressed Unstressed: Classic Poems to Ease the Mind

PAULA BYRNE

KICK

THE TRUE STORY OF KICK KENNEDY, JFK'S FORGOTTEN SISTER AND THE HEIR TO CHATSWORTH

WILLIAM
COLLINS

William Collins
An imprint of HarperCollins*Publishers*
1 London Bridge Street
London SE1 9GF
WilliamCollinsBooks.com

First published in Great Britain by William Collins in 2016

Copyright © 2016 Paula Byrne

1

Paula Byrne asserts the moral right
to be identified as the author of this work

A catalogue record for this book
is available from the British Library

ISBN (HB) 978-0-00-754812-5
ISBN (TPB) 978-0-00-817491-0

Printed and bound in Great Britain by
Clays Ltd, St Ives plc

All rights reserved. No part of this publication may be
reproduced, stored in a retrieval system, or transmitted,
in any form or by any means, electronic, mechanical,
photocopying, recording or otherwise, without the
prior permission of the publishers.

This book is sold subject to the condition that it shall not, by
way of trade or otherwise, be lent, re-sold, hired out or otherwise
circulated without the publisher's prior consent in any form of
binding or cover other than that in which it is published and
without a similar condition including this condition being
imposed on the subsequent purchaser.

MIX
Paper from
responsible sources
FSC™ C007454

FSC™ is a non-profit international organisation established to promote
the responsible management of the world's forests. Products carrying the
FSC label are independently certified to assure consumers that they come
from forests that are managed to meet the social, economic and
ecological needs of present and future generations,
and other controlled sources.

Find out more about HarperCollins and the environment at
www.harpercollins.co.uk/green

For my boys, Tom and Harry
(Kennedys through and through …)

and in memory of my grandfather, Robert Kennedy

CONTENTS

PROLOGUE

Kicking the Surf

Hyannis Port, Cape Cod, 1937.

Joseph Patrick Kennedy stood on the veranda of his newly restored ocean-front beach-house, watching his seventeen-year-old daughter, Kathleen, water-skiing on Nantucket Sound at breakneck speed. Of all his girls, she was the one whom he loved the most. She was as plucky and fearless as her brothers, imbued with the same restless energy and drive. One of the reasons her father favoured her was because she wasn't afraid of him. She wasn't afraid of anyone. As she approached the sprawling white clapboard house with its green shutters, the speedboat and its tow-line abruptly began to jackknife, veering this way and that in spiky, jerking movements. Joe's eyes narrowed as he watched the boat. Kathleen was dangerously close to the motor and he feared that she would be cut to pieces, crushed by the boat, carved up by the blades of the propeller. What on God's earth was she doing?

His serious face suddenly broke into that radiant Kennedy smile and his shoulders relaxed. He saw exactly what she was doing. She was spelling out her name in the foamy surf.

KICK

Kathleen Agnes Kennedy was born on 20 February 1920. Everyone, with the exception of her mother, who called her Kathleen, called her 'Kick'. It began when her younger siblings found it hard to pronounce her name. She became Kick.[1] Her moniker suited her perfectly. It was also said that K.K. was known as Kick because her ebullient personality reminded her father of a high-spirited pony.[2] She was vivacious and quick-witted. As a little girl she loved to kick off her shoes, loved to run barefoot in the sand. When she became a debutante in London in the late 1930s, and a guest at England's finest country houses, she would surprise polite society by her habit of kicking off her high-heeled shoes in company. Many a haughty aristocratic eyebrow would be raised, especially among the young debs put out by the unruly conduct of the Kennedy girl. But she soon charmed them all, winning them over with her jokes, her effervescence and her ease of manner.

She wasn't a girl whom it was easy to constrain. Part of a large, clever family, she had to fight to be heard. She could be as headstrong as her boisterous brothers, but she was never belligerent or aggressive, as the male Kennedys could be. There was a sweetness and gentleness about her. Kick, blessed with an open, happy disposition, was cheerful and sunny, rarely moody or sulky. She was kind but tenacious. Children who are quietly determined, though seemingly malleable, are often the ones to be anxious about. They tend to get their own way.

That day when she traced out her name in the surf, Kick was showing off for her father, whom she idolized. But she was also doing it for herself. She had a very strong sense of self. She knew who she was. She was a Kennedy. She also had a stubborn streak. She would need those traits for what lay ahead. She would turn out to be the rebel of the family. She would kick against family, faith and country. And her name in the Kennedy family history would one day be erased, just as her 'K I C K' in the surf lasted only a moment before disappearing back into the ocean's milky blue depths.

1

Rose and Joe

A very good polite Catholic.

Rose Kennedy

83 Beals Street, Brookline, January 1920.

Rose Fitzgerald Kennedy was eight months pregnant with her fourth child and she was about to walk out on her husband, Joe. Leaving her three little ones in the care of the Irish nanny, she packed a bag, slammed the door of her small townhouse in Brookline, Massachusetts, and returned home to Dorchester. She moved into her old bedroom, without saying a word to her parents. She was where she belonged, with her beloved father, and she said to herself that she was never going back. She had failed to heed his advice when he had warned her not to marry the upstart Joe Kennedy. After six years, her marriage was in crisis. Rose had made a big mistake.

But the child kicking so strongly inside her belly was a constant, nagging reminder that she was now a mother with responsibilities. Two of her small children were a cause for grave concern. Little Jack was sickly, in and out of hospital. Nobody could work out what was wrong; it was many years before he was correctly diagnosed. Rose's firstborn daughter, Rosemary, was also a worry. She was too quiet, didn't cry as much as her other two babies.[1] Rose was trapped, and she knew it. But she was teaching her husband a lesson.

Leabharlanna Fhine Gall

She was a Fitzgerald, the cherished eldest daughter in one of the city's most prominent Roman Catholic families. And now she was home.

Her diminutive father, John F. Fitzgerald, of Irish immigrant stock, was the first American-born Irish Catholic to be elected to the office of Mayor of Boston. What he lacked in height, he more than compensated for in energy. He was a gifted athlete and a good scholar and was accepted into Harvard Medical School. Just one year after his studies began, his father died. Fitzgerald left Harvard, took a job as a civil servant and raised his siblings. He washed their faces and dressed the babies.[2] He never complained. He just got on with it.

He was a man of extraordinary charm and vitality. So charming, with the Irish gift of the gab, that his nickname was 'Honey Fitz'. Other nicknames were 'young Napoleon' and 'the little General'.[3] In trying to describe her father's particular brand of charisma, Rose would one day write of the attractive mix of his 'abundant energy, vitality, physique, quick reflexes, and a psychological or endocrinological "x factor"'.[4] She noted that her father had the ability to walk into a room full of dull, bored people and within minutes the place would be buzzing with life and energy. This charm, this energy, this 'x factor', would be inherited, above all, by her daughter Kathleen and her son Jack.

When she came to publish her memoirs in her eighties, Rose called herself Rose Fitzgerald Kennedy. In her mind, she was always a Fitzgerald, and proud to be so. 'There was no one in the world like my father,' she wrote. 'Wherever he was, there was magic in the air.'[5] She quoted him so much that she earned the nickname 'Father says'.

Honey Fitz had an eclectic, wide-ranging mind and a habit of cutting out anything in print that interested him: news articles, quotations. He would pin them to his lapel. Rose inherited this trait and her children remembered her wandering around the house with notes pinned to her dress. Later, she put together scrapbooks full of photographs and clippings. She was an inveterate writer and always kept a notebook by her side to scribble down interesting ideas or quotations from books or plays. When her papers were released in 2007, there were 185,000 items stored in 253 boxes. Among those papers are Kick's letters and her own scrapbooks of cuttings, articles and photographs.

Rose Fitzgerald had grown up in the world of politics. Honey Fitz became a state Senator for the Democratic Party, spending his weeks in

Washington and returning home to the country at weekends and for vacations. Despite the fact that he was so often away working, Rose was far closer to her father than to her mother, Josie. Honey Fitz loved people, so long as they were interesting, whereas Josie was shy and preferred to surround herself with family members. She was the disciplinarian. She spanked her children if they misbehaved. She was also deeply religious and instilled her piety into her children. As a fervent and devout Roman Catholic she drilled the children in the catechism. During the month of May (the month of the Blessed Virgin) she kept a shrine and her children filled it with flowers and prayed every night. During Lent, the children would kneel in the dark and recite the rosary.[6]

Devoted wife Josie didn't know, or pretended not to know, that Honey Fitz had a string of affairs. 'Me for the pretty girls, brains or no brains,' he told a *Boston Post* reporter.[7] He would pick up any young attractive girl, particularly blondes, and barely bothered to keep it a secret. Josie Fitzgerald did a great line in denial. She learnt to smile graciously, dress stylishly and keep her feelings in check. This set a pattern for her daughter, who would repeat history when she made her own choice of a powerful but chronically unfaithful husband. Rose spent her life turning a blind eye, just as her mother had done. Trained well in the school of face-saving, she followed her mother in taking comfort from fashionable clothes and expensive jewels.

As the daughter of devout Catholics, Rose was encouraged to date only Catholic boys. A 'mixed' marriage was, in her parents' eyes, unthinkable. In her memoirs, she describes Boston as having two societies, one of them almost entirely Protestant (mainly of English descent) and the other Irish Catholic.[8] She recalled that 'between the two groups feelings were, at best, suspicious, and in general amounted to a state of chronic, mutual antagonism'.[9]

Protestant boys were a rarity at dances and social events. But even when a suitable Catholic boy caught her eye, her parents were unimpressed. His name was Joe Kennedy. Rose and Joe had met once as children when they were on vacation in Maine. Eight years later they met in Boston and what began as 'affectionate' friendship turned to romantic love.[10] Despite the opposition of her parents, who disliked Joe and thought him unworthy of their daughter, Rose continued to see him secretly.

Joe Kennedy should have been ideal son-in-law material. He had attended the prestigious Boston Latin School, Fitzgerald's alma mater. He was a brilliant baseball player, president of the senior class and a natural born leader. He was a fabulous dancer. He didn't drink or smoke, and was 'a very good polite Catholic'.[11] He was tall and handsome, with sandy-coloured hair, freckles and blue eyes. His best feature was a captivating smile. Rose said that when he smiled, he made everyone want to smile, too.[12] She recalled that he had a knack of getting along with people from all backgrounds: 'He could talk to anybody.'[13]

Joe was the son of P. J. Kennedy, a successful businessman and politician. But Fitzgerald was possessive of Rose, and no one was good enough for his daughter. The irony was that Joe Kennedy was all too much like Honey Fitz: tough, energetic, ambitious. In an attempt to keep the lovers apart, Fitzgerald forbade Rose to attend the renowned Wellesley College, where she had been offered a place. Wellesley girls often dated boys from nearby Harvard, and Honey wasn't having that. Rose later said that not going to Wellesley was the great regret of her life. She was entered instead into the Convent of the Sacred Heart, in downtown Boston.

The Order of the Sacred Heart had been founded in the early nineteenth century in France for the education of upper-class Catholic girls. It later spread to London, the Netherlands and America. Rose found herself entering a very different world: early-morning prayer, silence during class and serious study. She was still in touch with Joe, though he was due to start at Harvard. Despite her father's opposition to the romance, Rose refused to stop seeing Joe, and in order to separate them once and for all the Fitzgeralds whisked Rose and her sister Agnes to Europe for a two-month tour, after which she was deposited in the Sacred Heart Convent in Blumenthal, Holland.

She decided that she would surrender herself to her faith. But she was also determined to 'marry Joe, too, no matter what anyone thought or said'.[14] For his part, Joe was equally determined to marry the Mayor's beautiful daughter. Her newfound piety only added to her allure. He was furious that Fitzgerald didn't think him good enough for his 'Rosie'. He hated to be underestimated, and it drove him harder in his ambition to succeed. He was the first and only son in his family, with three sisters and a strong mother, who was also a devout Catholic. His father, P.J., a quiet and more benign figure, was rarely at home, busy with his bank and with the world of politics.

At Harvard, despite his sporting success and easy manner, Joe was not accepted into the more Brahmin clubs. His Irish roots and Catholicism saw to that. Rejection only fuelled his ambition. And to succeed he wanted to make money. And for that, it would help to have the right wife. With his good looks and his charm, he had developed a reputation as a ladies' man with a taste for 'actresses'. But they weren't the kind of girls you married. If he wanted the Mayor's daughter, he was going to have her. And Honey Fitzgerald was not going to stop him.

Joe graduated from Harvard and took a position in his father's bank, before leaving to become an assistant bank examiner, an auditor responsible for ensuring proper financial practice. His plan was to become the youngest bank manager in Boston. The time was ready. But Fitzgerald was still set against him.

Then in December 1913, something happened that changed the dynamic between Rose and her father. Fitzgerald was in the middle of a re-election campaign. Out of the blue a letter was posted to the Mayor, edged in black, demanding that he should withdraw from the campaign or his affair with a cigarette girl called Toodles would be exposed. In fact, Fitzgerald had done little more than kiss her on a dance floor, but he knew that the damage was done. This was a battle he was not going to win. The Toodles scandal had brought shame to his door.

Josie and Rose were united in their fury. Toodles was the same age as Rose. Fitzgerald had constructed an idealized image of home and family. Josie had put up and shut up as long as her home and family were inviolate. But now that the press was on to her husband, the lines had been blurred. Fitzgerald withdrew from the campaign for 'health reasons'. For Rose, this spelt freedom. Her beloved father, her idol, had feet of clay; he had been a coward and had run from a fight. She had lost respect for him, and he was never the same again in her eyes. A known philanderer was in no position to stop his daughter from making a good marriage to a man who was now cutting a figure: early in 1914, at the age of twenty-five, Joe Kennedy had become President of Colombia Trust Company, making him the youngest bank president in the United States.[15] Rose married him later that year, on 7 October. Cardinal William O'Connell, a close friend of the Fitzgeralds, conducted the ceremony. 'I'd always wanted to be married by a Cardinal and I was,' said Joe.[16]

Rose almost immediately got pregnant, giving birth to a healthy 10-pound boy called Joseph on 25 July 1915. He was known as 'young Joe', or 'Joe Junior'. Honey Fitz told a waiting reporter the happy news of his grandson: 'Of course, he is going to be President of the United States, his mother and father have already decided that.'[17] A year after Joe's arrival, Rose was pregnant again, and she gave birth on 29 May 1917 to another boy, though he was an underweight and sickly child. She called him John Fitzgerald Kennedy, but he was to be called Jack.

Rose now longed for a daughter, and she got her wish when she gave birth to a girl whom she called Rosemary. But the child seems to have been starved of oxygen at birth. The deadly Spanish flu epidemic was as its height. The family physician was worked off his feet and he arrived late. The midwife could easily have delivered the baby herself, but she followed instructions to wait for the doctor and she held back the baby's head until he arrived (he would receive his full fee only if he was present at the delivery). This decision was to have dire consequences for the baby. Though she was a lovely child, the most classically beautiful of the Kennedy daughters, it became increasingly clear that she was brain-damaged.

Soon Rose was pregnant again. But she was deeply unhappy. Joe was rarely home, and she was lonely. She missed her family, and her father, and the role she had cultivated as Mayor's daughter. There was also the problem of sex. As a devout Catholic, Rose believed that sexual intercourse was for the sole purpose of procreation. Canon law decreed that contraception was tantamount to murder. Kick would inherit this belief. Rose refused to use birth control and she had been pregnant almost constantly since she was married. But sexual intercourse during menstruation and pregnancy was frowned upon. Joe had embarrassed Rose one evening at dinner with close friends when he began discussing their sex life: 'Now, listen, Rosie, this idea of yours that there is no romance outside of procreation is simply wrong … It was not part of our contract at the altar, the priest never said that … and if you don't open your mind on this, I'm going to tell the priest on you.'[18] His sexual frustration is evident from this remark. And it no doubt gave him licence to have extramarital affairs and justify them to himself. Joe did not drink or smoke, but his vice was 'fornication'. Invariably he was drawn towards actresses, waitresses, secretaries and models. Like many powerful men, he had a high libido, and an appetite for 'fresh meat', which his son Jack would inherit. He compartmentalized his life, without compunction, into two parts, family and home on the one hand, and his affairs on the other. Rose felt utterly cheated by how her life was turning out. That was why she walked out and returned to her family home.

* * *

Rose stayed in her old bedroom, thinking about her future and, for a fortnight, nobody said a word to her. While there, she did agree to accompany Joe to the Ace of Clubs ball, an important event for her as she was President of the organization. Before she married Joe, Rose had founded a club for women who had studied abroad and were interested in current events. Every year she led the grand march in the charity ball.[19] She was determined that, despite her marital problems, this year should be no different. It was business as usual. Though heavily pregnant, Rose looked stunning in her 'black web dress'; one of the reasons she attended was to avoid being the subject of gossip. But after the dance the couple went their separate ways.

Shortly afterwards, her father came to talk and urged her to return to Joe. Divorce was never going to be an option. Rosie had made her choice, and she was going to have to live with it. 'What is past is past,' her father told her. 'The old days are gone. Your children need you and your husband needs you. You can make things work out. I know you can.'[20]

When she cradled her small daughter, Kathleen Agnes, in her arms in February 1920, Rose knew that she had made the right decision to return to Joe. Just as she had experienced an epiphany at Blumenthal to dedicate her life to God and to marry Joe, she now resolved to become the perfect mother and wife. Like Marmee in her favourite book, *Little Women*, she would learn to suppress her anger.

Rose Kennedy would apply to motherhood the exacting standards that she brought to bear in her thwarted intellectual life. She would pour her vast reserves of energy and ambition into raising her children, a job she took very seriously: 'I looked upon child-rearing as a profession and decided it was just as interesting and just as challenging as any profession in the world and one that demanded the best that I could bring to it.'

Furthermore, she wanted those children to be the best: 'I had made up my mind to raise my children as perfectly as possible.'[21] Rose would pay a huge price for her overweening ambition for her children. But she was steadfast in her beliefs: 'what greater aspiration and challenge are there for a mother than the hope of raising a great son or daughter?'[22]

2

A Beautiful and Enchanting Child

All my ducks are swans ... but Kick was especially special.

Joseph Kennedy

Kick was born, like her brother Jack and sister Rosemary, in the twin bed nearest the window in the upstairs master bedroom at 83 Beals Street in Brookline. From the start, Kathleen was a special baby. One of nine children, she would take on the status of eldest daughter, as a result of Rosemary's special needs which made her forever a child.

Rose doted on her baby, but on the day that she was born, Jack, just two and a half, developed a serious case of scarlet fever and was hospitalized. In those days, as Rose recalled, it was a 'dreaded disease, fairly often fatal, quite crippling in aftereffects'.[1] Joe proved himself to be an exemplary father, praying for his son and spending hours in the Boston City Hospital. He had 'never experienced any serious sickness in the family previous to this case of Jack's' and he had 'little realized what an effect such a happening could possibly have' on him.[2]

Jack of course did recover, and became particularly close to Kick. He returned home just before his third birthday, and he was shown his new baby sister. On the medical index cards that Rose kept for all of the children, she wrote that Jack seemed 'very happy' to see his sister.[3] Physically Kick resembled him the most, with thick golden-brown hair and blue-grey eyes. She would not grow up to be conventionally beautiful. She had her mother's strong jawline and short neck along with a somewhat square face that was unlike Rosemary's (which was heart-shaped), but she was a striking girl with lovely ivory skin. Kick's beauty was all within, and she would grow up to have the greatest sexual charisma of all the girls. Men would be utterly captivated by her.

She was a fearless toddler, always wanting to keep up with her two elder brothers in sports and physical activities. Rose noted in her journal that at the age of two and a half she went out in the snow by herself in her little sleigh.[4] She was already exhibiting signs of the independent spirit that would define her life. In a diary fragment, Rose wrote that her three-year-old daughter was 'a beautiful and enchanting child', with the soft, high colouring and beautiful skin of her Kennedy grandmother: 'Although we delighted in her, I don't think we could have spoiled her if we had tried.'[5]

Rose Kennedy has sometimes been presented as a somewhat cold and uncaring mother. Nothing could be further from the truth. She was a strict disciplinarian (one had to be with nine lively children), but her journals show a different picture to the one that is sometimes perceived. She had a keen sense of humour, and she clearly took great pride and delight in her brood. Like many a Catholic mother, she especially adored her boys. She noted down all the amusing things that Joe and Jack did: 'Joe Jr. and Jack have a new song about the Bed Bugs and the Cooties. Also a club where they initiate new members by sticking pins into them.'[6] Another entry recorded: 'Boys went to store and saw "No dogs allowed in this Restaurant" and they put in front of it "Hot".'[7]

Kick was also naturally funny. When she was a toddler, her mother tried to discourage her from sucking her thumb in the night by binding it with a plaster. Rose noticed the next morning that it had been removed and when she asked where it was Kick replied innocently, 'A little mouse took it.'[8] Her first surviving letter was written to Santa Claus when she was six: 'Dear Santa Claus i want a doll and a doll carriage tea set and paper doll little book and little blck board your little friend Kathleen.'[9] Throughout her life, she adored writing letters, always scribbling at high speed, with frequent slips of the pen, regular spelling mistakes and occasional bad grammar (as far as possible, I reproduce her exact words in all quotations, only correcting where there is ambiguity of sense).

With so many children in the house, Christmas was a special time. Rose recalled that it was always 'the greatest event in our house'.[10] The children all helped to select the Christmas tree, 'as big as our living room would allow'. Rose remembered them choosing presents carefully for one another, 'a story-book with large colorful pictures' for Jack, or a 'wind-up toy' or 'for the baby of the moment, a rattle, or teething ring, or jingle bells'. Then the children would excitedly wrap them and hide everything away in secret places until Christmas Day.

Rose would tell them the Christmas Nativity story and the children would sing 'Away in a Manger', then on Christmas morning they would look to see what Santa had brought. The house looked like a Fifth Avenue toy-shop.[11] She would also tell them the story about how her father had started the idea of public Christmas trees for those people who couldn't afford to buy their own. Honey put up a Christmas tree in the middle of Boston Common, 'and the idea spread, until thousands and thousands of cities and towns and villages all over the country have public Christmas trees every year'.[12]

Rose claimed that she was particularly close to her first four children. 'I spent more time with them. I knew their every thought and each personality fascinated me,' she declared in her memoirs.[13] In an entry in her journal for 1923, she seems less enamoured: 'Took care of children. Miss Brooks, the governess, helped. Kathleen still has bronchitis and Joe sick in bed. Great Life.'[14]

Rose, having made her decision to stick by Joe, was more content than she had been before, and she had all the trappings of wealth to reconcile her to the realities of her marriage. She took solace in her money and status. She was back, but it was to be on her own terms.

Joe had almost made his first million by the time Kick arrived. A few weeks after she was born, the Kennedy family moved into a large, newly built Colonial-revival house, at 131 Naples Road, which had all mod cons, including a washing machine and ice-box. Rose brought her cherished grand piano and her Sir Thomas Lipton crockery embellished with the Irish shamrock.

She had servants and a chauffeur. All the children had their own bedrooms, and so did she and so did her husband. This was an important symbol of Rose and Joe's increasingly separate lives. They also began vacationing apart, sometimes for months at a time. When they went to New York City, they always stayed at separate hotels.

The house had a wraparound porch, a key to Rose's management of her ever-increasing brood: 'the front porch is one of the greatest arrangements ever imagined for the benefit of mother and child'. She divided the porch into sections with folding gates, so that the children could play together but also be safe, and she could keep a close eye on them.[15] The children were entertained by the 'full panorama of neighborhood life … cars passing by, people walking along (many of them acquaintances who waved), the letter carrier, the milkman with his wire basket loaded full as he came to our house and empty as he left, the policeman passing by on his patrol, the grocery boy, tradesmen, visitors, and friends of all degrees and kinds – everybody with a smile and cheerful greeting for the children'.[16]

Kick's first school was the Edward Devotion School, a five-minute walk from her family home. Joe, Jack, Rosemary and Kick all attended the school, though Rosemary was kept back from first grade and stayed in a class with younger children. She was rarely teased because she was so beautiful and innocent, and she had siblings to take care of her.

Rose Kennedy was a natural teacher. Indeed, she was probably a better teacher than a mother. Not coddling the children, or being overly affectionate, teaching them to be strong and independent, was part of her code. The children lived by a strict routine. Fresh air and exercise were high on the list. They were encouraged to take part in sports, especially swimming and tennis, to eat the right sorts of food, to read the right sorts of books, to contribute to the right sorts of discussions. Rose kept a close eye on their diets. She was obsessed with their weight, particularly the girls'. Every Saturday the children were weighed, and Rose scrupulously made a note of the latest figures on the index cards that contained all of their medical information. At the age of just seven, Kick wrote to her mother, 'I gained a pound and a half. Eunice gained some too. Rose is as fat as ever.'[17]

Joe Kennedy wanted his family to be sleek and lean. He did not want his children to look like fat Irish peasants. The children were perfectly turned out, usually all of them dressed in the same clothes, as if their only identity was as a Kennedy – matching middy blouses and skirts for the girls and identical sailor suits for the boys.[18]

Rose hired an orthodontist to straighten out the children's teeth, giving them the famous 'flashing Kennedy smile'. For five years the children hopped into their father's Rolls-Royce to be driven down to New York to a 'superdentist' to have their braces tightened. Rose closely monitored the intake of candy (only one piece allowed per day after dinner); tooth-brushing took place after every meal. With the thirteen-year age spread in the family, the dentist visits covered a span of two decades.

Rose admitted that she had all the domestic help she required, and that her role in the household was more like that of an 'executive'. She recalled twenty years of 'rows of diapers hanging up to dry on the back-yard clotheslines'.[19] During the winter months, the diapers would freeze on the line, and would have to be thawed on the steam radiators.

Rose would think nothing of spanking the children with a ruler or a wooden coat hanger. She would never hit them in anger, but she believed in smacking, especially as she had such boisterous children. As she said, the mere mention of a spanking was enough to moderate a child's bad behaviour. In later years, her grandchildren retrieved all the coat hangers from the closet and threw them down the garbage chute, just in case. Rose thought this was hilarious. Spanking was a very Roman Catholic punishment – immediate, direct, not inflicted in anger, and with the lesson learnt everyone could move on. Rose's second method of discipline was to lock naughty children in the cupboard: 'Well, I put them in the closet, but ... they weren't scared of the dark. It would just get one or two of them out of the way for a while.'[20]

Rose's lack of emotional nourishment left its scars on her children. Jack, who was a sensitive boy, remembered: 'My mother never really held me or hugged me. Never! Never!'[21] The only time she touched them was to spank them. Kick, like Jack, was uncomfortable with physical demonstrativeness, which was another legacy of Rose's emotional sterility. Later in life, Kick sought out several maternal substitutes, most notably Nancy Astor, with whom she developed deeply affectionate relationships. Older women were drawn to her, sensing that she lacked that special mother's love.

Rose left the hugging and kissing to the children's nanny, a working-class Irishwoman called Katherine Conboy, known to the family as 'Kico'. Kick and her sisters adored her, and they would spend hours in the kitchen chatting to her. She in return adored the Kennedy children. Rose was perfectly happy with this arrangement. She simply did not see it as her role to kiss and hug for fear of '(s)mother love'. Respect was her by-word. The children always called her 'Mother', and they feared and loved her in equal measure.

Thus the Kennedy children were raised as upper-class British children were, by the nanny, and emotionally distant from their parents. It made them tough and independent, but it also left psychological wounds. Perhaps this was one of the reasons why Kick and Jack understood and sympathized with their English aristocratic friends. Rose's strategy was to encourage the eldest son and daughter to take on the role of nurturing and shaping the other children. Joe Jr took to this role of little father with aplomb. Jack later said, 'I think if the Kennedy children amount to anything now, or ever amount to anything, it will be due more to Joe's behavior and his constant example than to any other factor.'[22]

The surrogate-mother role was more difficult for Kick because of Rosemary. Kick had to assume the role of eldest sister and was encouraged to take responsibility for all of her sisters, but, although she loved them, she was not naturally suited to the role. She was too wild, too free-spirited. Eunice, just one year younger, was much more temperamentally suited to that role, and she felt especially responsible for Rosemary. All of the girls mothered Teddy, the baby of the family, who was born in 1932. 'It was like having an army of mothers around me,' he recalled.[23]

Kick worshipped her father. He was a forceful presence in the lives of the children, despite the long absences caused by his work. He approached his duties as a father with great seriousness, and he loved children, but only his own. When he was away from home, every Sunday the children would line up in order of age and speak to him on the telephone.[24]

When he returned from business trips, it was a moment of high excitement for the children. 'He would sweep them into his arms and hug them, and grin at them, and talk to them, and perhaps carry them around,' Rose recalled. As each child became able to talk he would 'want that child in bed with him for a little while each morning. And the two of them would be there propped up on the pillows, with perhaps the child's head cuddling on his shoulder, and he would talk or read a story or they would have conversations.'[25] Joe struggled with Rosemary's mental incapacitation. He wanted his children to be perfect Americans, and that was one of the reasons he especially doted on Kick, who was so lively and smart. She later called him a 'powerhouse, a force of nature'.[26]

He believed in treating the small children as young adults, refused to talk down to them and was plain-speaking and blunt, though loving. He was very tactile with the children, unlike Rose. They knew, however, not to overstep the mark, and if they did, one 'Daddy's Look' was all it took: 'ice-cold steel blue, piercing right into and through you and stripped you to the soul'.[27] But if the children were ever in trouble, Joe insisted always on hearing the truth: 'tell me the truth. Tell me everything about it, the whole truth. Then I'll do everything I can to help. But if you don't give me the truth, I'm licked'.[28]

Joe had his own inimitable way of speaking, which the children long remembered, with amusing phrases and aphorisms that became part of family lore: 'applesauce' (bullshit) was not tolerated, nor would he accept 'monkey business'. 'He doesn't have the brains of a donkey' or 'He doesn't have enough brains to find his way out of a telephone booth' were Daddy expressions. 'All my ducks are swans,' he would say of the children, adding that Kick was 'especially special'.[29] 'No crying in this house' was another favourite, along with 'You'd better believe it', 'Things don't happen, they are made to happen' and 'I don't want any sour pusses around here'.[30] In later years, the children, now adults, would have cushions made with his aphorisms embroidered on them.[31]

Joe was not one for self-pity. Teddy revealed the key to his character when he described his father's support and optimism, especially when things went wrong: this was when Joe was at his best. 'The greater the disaster, the brighter he was.' When things went really badly, Joe would declare, 'That may be one of the *best* things that ever happened to you!' But, most of all, Joe wanted his children to strive. Not necessarily to be the best, but to 'strive' for excellence. And then: 'After you have done the best you can, the hell with it.'[32]

This interest and devotion exhibited by a father towards his children was highly unusual in those days, when fathers were often remote and women were left to run the house and family. As well as the telephone calls, the children were encouraged to write letters to their father, and he admonished them whenever they forgot to write. Kick's earliest letters to him are full of affection and love, funny stories, and kisses, hearts and pictures. In preparation for writing her memoirs, Rose looked back over her papers and noted that Kick's 'early letters seemed so warm and affectionate, perhaps more so than the other children'.[33]

Kathleen also missed her father and worried about him when he was away: 'Dear Daddy, I hope you have got rid of your cold … We are all fine and we miss you very much.'[34] She told him jokes, reported that she had joined the Girl Scouts, that there had been 'peachy skating' at the Field Club, and asked 'are you coming home soon?'[35] Her letters to Rose were much less effusive.

In 1925, Joe set up a trust fund for each of his children that would increase to $10 million by the mid-1940s. All of the children were 'trust fund' babies. They had the cushion of money, which also bestowed confidence, but also carelessness.

In May 1927, when she was seven, Kick made her first Holy Communion. Her parents were in California, but she wrote to tell them that she had been preparing for it by going to church every day for the week leading up to the ceremony. It's surprising to discover that Rose and Joe were absent. For Catholic children it's a very special ceremony, a watershed moment in which the Holy Eucharist is taken for the first time. Little girls are dressed to look like mini brides in white dresses and veils, symbolizing purity. Shortly before Holy Communion, the child makes their First Confession, a daunting experience in which the heart is opened in a dark booth. The priest, who sits behind a screen or grille, gives absolution; the child says an act of contrition and is given penance in the form of prayers.

It was left to Joe Jr to take on the paternal role, writing to his parents to inform them that little Kathleen was preparing herself for the sacrament.[36] By this time Rose had seven children and was pregnant again. Joe Sr was about to become even busier, and Hollywood was beckoning.

3

Forbidden Fruit

A real-life Jay Gatsby, ever-reinventing and legitimizing himself.

Amanda Smith, Joe's granddaughter[1]

September 1927.

They tumbled out of the silver Rolls-Royce with blue fenders, like characters from F. Scott Fitzgerald's *The Great Gatsby*. The glamorous woman and the tall, handsome, impeccably dressed man in his white flannels. Then came the children. There were seven of them, good-looking, beautifully turned out, barely able to conceal their excitement. Mother and children had taken a private train from Boston, where Joe met them, and they were now arriving at their newly rented home in Riverdale, an affluent suburb of New York. The Kennedys always knew how to make an entrance.

The move was crucial for Joe, who knew that however much money he made, he and his family would never belong in Brahmin Boston. They would never be welcomed at the right sort of country club. Joe later said that he had moved because he felt that his daughters would never be invited to the best coming-out parties in Boston. He knew that New York was a meritocracy in a way that Boston could never be.

Joe's rise to the top was carefully orchestrated. He had the big house; he wore tailored suits and custom-made shirts and refused to ride the streetcar to the office, preferring to drive in his Cadillac. He gave up baseball for golf, through which he could make important connections. He was still an outsider. But there was one place where he could use his outsider status to his advantage, and where he would make his fortune. Hollywood.

In November 1919, Joe, seeing the opportunities in the new world of moving pictures, had set up his own film-distribution company, Columbia Films Inc. By 1926 he was a movie mogul, and owned his own motion picture company, FBO (Film Booking Offices of America). One of his strategies had been to convince the studios that he was the man who could clean up Hollywood. In the early twenties Hollywood had been rocked by sex scandals and charges of immorality, such as the notorious Fatty Arbuckle affair, when the actor was accused of the rape and murder of a young starlet.

Film titles such as *Loving Lips*, *The Restless Sex* and *Short Skirts* give an idea of the way that Hollywood was going. Joe would give Hollywood good clean family films. Furthermore, there was widespread anti-Semitic distrust of the studios, which were mainly run by Jews. Joe, by contrast, was 'a Harvard graduate, a Boston businessman and banker, a family man, a practicing Christian, and decidedly not a New York City Jew'.[2] As studio head, Joe instituted new accounting procedures and fired several of the overpaid executives. While the films were produced in Hollywood, the major decisions were made on the East Coast. Kennedy moved into the FBO offices at 1560 Broadway off 24th Street in New York City.

Joe was known in the studio world as the 'blond Moses', leading the way for film companies converting from silent movies to talkies. His charisma and charm were remarked upon time and time again. The actress Joan Fontaine said, 'You felt not just that you were the only one in the room that mattered, but the only one in the world.'[3] What he took from his time in Hollywood was the art of performing as a public personality, and the importance of image. In a stroke of PR genius, he invited in a group of newspaper reporters and explained his vision for the movie industry. 'Wholesomeness, Mr Kennedy pointed out to his guests, is intended to form the keynote of the pictures … and there is to be a very general elimination of the sex problem movies and of those which depend upon sex appeal,' announced the *Boston Daily Globe*.[4]

The Kennedy children were a key part of his image as a family man. From their perspective, to have a father in the movie world was thrilling. They had access to the latest Hollywood films, much to the envy of their friends. Kick's early letters are full of references to the movies that she had seen. They provided the backdrop to her life. All the movies were checked in advance for their suitability: 'if there was a slip-up and the plot became lurid, the projector was switched off and the audience was sent out'.[5] The boys loved the cowboy films that Joe sent over. Kick and her sisters watched Douglas Fairbanks movies and films with titles such as *Welcome Danger*.

Kick attended the Riverdale County School, along with four of her siblings. As Catholics, the Kennedys were outsiders. They were a tribe and they stuck together, but Jack and Kick found it easy to make friends, and were keen to establish their own identity outside that of being a Kennedy. After school, the children played touch football in the field behind the Presbyterian church, Kick joining in with her brothers. A friend remembered that 'Kathleen was one hell of a football player. She was on top of everything.'[6]

She was especially close to Jack, a thin, underweight child who continued to be plagued with illness. Like many clever, sickly children who miss a lot of school, he devoured books and had a precocious intellect. His passion was for history and reading literature and poetry. One of his defence mechanisms was a highly developed sense of humour. Kick was the butt of many a brotherly joke poking fun at her lack of intellect, but this was part of their teasing relationship. A schoolfriend from Riverdale days observed that 'Kathleen was bonded to Jack with a profundity that mere blood seemed insufficient to describe.'[7]

Kick was given a very special birthday present for her eighth birthday: a new baby sister. She was to be called Jean. Kick wrote to 'Dear Daddy' and told him, 'I like Jean very much.'[8] Her father was taking his usual long vacation in Palm Springs. 'I hope you are having a nice time in Florida. Do you go in swimming? Is the water cold?' she asked in one of her earliest surviving letters.[9] In her neat, bold hand, she described a funny moment when she was given a present of a little box of powder for her doll, which she managed to spill over herself. Neither of Kick's parents was home that winter. Rose had returned to Boston to have the new baby, and Joe refused to sacrifice his annual vacation with his male buddies and business associates.

There was a team of nannies and nursery maids dedicated to looking after the children in the absence of the parents. Joe's closest friend and adviser was an old friend of Honey Fitz, a man called Edward Moore. He and his wife Mary were childless and they became surrogate parents to the Kennedy children. When Rose and Joe were away, the Moores stepped in to help.

In the days after Jean's birth, a huge bouquet of flowers was delivered to St Margaret's Hospital from the actress Gloria Swanson, congratulating Rose on the birth of her child. Joe finally arrived from Palm Springs at his wife's bedside, carrying three expensive diamond bracelets. This was not just a gift for having the baby, it was a guilt present. What did Rose really think when she looked at Gloria Swanson's bouquet of flowers and the diamond bracelet glittering on her arm? It was an open secret that Joe and Gloria Swanson were in the throes of a passionate affair.

They had met for the first time in November 1927. Gloria was just twenty-eight, beautiful, charismatic and perhaps the most famous movie star in the world. She looked like a younger, more glamorous version of Rose. She had the same black, glossy hair, luminous skin and sapphire-blue eyes. Joe was utterly captivated. She could further his reputation as a serious studio head. He was tired of making B movies and cowboy films. He saw the way Hollywood was going – talkies. He wanted a business partnership with the screen goddess and he wanted her for himself. When they first met for dinner to discuss their partnership, Joe assured her, 'Together we could make millions.'[10] He offered to manage her, promising that he would reduce her debts and make her an even bigger star.[11]

The affair was to be a lasting one, and it posed a serious threat to his family. Gloria was utterly unlike the usual chorus girls that had previously attracted Joe. Before her, it was easy for him to compartmentalize his sexual affairs and his love for Rose. Rose was his wife, the mother of his children; the showgirls were there just for sex and for fun. Gloria was in an entirely different category.

Joe, more than ever, began to lead a bifurcated life, between his wife and large brood of handsome children and the glamorous movie star, the ultimate trophy mistress. In October 1928, he invited Gloria to a Halloween party in Riverdale along with her children. Gloria initially refused to meet the wife of the man she was sleeping with. But she did allow her children to go to the party. Her daughter, known as 'little Gloria', was the same age as Kick. She remembered the party with the decorations and all of the Kennedy children.

Kick was intrigued to meet the daughter of the world's most famous movie star. She liked little Gloria, and took her to Riverdale to meet her schoolfriends. She introduced her guest as 'Gloria Swanson's daughter'. The other girls laughed and thought it was a joke: 'After all, Gloria Swanson was, to them, practically a supernatural being, so she wouldn't be in Bronxville.'[12] Kick was indignant that nobody believed her story.

She liked her new friend, but she longed even more to meet the beautiful star herself. She wouldn't have to wait long. The seriousness of the love affair was evident from Joe's deliberate and highly risky merging of his two lives. He was adamant that his star, Gloria Swanson, should meet the family.

4

Hyannis Port

Our whole lives were centered in this one place.

Teddy Kennedy[1]

August 1929.

A chorus of residents and vacationers in the small seaside-resort town of Hyannis Port huddled excitedly around the harbour overlooking Nantucket Sound. In the distance they heard the buzzing of the Sikorsky amphibious plane, watched it flying low over the sea before it landed gracefully on the water and came to a halt: a more dramatic entrance could not be imagined, but then again, the flying boat was carrying one of the most famous women on the planet, and she was known for her love of drama.

Out from the tiny plane stepped Gloria Swanson. There was her lover, Joe Kennedy, in his launch, piloting her back to the shore where his wife waited to greet her. The women looked so eerily alike, except that the guest was nine years younger than the hostess. Joe was ecstatic at having Gloria on his arm, and, in the throes of his obsession with her, paid not the slightest attention to the whispers of his neighbours and friends. Nor did he care what his wife was thinking.

Rose was far too intelligent not to be aware of the gossip that circulated about her husband and Gloria, but she was not about to confirm the rumours, and certainly not to the nosy rubberneckers who clustered around the harbour waiting for a glimpse of the actress. Rose warmly welcomed her husband's mistress. Gloria later mused on her rival's sang-froid: 'Was she a fool, I asked myself … or a saint? Or just a better actress than I was?'[2] Rose was neither fool nor saint. She knew exactly what was going on and, if she thought Joe was going too far expecting her to befriend his mistress, she didn't show it. As usual, she held her head high, dressed impeccably and put on her best show. Gloria might be Joe's mistress, but Rose was his wife.

Nine-year-old Kick was especially excited to be meeting Gloria Swanson. She and her sisters had converted a room above the garage into a club-house. They pasted movie posters on the walls and discussed their favourite stars. Gloria paid a special visit and scrawled her name on the wall. Kick may have intuited that something was not as it should be. Her best friend Nancy Tenney later recalled that the girls at school had two fan clubs, one for Constance Bennett and one for Gloria Swanson. None of the Kennedy sisters wanted to be in the Swanson camp: 'Kathleen never discussed the reason she was so adamant. I didn't know what it was all about until years later.'[3] However, Kick's letters to her father suggest that she worshipped Gloria Swanson. Or perhaps she was following her mother's example in pretending that Gloria was nothing more to her father than a business asso-ciate. She treasured a signed photo and constantly asked after little Gloria, with whom she began a correspondence.[4]

Joe was overstepping the mark in bringing his mistress to Hyannis. It was a place that was associated with family. The Kennedys considered it their true, spiritual home, the epicentre of their lives. A decade later, in 1939, Rose gave an interview to *Reader's Digest* in which she set out the Kennedy family manifesto: 'Years ago, we decided that our kids were going to be our best friends and that we could never see too much of them.' Rose explained that, with her husband's hectic schedule, it wasn't possible to have friends, and go to dinner parties. Because Joe was often away from home, when he was with the family they didn't want to share their precious time with outsiders. The substituting of children for friends meant that outsiders, close colleagues and, later, in-laws often felt excluded. The family was at once cohesive and suffocating. What Rose failed to understand was that her children needed friends with differences to kick against, in order to find out who they were. For her, family always, always came first. As she told

Reader's Digest: 'as a result the Kennedy children became natives of the Kennedy family, first and foremost, before any city or any country'.[5]

Every summer, for the duration of the holidays, the whole family assembled at Hyannis Port. It was their playground, the backdrop to their lives. For generations, it would be the place to which they would return in times of triumph and tragedy. They all looked back on summers on the Cape as providing their happiest memories – the long summer vacation stretching out before them, the lazy hot days of sports and fun. The family had begun holidaying in Hyannis Port in 1924. In those days, it was not a fashionable place. The 'Kennedy Compound' lay far in the future. But there was good railway access, lovely sandy beaches and a golf club that was more than happy to accept Joe Kennedy as one of its members. Equally important for the Kennedys was that Hyannis Port had a Roman Catholic church. St Francis Xavier, located on South Street, was a pretty structure, built in 1874. Once called St Patrick's Church, it changed its name to avoid giving the impression that it was an 'Irish only' church. This was the summer parish for the Kennedy family. Joe Jr and his brothers became altar boys.

The family rented Malcolm Cottage, a large white clapboard house with green shutters, at the end of Merchant Avenue, just a block from the sea. It had an extensive lawn where the children could play and it came with its own private beach. After renting the house for several years, Joe bought it in November 1928 and instructed the original architect Frank Paine to remodel it. Extra rooms were added, windows were widened to take in the sweeping ocean view and a large RCA sound movie theatre was built. Hyannis Port had only just got its own theatre for the talkies, so it was very spectacular that the Kennedy family had their own private facility, which showed the latest films shipped in from Hollywood.

The house was spacious but it was not grand. It was a lovely family home. Rose loved her Cape Cod garden and planted 'old-fashioned blooms' such as asters, chrysanthemums, calendulas, black-eyed susans and marigolds. The glorious riot of colour contrasted with the dazzling white of the clapboard house and the rich green lawn. There were butterflies, and innumerable birds: seagulls, oystercatchers, bobwhites and the beautiful red cardinal. Eagle-eyed children could spot chipmunks foraging for food. The beaches were lined with a profusion of wildflowers, in particular the hot pink wild beach rose, which emitted a strong and sweet fragrance. The family would hunt for beach plums, rose hips, elderberries, chokeberries and wild grapes.

One morning Rose bundled the children into the station wagon. They were off to forage for wild blueberries, each child carrying a tin pail. Ten miles into the wilds, they spotted a sunny patch of bushes with ripening berries and began to fill their buckets. Suddenly Eunice began screaming. A wasp had stung her, and all of the other children suddenly imagined that they, too, had been stung. Seconds later, Jack ran up yelling and waving his arms. He had sat on an anthill and ants were swarming all over him. Rose packed up the children 'with a small harvest and my deflated educational ideas'. On the way home, they stopped off at the store and bought three quarts of blueberries: 'I never mentioned picking blueberries again.'[6] Rose had her issues, but she certainly didn't lack a sense of humour.

Food was an important part of the Cape Cod experience. The children loved to picnic on the beach, and they would set off with a thermos jug with creamed chicken, fresh fruit, lollipops and always a chocolate cake with thick, gooey icing. They bought ice cream from the store along with a pack of cones.[7] One of the favourite Kennedy desserts was Boston cream pie, a luscious confection of light fluffy sponge sandwiched together with custard cream and frosted with chocolate. There were healthy snacks, too: carrot and celery sticks, and in the evenings roast chicken, apple jelly and acorn squash.[8] Alcohol was not permitted in the Kennedy household.

Above all for the sporty, wholesome clan there were the outdoor games. The children played touch football on the beach, went swimming and played competitive tennis. Rose colour-coded the children's bathing caps so she could recognize each child in the water. Each of them (except for Rosemary) had their own sailing boat. When they raced on Nantucket Sound, Joe would follow in his own boat, shouting out their mistakes. After every race the station wagon would be dispatched to collect the trophies. When Rose wanted the children to bring the boats in, she would lower the flag from the flagpole in front of the house.[9] Joe later had a pool built, and an outdoor shower was installed by a side entrance. The children could practise their diving and splash about after a day on the beach.

Kick loved to run around barefoot. She was by nature a free spirit, and she and Jack chafed against Rose's disciplined regime. Clocks were installed in every room and the children knew not to be late for mealtimes, or they would go without. They would learn to charm the cook behind their mother's back.

Joe would sit in his favourite chair in the corner of the living room or on his bedroom balcony (nicknamed 'the bullpen'), looking over his brood. If the children fought or dissolved into tears over a quarrel with a sibling Joe would clap his hands in steady rhythm: 'No – crying – in – this – house! No – crying – in – this – house!'[10] He hated tears and impressed upon the children that crying accomplished nothing. Kick and Jack invented a family motto: 'Kennedys never cry'.

On cold days they played indoor games. A favourite was 'categories', a trial of intellectual trivia. The children always had to be doing something.

On Sundays, they would troop downstairs in 'Sunday Best'. Rose would be waiting at the foot of the stairs to inspect them.[11] They would set off for mass at St Xavier's, the boys preparing to do their altar-boy duty, the girls clutching Bibles and rosary beads. They were the ideal Catholic family.

5

Bronxville

Kathleen ... was such a beautiful and lively and outgoing child and girl that I became convinced she never felt neglected at all.

Rose Kennedy[1]

In May 1929, six months after the renovation of Malcolm Cottage, the Kennedys left their rented home in Riverdale and bought an imposing, luxurious red-brick Georgian house in the Westchester community of Bronxville, called Crownlands. The family had never been really happy at Riverdale, and never felt that they belonged. Bronxville was a leafy, affluent suburb, 15 miles north from central Manhattan, only 1 square mile in area. It had the all-important (recently built) Catholic church, St Joseph's, good schools for the children and an easy commute for Joe, whose main offices were in Manhattan.

Crownlands at 294 Pondfield Road was a twenty-room house set in 6 acres of lush lawns high on a hill. It had a grass tennis court, a tea-house and a greenhouse. Outbuildings included a five-car garage for Joe's fleet of ostentatious Rolls-Royces, as well as gardener's and chauffeur's cottages.

Rose set to work redecorating the interior. She placed her beloved grand piano in the hall. The main drawing room, impressive with two fireplaces, was adorned with cream carpets, walls painted in antique green and white calla lilies in large vases. Complete sets of Hardy and Shakespeare lined the bookshelves. On the children's bedside tables, rosaries and crucifixes merged with toys and books.[2]

The small children occupied the second floor, and the older ones the third. Joe had a large study on the ground floor, and though he was not often home, his door was always open to the children when he was there. They would sprawl on his sofa bed and talk to him about their problems with school or friends, and he would focus on each child directly, giving them the full beam of his attention.

Bronxville was a friendly place, and a perfect one in which to raise a large, lively family. In winter the children skated on the ponds and went sledding and tobogganing on the many hills and open spaces. There was a popular drugstore with a soda fountain on the corner near to the children's school. When the owner turned away, they would filch gum and Life Saver mints. Kick's school was the Bronxville Elementary, a short walk from Crownlands. She liked art and took an interest in textiles, asking her parents to be sure to attend her exhibition.[3]

Kick adored her brothers but she was also a girls' girl. She spent her allowance on swing records and clothes, shopping for skirt-and-sweater sets at Saks Fifth Avenue with her friend Alice Cahill.[4] She loved summer camp, and even though she felt a bit homesick, she threw herself into the experience, riding horses and swimming and gossiping with her friends. She asked Rose to send her cakes and bobby pins and her 'jadpaws' for riding.[5]

When she was ten, Kick went to Washington to visit the White House. She was given a sense of her father's importance when one of the Senators stopped her and asked her to send his regards to Joe.[6] Another Congressman asked after her grandfather and her mother.

Her father had recently decided to get out of Hollywood and Wall Street and turn instead to politics. The year 1929 was a momentous one for Joe Kennedy. He had been consolidating his wealth in Hollywood and on the stock market; he had purchased two vast homes for his ever-expanding family; his father had just died, and his obsession with Gloria Swanson was reaching a critical point. She was often at the new house in Bronxville. As Rose left town in one car, Gloria would arrive in Joe's Rolls-Royce. The actress stayed at the Gramatan Hotel, and the townspeople gossiped.

Rose was troubled, particularly as the word was out in Catholic circles. After returning to New York City in 1929, Gloria recalled being taken to a meeting with Rose's friend Cardinal O'Connell, who tried to talk her into ending the affair. O'Connell told Gloria that Joe was talking to senior church officials about seeking a divorce. Did she not realize that his reputation would be ruined and she would be publicly tainted? The affair didn't stop instantly, but it began to cool.

Joe knew that it was time to get out of Hollywood, and he also began to take his money out of the stock market. He had guessed that the bubble on Wall Street was going to burst. As Rose said of her husband, 'Part of his genius was an amazing sense of timing.'[7] He did indeed always seem to know exactly the moment to get into an investment and the moment to get out. When the market crashed in October, he remained unscathed. He left Hollywood a multi-millionaire.

In February 1932, Kick was given a twelfth-birthday party. Rose was in Boston, about to give birth to her ninth and last child. 'Daddy did not come home last night,' Kick wrote to her mother. 'We do not know when he is coming.' She told her mother to send games for her party. She had been at a school dance, where she had danced with a boy: 'I had my hair waved and it looked hot.'[8]

When she wrote to her father, a few weeks later, she told him, more primly, that she had been to a party but 'There were no boys.' She hinted that she would like to have her own horse and that she wanted to go to see the musical comedy *Hot-Cha*. She showed off the typewriting skills she was learning and told Joe that she was pleased with the arrival of her new baby brother, Teddy: 'Every body thinks that the baby Should have been called George After Washington mother said she didn't like it though.'[9]

In her letter Kick asked if her sister Rosemary was coming home for her birthday party. Rose and Joe had bowed to the inevitable, acknowledging that Rosemary was brain-damaged and unable to cope with mainstream school. She was sent away to a specialist private institution, the Devereux School in Pennsylvania, where she began to make slow progress. But after two years she was brought home. In her memoirs, Rose wrote of her sorrow at her eldest daughter's plight, but also of her determination that everything should be done to make her feel a normal and valued member of the family.[10] Some friends wrongly assumed that Rosemary's problems arose from her being in her vibrant sister Kick's shadow, but this was not so. Nevertheless, it was difficult for Kick, who was forced to accept responsibility for her elder sister, to protect her from whispers about her slowness.

Kick at thirteen, her mother recalled, was 'a very attractive lady, with a beautiful, pink Irish complexion – intelligent at school – radiant, a glowing personality – no illness like Jack as she matured, a lovely interest in all that was happening around her'.[11] Rose also emphasized her daughter's deep spirituality. Kick would make 'Spiritual Bouquets' for family members. This involved weeks and weeks of special prayers, going to mass and communion, after which the beloved person would be sent a card listing all the prayers and devotions that had been offered up on their behalf.

Though Kick was a devout girl, she was also at the age where she was beginning to take an interest in boys. Her mother worried about her popularity and the fact that she was spending so much time going to the movies or on the telephone chatting to boys. As Rose remarked rather drily, 'she had a keen interest in social life'.[12] Worried that she was being distracted from her schoolwork, Rose decided that it was high time that Kick received some of her education in a Sacred Heart convent school, as she had done herself.

In her memoirs Rose recalled that 'Joe and I had agreed that the responsibility for education of the boys was primarily his, and that of the girls, primarily mine'.[13] Joe set the course for Joe Jr and Jack to attend the prestigious Choate School in Wallington, Connecticut, and then, following their father, to go on to Harvard. Rose was determined that her girls would, above all, have a Catholic education. Kick was sent off to a Sacred Heart convent in Noroton-on-the-Sound, also in Connecticut.

6

Convent Girl

Now I suppose you are glad you have me stuck behind convent
walls.

Kick Kennedy

The journey from Bronxville to Noroton, Connecticut, was only 30 miles
but for thirteen-year-old Kathleen Kennedy, she might as well have been
travelling back in time. The Convent was an imposing mansion, a former
governor's residence, on the edge of a 10-acre estate. It was set behind walls,
situated on a tiny peninsula, surrounded by the waters of Long Island
Sound. A more isolated spot could hardly be imagined. If ever Rose
Kennedy wanted to remove her headstrong, independent daughter from
unsuitable boys this was the place to do so. Noroton Convent was the strict-
est and most exclusive of the Sacred Heart schools. Only girls from the very
best Catholic families were accepted.

The nuns had converted the ballroom into a chapel; the elegant high-
ceilinged bedrooms with parquet floors were now classrooms. Religious
paintings and statues saturated the Convent. The girls rose at six every
morning, and washed in cold water, often having to break through a layer
of ice, before attending morning mass wearing black veils. They were taught
to make a sweeping curtsey to the nuns. Silence was often imposed at
meals.

The nuns, wary of lesbianism, discouraged close friendships; the girls were never permitted to go 'two by two'. The school motto was 'noblesse oblige'. Sacred Heart girls were taught French literature, Christian doctrine and needlepoint. The nuns were called 'Madame' or 'Mother'; afternoon tea was *goûter* and holidays were *congés*.

Kick loved beautiful clothes, but here she was expected to dress in a plain brown woollen uniform (on Thursday afternoons and Sundays, the girls wore wine-red jumpers). For swimming, they had to wear a large woollen bathing suit under a short skirt. Even Kick's underwear had to be woollen, which she loathed, but at least it kept her warm in the freezing conditions.

Kick's letters home show how much she put on a brave face. She wrote to Rose telling her that she was performing in a Christmas tableau: 'I am an angel. I'm decked out in a pink affair and wings. I'm perched up on this ladder looking down at the crib. Some fun.'[1] She suffered from asthma, and disliked the harsh, damp climate of Noroton. She told her mother that she was unable to take part in the school walking race as she got out of breath. Her letters are full of longing for home.

The Noroton girls found their own small ways to rebel. The nuns insisted on reading all of the mail, which the girls resented. Kick found a way of making a mailbox drop that circumvented the censorship. 'It is perfectly alright,' she wrote to her mother, 'and the whole school is doing it.'[2]

Kick railed against the school and its strict discipline, and longed for Sundays and Thursdays, the days when the girls were allowed visitors. The girls wore formal dresses and were served tea in the visitors' cabin by the sea. That fall, Jack, who had started at Choate, often visited Kick. He brought along his schoolmates who invariably fell in love with his cute kid sister, a female version of Jack, with the same sense of humour and a dimpled smile.

Jack, in common with Kick, had a gift for friendship. His mother called it 'his outstanding talent … making friends and enjoying friendships'.[3] He would bring home numerous friends, known in Kennedy lore as 'Jack's surprises'. They never knew how many would turn up at any time, but the best of them was Kirk LeMoyne Billings, known to the family as 'Lem'. Jack called him 'LeMoan', 'Pithecanthropus', 'Ape man': the Kennedys loved nicknames. He would remain Jack's lifelong and most trusted friend and ally.

Lem was tall, blond, simian and athletic. He and Jack were drawn together by their mutual dislike of the strict discipline of Choate. They shared the same ribald sense of humour and trusted one another implicitly. Jack was utterly devoted to Lem. Lem's father died while he was at Choate, leaving him no money. It was the Kennedy family who looked after him financially, and they practically adopted him. Joe Kennedy described him as 'my second son'.[4] Lem was probably homosexual; he never married and admitted that his devotion to Jack overshadowed everything else in his life. He adored Kick, who was so like her brother, and he did fall in love with her, though she, perhaps sensing his inclinations, only ever treated him as a brother.

At Christmas, the Kennedys took possession of a newly acquired Palm Beach house in Florida, on Millionaires' Row. Rose loved Florida and she persuaded Joe to buy the imposing mansion at 1095 North Ocean Boulevard. The Kennedys installed a tennis court and a swimming pool and added an extra wing. It had fabulous ocean-front views. They would now make a habit of spending every Christmas at Palm Beach and summers at Hyannis Port.

Lem spent his first Christmas with the Kennedys in 1933, and wrote to Kick when she returned to the Convent. 'I hope Mother Superior enjoys my letters,' he teased, knowing that all letters were read and censored.[5] Kick had loved her Christmas vacation at her new home, and was miserable about returning to Noroton. 'Daddy dear,' she wrote, 'Now I suppose you are glad you have me stuck behind convent walls I am all safe and sound now and can't go skipping around to "El Studio" or the Everglades ... I feel very rested and everyone thinks I look very well so a few parties never did anyone any harm.'[6] She was homesick, and struggling with the cold weather. She wrote to her mother separately: 'I miss you all like anything in fact worse than I ever have. Every day this week I'd sit in the study hall and think a week ago today I was basking in the sun and now I am in a fire trap trying to study. It's a great life if you don't weaken.'[7]

That was the Kennedy mantra: be strong, fight harder, don't give in. In fact all of the children, with the exception of Joe Jr, were beset with health problems. Jack was still by far the sickliest child. Bobby, Kick's favourite little brother, born when she was five, joked that Jack was so poorly as a child that if a mosquito bit him, the insect would immediately perish from having tasted his brother's tainted blood.[8]

Kick was deeply worried about Jack's health, while herself continuing to suffer from increasingly bad asthma, and allergies, for which she took injections. 'The asthma is coming,' she wrote to her mother in January 1934, 'I can feel it.'[9] Kick starred in a play in which she cross-dressed as the hero and had to kill the villain. 'I had ski pants on and Mother Fitzgerald wouldn't let me appear without a coat over the pants,' Kick complained to her mother; '... she thinks pants are immodest. Ski pants, mind you. If she only knew.'[10] She asked her mother to give her love to everyone 'and tell them they are not missing a darn thing in this Iceland'. She talked about plans for Easter, and flying south for the holidays. The Kennedys, with their vast wealth, thought no more of taking flights than lesser mortals would of bus journeys.

In February 1934, Kick was operated on for appendicitis and recuperated in Palm Beach. She seriously contemplated leaving Noroton and its damp climate, but she stuck it out. She was beginning to make some good friends and, like Jack, she made friends for life.

One of her closest friends was a pretty petite girl, with long blonde, wavy hair. Her name was Charlotte McDonnell, and she was from one of New York's prominent Catholic families. She was as spirited as Kick, and likewise hailed from a large, boisterous family. She was one of fourteen. Charlotte was constantly in trouble at Noroton. The nuns excluded her for several days for possession of a dirty-joke book.[11]

Lem and Jack came to visit the girls whenever they could for Thursday tea, and a flirtation took place between Jack and Charlotte. She wrote to thank him for the jigsaw puzzles that he sent to the girls, and told him that it was so cold at school that she had to chop a hole in her inkwell in order to write to him.[12] Jack would over the years flirt with and have affairs with several of Kick's friends.

Kathleen was extremely popular at Noroton. One of her schoolfriends who later became a nun recalled her vivacity and charm: 'wherever Kathleen went, sunshine followed'.[13] She was rarely moody or temperamental, always sunny and full of jokes, always quick to laugh.

In May, Kick sent her mother another Spiritual Bouquet, for Mother's Day with an affectionate card: 'To the sweetest, youngest mother in the wide world ... may this bouquet give you many graces. I love you.'[14]

At Whitsun, there was a raffle for 'gifts and fruits of the Holy Ghost', and Kick remarked pithily, 'I got Wisdom which I need for these final exams and Patience, which I sure need too.'[15] She was preparing herself for a one-day spiritual retreat 'which I know you will not want me to miss'. But she longed to go home for the summer holidays. Her asthma was bad and she was continuing to have injections, and she told Rose that her doctor had ordered chest X-rays. 'I go to Mass every morning,' she added dutifully.[16]

In June 1934, as a reward for his involvement in Franklin D. Roosevelt's campaign for the presidency, Joe had been offered the position of Chairman of the newly formed Securities and Exchange Commission (SEC). That summer, he befriended the prestigious *New York Times* political journalist Arthur Krock, who would become one of his most powerful supporters and allies. Joe was setting his sights on the White House, and he leased Marwood, a huge, faux-French mansion in Washington, as his political base. The family would continue to live in Bronxville. At his new base, Joe held spectacular parties and dinners, shipping in lobster from Maine and oysters and clams from Cape Cod, washed down with plenty of the best Scotch.[17]

Kick was relieved and delighted when she finally left the Convent for the long summer vacation at Hyannis: the coldness and the austerity would be temporarily forgotten with the promise of the sunshine of the Cape and reunion with the rest of the clan. Weeks and weeks of sailing, tennis, touch football, dancing and fun lay ahead. Kick was especially looking forward to spending time with Jack, who was bringing Lem for the vacation.

Kick and Lem stuck together, worried about Jack, but also determined to enjoy the summer as best they could. Lem found the relationship between the Kennedy parents extremely odd, and saw at first hand how Joe dominated Rose. He was also struck by Rose's obsession with good manners and social form, table manners, punctuality, appearance: 'Don't wear white socks with dress suit. Wear dark shoes with blue or gray suit, not brown shoes.' She forbade the children to address people with 'hi'. Nobody could leave the dining table until Rose had left.[18]

Jack's persistent and myriad illnesses were one of the reasons why he lived for the moment, and this was one explanation for why he loved sex and women. For Kick, it was another odd mixed message. She was a convent girl, expected to behave well at all times, to obey her mother's commands and her insistence on etiquette and social form. Conversely, her brothers, to whom she was so close, were beginning to lead active sex lives. One friend reported that Joe Sr left carefully opened pornographic magazine centrefolds on Jack's bed. 'I think it's Dad's idea of a joke' was Jack's response.[19]

While Joe was encouraging his sons to sow their wild oats, Rose continued to impress upon her daughters the importance of a religious life. In notes she made entitled 'Advantages of Catholic Education', she wrote about the benefits of a convent:

> If she is in a convent school, she is taught by women who have devoted their lives to the spiritual welfare of children. They themselves lead unselfish, exemplary lives, devoted to loving and worshipping of God. They give the girls the Catholic point of view about why they are in this world and their obligations to God, to themselves and their neighbor, and inspire them with the love of God … They teach the girls to be gentle, unselfish and charming in their manner and behavior, and it seems to me that I can tell a convent girl in any part of the world.[20]

'Gentle, unselfish and charming' with a devotion to God and the Catholic Church: that was Rose's mantra for her girls. After a summer of sunshine, dancing and boys, Kick returned to Noroton: 'Here I am back in this _____ I had better not say,' she wrote to her mother. 'Its lovely here now but its awful to be back.'[21]

7

Muckers and Trouble

She thinks you are quite the grandest fellow that ever lived and your letters furnish her most of her laughs in the Convent.

Joseph P. Kennedy to John F. Kennedy

Kick embraced her academic work at Noroton. She was an able scholar. Her school report for Christmas 1934 suggests that she was near the top of the class. Pass mark for examinations was 75 per cent and she attained high marks in all of her subjects, especially in Christian Doctrine (91 per cent) and History (90 per cent).[1] She wrote to her mother to enquire about her school report: 'I hope it wasn't too bad.'[2] She told Rose that she was studying hard, but longing for Christmas at Palm Beach. There was nowhere to shop at Noroton and she badly needed 'a bath-robe, bathing suit, underwear, shoes etc.'[3]

She told Rose that she had received her 'aspirantship to the Angels' and that four of her friends had got their 'Child of Mary' medals in a 'beautiful ceremony'. Unlike her mother, Kick had not achieved membership of that exalted and exclusive sodality. She also wrote to 'Daddy Dearest', thanking him for a trip to New York to see a show. She was taking sewing classes and otherwise cramming for exams: 'I am sitting in the Study Hall waiting for my dear brother, Jack, to show up. I only hope he does.'[4]

Kick remained close to Jack. He knew that she was unhappy at the Convent and spent as much time as he could visiting and writing her amusing letters. Her relationship with Jack was based on jokes and banter. But she admitted to her father how much she adored and admired him. 'She really thinks you are a great fellow,' he told Jack. 'She has a love and devotion to you that you should be very proud to have deserved. It probably does not become apparent to you, but it does to both Mother and me. She thinks you are quite the grandest fellow that ever lived and your letters furnish her most of her laughs in the Convent.'[5]

That February, Jack had got into serious trouble at Choate and was almost expelled. Kick had become involved in the story, incurring, for once, the wrath of her father. Jack had long clashed with his teacher and housemaster J. J. Maher. Maher disliked Jack, and believed that he was a bad influence on Lem, who slavishly followed every move he made and endorsed his every whim. Maher recommended that Jack and Lem be kept apart.[6]

The headmaster, George St John, had a derogatory term for boys who refused to follow the Choate line: they were called 'Muckers' (a thinly veiled insult for Irish labourers). Jack and his friends decided to form a renegade society rebelling against the school's values and ethics: it was to be called 'The Muckers Club', to, in Jack's own words, 'put over festivities in our own little way and to buck the system more effectively'.[7] There were thirteen members, and each member proudly wore a tiny gold pin in the shape of a shovel with their initials inscribed alongside the logo of CMC (Choate Muckers Club).

The club planned pranks, one of which was to spread a pile of manure on the school dance floor and have their pictures taken shovelling the muck. The headmaster got wind of the plan and was furious, threatening to expel the boys involved. Jack, the ringleader, was in the most serious trouble. Joe Sr was called to the school for a meeting to discuss Jack's future. In the meantime, Jack wrote to Kick telling her all about the incident. Kick immediately sent Jack and Lem a congratulatory telegram, which was intercepted by the school staff:

DEAR PUBLIC ENEMIES ONE AND TWO ALL OUR PRAYERS ARE UNITED WITH YOU AND THE OTHER ELEVEN MUCKS. WHEN THE OLD MEN ARRIVE SORRY WE WONT BE THERE FOR THE BURIAL

Kick's telegram made everything worse. Joe was not pleased. He wrote to her: 'I know you want to do all you can for Jack,' he began, but then told her that there was a genuine chance that he could be expelled from school: 'I want to urge you to stop all this talk [in] letters and telegrams to him and LeMoyne, so that we can dismiss the whole matter.' He told her that, by sending the telegram, she had added 'fuel to the fire'.[8]

It was Kick's fifteenth birthday, she was far from home and clearly her father was angry. She wrote back, secretly: 'I wanted to write you privately about the letter you wrote me. (in case you have not told Mother).' She apologized for her part in the fiasco and confessed that Jack was angry with her. 'I hope everything is OK now and I really want to help Jack.'[9]

She was deeply upset by her rift with Jack, especially as it was her birthday. Her parents sent her perfume and money and she wrote to them that she had had a 'very happy birthday although I missed everyone too much. It was the first birthday from home and its quite hard.'[10] She kept up the pretence with her mother that all was fine, telling her she had had a birthday cake, and a birthday lunch with her roommates at Maillard's in New York City; she and her friends also went to Radio City and watched Leslie Howard in *The Scarlet Pimpernel*. She told her parents that her birthday present from her eldest brother Joe was a visit to the Convent: 'he is driving up here today on way to New York so am looking forward to seeing him'.

She asked her mother to prepare 'Palm Beach for my arrival around March 20th'. She also asked if her parents could send a film for the 'Shrove days before Lent. They are the last two days we are allowed to have candy, dancing etc.' She and her friends wanted *David Copperfield*. It would be the last fun time before the austerity of Lent.

Kick and Jack made up. After the Muckers fiasco, Jack began to take his work seriously, urged on by the promise of a year in England in the footsteps of his brother Joe, who was studying under Professor Laski at the London School of Economics. Jack graduated from Choate, voted by his class as 'most likely to succeed'. Kick was to take time away from Noroton, and plans were under way for her to spend time in Europe as well. Rose was determined that Kick should go to France, to improve her competence in the language and to undergo the experience of a French Sacred Heart convent.

Perhaps Rose hoped that her headstrong daughter would experience a similar religious epiphany to the one she had had in Blumenthal, which had so shaped the course of her life. Rose decided on the Sacred Heart Convent in St Maux, north-east France. Kick and Jack would sail for England with their parents in September.

As the children grew older, they insisted on bringing their friends to the Cape. The house was a hive of activity, with sports and picnics during the day and dances and movies at night. Several friends expressed their surprise at the disciplined way that Rose ran the household. Every lunchtime the family would head to Taggart's Pier for swimming and diving.[11] On the way to the dining room, Rose would pin a newspaper article or a theme to discuss on to her bulletin board and encourage the children to debate the issue of the day over dinner. History, geography and religion were at the top of her agenda. She later thought this contributed greatly to the prowess Jack showed in his televised debates with Richard Nixon in 1960. All of her children turned out to be brilliant public speakers.[12]

Rose recounted in her memoirs that she could be strict, but that she always tried to temper this with a sense of humour: 'People told jokes, made wisecracks, hurled friendly insults, and hooted and hollered at silly mistakes. They joshed and kidded and made faces and fooled around (within limits) and talked about things that popped into their minds: things that happened at school, news of friends, opinions, likes and dislikes, a certain amount of chatter and gossip: the stuff of life, well spiced ... there was no lack of laughter or fun.'[13]

One of Kick's friends said that being at the Kennedy dinners at Cape Cod reminded her of being in a classroom. Everyone was expected to have an opinion. Kick was as 'vociferous and opinionated as her brothers'.[14] Over the dinner table, each child was expected to recount their day's activities, and report on whether they had lost or won.

One of Jack's schoolfriends, Paul Chase, remembered how important it was for the Kennedy children to be winners: 'Mr K. really did preach that winning was everything.'[15] Whether it was card games, Monopoly or physical sports like tennis and sailing, winning first place was what mattered. If any of the Kennedy children lost, the reasons were carefully and methodically analysed.[16] The children teased their father over his favourite aphorisms: 'We don't want any losers around here. In this family we want winners.' 'Don't come in second or third – that doesn't count – but win.'[17] But they believed in his vision wholeheartedly.

In the summer of 1935 the Kennedy children came away from the sailing competition at the Hyannis Port Yacht Club with fourteen first prizes, thirteen seconds and thirteen thirds in seventy-six starts.[18] Eunice remembered racing fourteen times a week when she was only twelve years old.[19] Rose and Joe ensured that the children had proper coaching for swimming and for tennis.

Joe was king at Hyannis. He would sit in the bullpen, usually on the telephone to the White House or to a business associate, but always with an eye on the children. He would watch them out in their sailing boats or on the beach. One of Kick's friends recalled: 'He ruled the roost. And, oh, God, did they love him. But they were scared to death of him, too.'[20]

The children's friends were surprised by their competitiveness. 'Which of us is the best looking?', 'Who has the best sense of humour?' All agreed that Kick was the nicest Kennedy.[21] Jack was the most intellectual and witty, Joe the most handsome and athletic, and so it went on. As the years went by, brain-damaged Rosemary became more lost and left behind, until the moment came when Joe began to believe that her presence was harming the rest of the children.

Even the liveliest guests were overawed and subdued by the ebullience of the Kennedys. Often it was hard for outsiders even to get a word in edgeways. Large families are entities unto themselves. They create a shorthand, private language, a code of behaviour, in-jokes, nicknames, family anecdotes, which bind them together, but also isolate those not in the know or in the fold. Years later when Jackie Bouvier met the family for the first time at Hyannis Port, she described them as 'like carbonated water' where 'other families might be flat'. She was struck by their collective energy, enthusiasm and 'interest in life … it was so stimulating'.[22] Lem observed, 'With them, life speeded up.'[23] Video footage of the family at Hyannis Port shows the children pushing, jostling, racing one another, showing off. But always having the greatest fun. Their friends appeared happy to float in their orbit, perhaps hoping that some of the Kennedy glitter would rub off on them.

Kick and Jack grew closer and closer. Like all the Kennedys they bickered and bantered, friends remarking that they were like Rosalind Russell and Cary Grant in *His Girl Friday*.[24] Jack, the great reader of the family, would tease Kick for her philistinism. She would tease him back for being skinny and vain. But Jack adored Kick, and it was of vital importance that his favourite sister sanctioned any girlfriend of his. She was so popular and easygoing that it was almost impossible for anyone not to get along with her. If she had disapproved of a girlfriend of Jack's, that would have been the end of the relationship.

Jack had now got his driving licence and they would take off together to a dance at the Yacht Club or a movie at Idle Hours, the local theatre. If Kick stayed out late, at the golf club or the drugstore (the favourite hangout for American teenagers with ice-cream sodas), her mother would come looking for her in her little blue car. 'Dear, it's time to come home,' she would say. The children always recognized the headlights on her car, and knew that it was time to go home.[25] If Jack and Kick were very late home, they would crawl into the drive, turn their own headlights off, be careful not to slam the doors, take off their shoes and creep into bed. In the morning, Kick would find a note pinned to her pillow: 'The next time be sure to be in on time.'[26]

When she was at her friend Nancy's house, over the road, staying beyond her curfew of nine o'clock, Rose would lean out of the window and summon her home calling out 'Kaaaathleen!' in her whiny Boston drawl.[27] The Kennedy children thought it a great tease to call out their sister's formal name in imitation of their mother.

Despite their great wealth, the Kennedys were often scruffily dressed and rarely carried cash. They would put their ice creams and drinks on account at Megathlin's Drugstore. Kick was usually barefoot and dressed in cut-off shorts and T-shirt. On rainy days, she would cycle the 3 miles to the movie theatre, where she loved to watch romantic films.

Kick chafed against her mother's efforts to turn her into a proper young lady. One sunny day, Rose called her in from the beach to give her a flower-arranging lesson. Kick was torn between giggles and being horrified. Her mother gave her a basket and a pair of scissors and told her to go and cut flowers and then arrange them. Kick cut the flowers the wrong length and then put the basket down, absent-mindedly, leaving the flowers to dry out in the heat of the sun.[28]

Kick, like Jack, was untidy and disorganized. Her clothes would be strewn over her bedroom floor, just waiting for someone else to pick them up. Make-up and the latest records were scattered over her dressing table. She would retire for the evening to find another of her mother's interminable notes pinned to her pillow telling her to be sure to wipe her lipstick off her mouth before going to bed.[29]

* * *

A hierarchy was established within the family with Joe Jr, Jack and Kick firmly at the top. Kick would introduce her brothers to her girlfriends for dates, and their friends in turn would fall in love with her. She would tease her brothers when she found bobby pins in between the car seats.

Kick and Jack shared a sense of irony and got through life on their charm, whereas Joe was strong and opinionated, with an explosive temper. But he rarely lost his temper with his youngest siblings. People remarked that he treated little Teddy like a son. In video and photographic images of the Kennedys in Cape Cod, Joe is often seen with a small child on his shoulders, or cuddling one of his younger siblings.

But Joe Jr could be tough with Jack and Kick, and in many respects they feared him more than their father. He was the one who often meted out discipline. He was over-protective and obsessed with the family honour.[30] Jack did not try to be the favoured son. He knew how difficult it was to compete with Joe the Golden Boy, so he rarely bothered. 'Jack did the best on the intellectual things and sort of monopolized them,' Eunice recalled.[31] It was also a way of rebelling against his father who rather disliked intellectuals. Kick recognized that Jack, like her, was a rebel, and that rebellion could take many different forms. For the moment, she was content to flirt with her brother's friends, play her records on her Victrola, tease her siblings, show allegiance to the Kennedy code. Kick was biding her time.

Friends noticed the especially tight bond between Joe Jr, Jack and Kick. They were an unbreakable trinity, talented, good-looking and most of all good fun. A friend of the family said that the three were like a family within a family: 'They were the pick of the litter, the ones the old man thought would write the story of the next generation.'[32]

8

Mademoiselle Pourquoi

Every time I think of that darn brother of mine I burn.

Kick Kennedy

September 1935.

They boarded the *Normandie*. This was the golden age of the ocean liner, and the *Normandie*, finished entirely in Art Deco style, was extremely popular among wealthy Americans. It was the fastest ship, and in June had broken the transatlantic speed record, averaging nearly 30 knots.

It boasted a huge swimming pool, a theatre, a winter garden, a gym, a chapel and a nightclub. Among its magnificent interiors was a huge, luxurious first-class dining room, illuminated by twelve pillars of Lalique glass, and with thirty-eight matching glass columns; comparisons were drawn with the Hall of Mirrors at Versailles, which earned the liner the nickname 'The Ship of Light'. The room could seat 700 people, and served the very best French cuisine. 'The food here is very pimp-laden,' said Jack in a letter to Lem in reference to the gorgeous French puddings that he was devouring. Joe was constantly criticizing Jack for his spotty complexion, but the boy comforted himself with the knowledge that Kick also had a huge pimple on her chin.

Joe Sr had recently resigned his chairmanship of the SEC in the hope of getting a better position, though he had declined all the posts that Roosevelt offered. What he wanted was to become Secretary of the Treasury. Before setting off for Europe, he had announced to the press that he was 'through with public life'.[1]

It was Jack and Kick's first trip to Europe. He was en route to the London School of Economics, she to the Sacred Heart Convent in St Maux. But, for now, they had a few days of fun to look forward to on the world's most glamorous ocean liner. Jack twirled Kick around the dance floor of the Grille, and they swam and played deck tennis and promenaded the liner, discussing and planning their year together in Europe, the places they would visit during the holidays.

Kick arrived at the Sacred Heart Convent in St Maux. She loathed it, and was determined that nothing was going to make her stay. Rose later admitted that the school was 'so strict in its rules and so remote from the general life of the country' that Kick was 'forlorn'.[2] Kick pleaded with her mother to let her transfer to the Holy Child Convent at Neuilly in Paris. Rose, for once, gave in.

Rose had endured the strict regime of Blumenthal, and she had expected her daughter to do the same at St Maux. Kick felt she had had a lucky escape. The Holy Child Convent in Neuilly was liberal and sophisticated, located in an affluent suburb, just 4 miles from the centre of Paris. In many ways, it was a finishing school for wealthy Roman Catholic girls. Its close proximity to the art galleries, museums, restaurants and shops of Paris meant that Kick could reach beyond the cloisters in a way which had been impossible at Noroton.

At Neuilly, she threw herself into the life of the Convent, studying Latin in the morning and skating at the outdoor ice rink in the afternoon. Her favourite nun was Mother Bernadette, who taught her History and Latin. One of the other nuns took her out to distribute leaflets about Sunday school: 'We talked French all the time, so it was not a waste of time.'[3] Kick found some of her schoolfriends catty. She had her hair cut shorter and was told by one of the girls that she looked less intelligent with her new style. 'You can have my full share of her,' she remarked to her parents. Her roommate was English: 'she seems very nice'. Kick thanked Rose for sending clothes: 'my red velvet hat arrived and it is very cute'.[4]

She enjoyed seeing the sights of Paris. She saw the cell where Marie Antoinette was incarcerated, and the Palais de Justice where she was tried. She thought the Sainte-Chapelle 'the most lovely thing I have ever seen'.[5] She loved the Louvre, where she gazed at the *Mona Lisa*. 'Am really getting too cultured for words,' she wrote. The girls made fortnightly visits to the Louvre to study the paintings: 'I shall be the official Parisienne guide for the Kennedy family.' She told her mother that she was going to Solemn High Mass at Notre Dame for All Saints Day.[6] She loved the circular rose windows at the great cathedral: 'Think I know every monument and church in Paris by this time.'[7]

Her friend Hope was on her way to visit, and they planned to ice-skate together. Hope was enrolled at St Maux, and returned after her weekend with Kick. Kick wrote to her mother as if to vindicate her own decision: 'Mother, Hope looks simply ghastly. She hates the convent like anything and when she had to go there last nite she was crying terrifically. It is a crime to leave her there …' She added, melodramatically, 'if she stays there much longer she will honestly kill herself. Every night I thank God I am not there. The head nun is always trying to turn Hope against me because I left and didn't have the spirit to stay.'[8]

Kick was obsessed with not gaining weight: 'Am eating plenty and getting very fat.'[9] She worried that she wouldn't be able to fit into her evening clothes ('by the way, the red velvet and blue silk are darling'), and she told Rose that the nuns were trying to fatten her up. She did not want to put herself on a diet the minute she returned to America.

Kick told her parents that Joe Jr had written to her but she had been surprised that Jack had gone quiet. 'Please tell Jack to drop me a line.' Jack's time in London had not been successful. He had been hospitalized in October and was gravely ill, though once again he made an unexpected recovery. Then, having told Lem that he planned to spend Christmas in St Moritz, he fell ill again and decided to return home to America. Kick was furious that he was returning. The news about Jack hit her hard. As he was always the one to share her quick wit and sense of fun, she had looked forward to spending time with him and he was now leaving her alone in Europe. Jack sailed back home and was hospitalized for suspected hepatitis. Then, to her horror, she heard that her best friend Hope was ill and returning home. Kick was devastated: 'I do not know all the details but she will rest for a while and may have to wear a belt on her stomach for two years. All I can say is a fine lot I came over with. First Jack, then Hope. I shall probably contract something sooner or later.'[10] She had lost her two lifelines, but it was Jack's loss that she felt most keenly: 'every time I think of that darn brother of mine I burn'.[11]

She masked her deep love for him by mock anger, that he had ruined her plans and let her down, but she was in fact deeply worried about him. Like Jack, she found it hard to express her feelings and disliked sentimental talk, but underneath the tough exterior she was a deeply emotional girl. When Jack finally got out of hospital she was immensely relieved. But she didn't reveal her anxiety to her younger siblings. When she wrote to Eunice, who was now at Noroton, it was in her usual jocular, teasing voice, addressed to 'Puny Euny': 'You should write your lonely little sister at least once a week. Boy, I could just see you over here. Lots of time I wished you were here. Now isn't that sweet of me.'[12] To Bobby, she wrote a sweet letter, enclosing stamps for his collection. She told him about the electric animals on the *Normandie*: 'you pressed a little button and the horse would trot and then another button and then he would gallop'.[13]

She missed her siblings, telling Bobby that she would watch from her Convent window and see the little French boys and girls ('about Teddy's age') going to school wearing blue smocks and hats and carrying briefcases laden with schoolbooks. She added that they went to school from 8.30 until 4.30: 'I don't think you would like to be a French boy, Bob, because they don't play football, baseball or any games like that.'[14]

She confided in Bobby and Eunice her difficulty in speaking French. She was not a natural linguist: 'It is rather hard at first not to talk English but everyone is supposed to talk French all the time.'[15] The nuns forbade the English-speaking girls to go out together without a French girl being present for fear they would start to chat in English. Kick was allowed to speak English for only one hour each evening. It was extremely difficult, but she made the best of it and worked hard, reading a French edition of *A Tale of Two Cities* and trying not to lapse into English: 'The French is going quite nicely but it is still rather discouraging at times. Time will tell though. I am trying to read as much as possible as I think it is the greatest help besides talking.'[16]

She didn't much like the French girls but bonded with a Belgian girl. She felt frustrated by her accent: 'It is quite disheartening though to go into a shop and ask for something in perfect French and they don't understand and when a French girl says seemingly the same thing and they do understand her.'[17] Nevertheless, the Kennedy stiff upper lip was in place: 'All the Frenchies including the nuns say I have made great progress … everything is daisy.'[18]

Kick was a success at Neuilly, charming everyone with her good humour and curiosity. The nuns called her 'Mademoiselle Pourquoi', because she was always questioning the rules. This was of course how she had been brought up around Joe Kennedy's dinner table, but it was an apt nickname, and a key to her character, because Kick was always one to question and, if possible, break the rules. She was Joe Kennedy's daughter more than she was Rose's, and she fought against the nuns in a way that Eunice, more sensitive, more academic, more spiritual, never did. Eunice was very much her mother's daughter and the family thought that, of all the Kennedy girls, she would have been the one to make an ideal Sacred Heart nun.

Kick was moved by the parades for Armistice Day. 'Saw all the parades and soldiers and was in Paris during the two minutes silence. It really was marvelous.' The girls couldn't get within a mile of the Arc de Triomphe: 'I have never been so squashed in my life.'[19] In the afternoon, she saw lots of Communist parades, 'and policemen lined all the residential parts of Paris'.

She was enjoying Paris, lunching at the Ritz and the Café de Paris, and going riding in the Bois de Boulogne, 'the biggest park in the world'. She joked to her family that 'I haven't ridden for a year so my derrier was plenty sore afterwards'.[20] A family friend, Mrs Wilson, took her window-shopping at the House of Paquin. 'I wore my red velvet and coat … she told me to be sure to tell you how nice she thought I looked.'[21]

For Thanksgiving, she was invited to dinner 'with all the trimmings' with Mrs Larkin, Hope's chaperone, and attended a Thanksgiving mass at the Madeleine Church: 'Nearly all Americans in Paris go.' She was invited to London for Christmas by her parents' friend Lady Calder, but revealed to Eunice that she had decided to go skiing instead. She asked Eunice to send her photographs from home, 'as I love to see how everyone is looking'. Kick was always to be found carrying her beloved camera. She had tried to take snapshots of the Paris sights to send home, but was cast down by the awful weather: 'It is very difficult to take pictures here as the sun is never out. It is nearly always raining or foggy.'[22] She was missing home, and all things American: 'You should see the football they play over here … dressed in little shorts and kick a ball around. Very sissified I think.'

She told Eunice that the French priests looked very funny: 'They all wear little hats like saucers.' As Christmas approached, she was homesick for her family, who, as usual, were gathering at Palm Beach. For once, she was sentimental, writing to Eunice: 'I miss you very much and would give my right arm for a glimpse of your funny-looking mug.'[23] She told her parents that there were times when she felt like 'jumping the next boat'.

One of the attractions of Neuilly was that the girls were encouraged to travel in their vacations. Kick planned to ski at the Winter Palace in Gstaad and wrote to her parents to discuss the financial side of the trip. Rose and Joe encouraged frugality, and Kick convinced them that because the trip was in Switzerland, she could practise her French (though in reality Gstaad was in a predominantly German-speaking canton). It was her first Christmas without the family, and far from home. She told Bobby, 'I shall be skiing through all the mountains while you are swimming in Palm Beach,' but she hoped that 'Daddy will call up on Xmas so I can talk to you all'.[24]

9

Gstaad and Italy

Hope you don't think I'm gallivanting like a chicken over here.

Kick Kennedy

It was a magical Winter Wonderland and Kick felt as if she was in another world as she gazed at the rows of snow-capped pines and the enormous fairy-tale hotel nestling under the Swiss Alps, which loomed over the tiny village of Gstaad. Horse-drawn sleighs draped in soft furs carried the girls to their destination: the famous Winter Palace Hotel. The view was breathtaking. The Palace, lit up at night, encircled a huge skating rink, and was set on a hill. The heavy snow muffled the sound, creating a peaceful, tranquil atmosphere.

Kick was looking forward to the winter sports – tobogganing, ice-skating and skiing. She had spent the week before Christmas planning her winter vacation, going to the hairdressers for a 'permanent', having her asthma injection and buying all her skiing things. 'My allowance dwindles like sand,' she told Rose.[1]

On Christmas Eve the girls attended Midnight Mass. The cold, fresh air made them hungry and when they got back to the Winter Palace they arranged a late-night feast. Kick's French perhaps wasn't quite as good as she thought it was: when she ordered five egg sandwiches from room service, she was surprised when the waiter arrived with sixteen ham ones. The girls ate them and then felt sick.[2]

Kick got a suntan from skiing, which she confessed to Bobby was now her favourite sport: 'The best part of all is when the snow is very deep and you fall in a nice, soft white bed.'[3] She joked that she had nearly killed herself a couple of times. She told Bobby about the special sleds that took the girls to mass, and the horse races in the snow: 'The horses jump beautifully.' And to her sister Jean she wrote about the little girls who were the best skiers she had ever seen. She bought a new Swiss sports watch as a Christmas present to herself.

On Christmas Day a man dressed as Santa Claus came and delivered presents. In the evening there was a Winter Ball. She told Jean that they travelled everywhere by sleighs: 'You should have seen us flying down the hill every morning to the village.'[4]

Rose had sent Kick snapshots from home: 'The pictures of the family are adorable.' One of them was of the other Kennedy girls on their ponies: 'none of you look different yet. I wonder if you will be when I come home.'[5]

Rose had suggested that they ship over her favourite records for her Christmas present. Kick was delighted: 'The record idea is swell.' Her mother sent a list of the latest songs, and Kick added some extra: 'I should really like the new songs of "Cole Porter" ... also I found a Dream, Thanks a Million, Let's Swing it, Now You've Got Me Doing It.'[6] She also asked for charms for her bracelet, skirts and sweaters in pastel shades and 'one of those evening bags that have everything in them.'[7]

Jack was once again seriously ill. He had returned from England with offers of places at both Harvard and Princeton. He chose Princeton in order to be with his Choate friends. But after a brief stint he returned home to be under the supervision of his Boston doctors, who suspected he had leukaemia. His skin was yellow and brown and he was frighteningly thin. Lem and another Princeton friend sent a cable: 'Tell us what time to arrive for funeral.'[8]

Meanwhile, his favourite sister was living the high life in Gstaad. Kick noted the presence of the Earl of Dudley, his sister Patricia and his son William. The boy was a year older than Kick, and took a fancy to one of her Irish friends. Kick also bumped into Derek Richardson at Gstaad. He was an American studying at Cambridge University. She had first met Derek at the home of Charlotte McDonnell in Southampton in the Hamptons.

Derek was instantly attracted to Kick and invited her to a Cambridge vs Oxford hockey game on 22 January 1936. She wrote to her parents asking for permission to visit Cambridge: 'this is a rush note to give you more details about why and where I should like to go to England ... I could fly over quite easily from Le Bourget ... I suppose this sounds fantastic and I wouldn't miss anything as Thurs is free ...' She assured Rose that she would stay with Lady Calder: 'will you please cable immediately so I can let him know'.

Joe was unimpressed and sent a telegram: 'MOTHER AND I BOTH FEEL YOU SHOULD NOT GO TO LONDON THIS TIME PLENTY OF OTHER OPPORTUNITIES AND WE'LL ARRANGE IT LATER EXPLAINING MORE FULLY IN LETTER LOVE DAD'. He sent a follow-up letter from Palm Beach, explaining their position: 'you know mother and I have no objection to your seeing as many things as you can over there and we want you to, but the idea of merely going over for a game was not quite the thing to do'.[9] He also explained that his 'business relationship' with Sir James Calder was under strain: 'I am sure you will understand this'. Calder owned Haig & Haig whisky and exported via Joe, who had the concession in the United States. Joe reassured Kick that there would be ample opportunities to visit Oxford and Cambridge in the future 'and see all there is to be seen'.

Always loving and kind towards Kick, he told her that Palm Beach had been unseasonably cold and that she hadn't missed much, and that Jack had been in hospital for two months: 'we are trying to find out what is the matter with him'. Then he wrote, 'I am terribly proud of the way you handled yourself over there and your whole attitude towards everything and I am sure you will get a great deal out of your year abroad ... Try to get all you can out of this trip, because it will be of great help to you in everything you do hereafter'.[10]

Kick wrote back uncomplainingly: 'Understand perfectly – Really didn't expect to go but thought I might as well ask'. She wasn't, however, about to give up on her dream of Derek and Cambridge. 'It would be more fun to go later when everything could be arranged. Everyone says the crew races are better than the hockey match anyway'.[11] She kept her letters home breezy and cheery. 'I still have no asma so everything is daisy'; 'It has been raining nearly every day since we have been back'; 'Going to see La Boheme this coming Sat. Really, I shall be educated'. She went to lectures on Queen Elizabeth I and Shakespeare's *Henry V*: 'it was excellent and I understood it quite well'.[12]

But she was also determined that Rose should not spoil her summer plans. Her hint about the boat races disguised the fact that Richardson, persistent and not prepared to give Kick up easily, had issued an invitation for her to be his date for his college's prestigious May Ball at Cambridge (which actually takes place in June).

The only problem was that Rose was planning to visit Kick in Paris at that time. Kick knew that her mother's presence would stop her from going to the May Ball, and she was determined not to let this happen. It was the first time she defied her in matters of the heart. It would not be the last. She tried to persuade Rose to visit earlier in the spring: 'School lets out the tenth of July and by that time think I shall be quite ready to get home. So it would be rather silly just to come over and go right home for you.'[13] She did, however, drop in that Richardson was writing to her. She had promised that she would stay away from French men, having decided, though, that they were 'really not as bad as they are made out to be'.[14]

Kick still suffered from homesickness. She was only fifteen, a continent away from her beloved family, and surrounded by people speaking French. Mother Superior wrote to Rose with an update on Kathleen's progress, on her 'home-sickness' and on her French, which she still found so difficult. Despite not wanting Rose to spoil her Cambridge plans, she desperately missed her: 'If it is not too much trouble Mother please come over because it will be so much easier to get through this year.'[15]

Kick was clashing with the Reverend Mother, and told Rose that she had been criticized for being 'rather stuck on my own ideas and won't listen to anyone else'.[16] The Reverend Mother was right to see that she had a stubborn streak and would stick to her guns if she thought she was right.

One of Kick's Noroton friends, Marie Celeste O'Malley, was visiting Europe with her sister. Marie Celeste was then staying on at Neuilly to get some extra tuition in Latin and Maths before attending Manhattanville College. Kick told her mother that the two girls were on their way to Garmisch for the Winter Olympics. Reich Chancellor Adolf Hitler had presided over the opening ceremony on 6 February.

Kick's friendship with her English roommates continued to flourish. They were her first taste of England and she was intrigued. Derek had written to her from England telling her all about the funeral of King George V who had died on 20 January. His eldest son, David, had succeeded as Edward VIII. Kick reported to her mother that Derek thought the funeral 'the most impressive sight he had seen while in London'.[17] Kick had listened to the coverage of the funeral over the radio. Her English friends attended a service, and Kick reported to Eunice that they now wore black bands on their arms. She was genuinely amazed at their response to the King's death: 'Have never seen anything like the love they had for the old king and more than love for the new king.'

She was also aware of the gossip that circulated about the wild new King: 'Mrs Larkin herd some stories of the new Prince [crossed out] King – She has plenty of Scandal.'[18] All the girls knew that the dashing Prince of Wales had been in a relationship with the married American Mrs Wallis Simpson. Having so much enjoyed the lecture on *Henry V*, the play about the former wild and dissolute Prince of Wales, Kick loved the idea of the handsome raffish Prince falling in love with a twice-divorced American, who was fashionable but not especially beautiful. Kick was beginning to express an interest in the English aristocracy. She told her social-climbing mother that 'the Earl of Dudley and [his sister] Lady Patricia Ward' were at Gstaad.

Kick was approaching her sixteenth birthday and she wanted some fun. 'Just think am almost 16 years old. Sweet Sixteen. Oh My,' she wrote to Eunice.[19] She was always finding funny stories about Convent life to amuse her siblings. She was given the honour of being sacristan at mass, which involved 'laying out the Priest's things and fixing the altar'. By mistake she poured oil rather than wine into the priest's bottle. Luckily her mistake was discovered before the priest got round to drinking the oil.[20]

She was also learning just how attractive she was to boys. Rose intuited that Kick was up to something with Derek. Just before Kick's birthday on 20 February, she cabled her parents to suggest a time for a birthday phone call. There was a mix-up and she forgot to put in the word 'birthday'. Rose feared the worst, panicked and telephoned immediately. Not because she thought Kick was ill or homesick, but because she feared that her head-strong daughter had eloped. Kick wrote: 'When you said you thought I had eloped I didn't know what to think. Hope you don't think I'm gallivanting like a chicken over here. Thought something dreadful had happened when I heard you were calling.'[21]

She had a lovely birthday. Honey Fitz had sent her candy, which she couldn't eat until Lent was over, as she had given up sweets. Her English friends gave her a picture frame, a Spanish friend a compact, and she got a huge box of crackers 'from the Irish girls'.[22] She went to a movie and then enjoyed a birthday chocolate cake and read her cables from her parents and several of her Noroton friends. She kept them all.

The rain continued to pour down throughout February. Kick was depressed about hardly seeing the sun, and longed for 'Paris in the Spring'.[23]

She had heard from her family about Jack's serious illness, and she was delighted when he was well enough to write to her. 'Thought you might have died off,' she wrote, disguising her deep anxiety about him. 'Glad to hear you are finally out of hospital and getting very tan under Florida's sunny skies.'[24] She gossiped about all the girls who had been asking after him, and teased him about them finding 'Jack Kennedy the cutest thing'. She told him that she was planning a trip to Italy and that the following year she wanted to go to Germany to learn German.[25]

In February, shortly after her birthday, she attended a magnificent ball at the Paris opera house. She was dazzled by the gowns, the jewels and the women wearing plumes in their hair. She wore a white gown trimmed with velvet, and danced with a young officer who later called at the Convent to ask the Reverend Mother if he could take Kick to an Aviation Ball: 'Of course she said no.'[26]

Kick subtly mentioned 'the boy from Cambridge'. Derek Richardson had been writing to her, and in March she went sightseeing in Paris with him and his mother. They climbed the Eiffel Tower, had lunch at a little bistro and went to the races at St Cloud. She told Rose that Mrs Richardson came to the Convent each time to collect her.[27] The weather was finally improving: 'Mother, Paris is really heavenly in the Spring.'

Her French was also slowly improving. She was reading classic novels, and made her 'confession' entirely in French when she was at retreat. She joked: 'Finished the jolly old Retreat yesterday so feel very holy at this point.' She enjoyed her confessor, a Belgian Jesuit whom she thought 'very inspiring'.[28] She told Rose that she longed to go to Lourdes, the home of St Bernadette, the girl who had seen visions of the Virgin Mary, which was now a place of spiritual retreat and pilgrimage for the sick and dying. She had been warned that it would be very hot in July, and also distressing to see so many sick people, but she was keen to go: 'the sight is really worth seeing'.[29]

She added that she had received her 'aspirantship to the Children of Mary ... Feel very well that I have finally succeeded in getting it.'[30] She worried about the storms and the bad weather in the United States: 'Hope the floods aren't too bad around the various Kennedy mansions – Sounds terrible from this side of the Earth.' She reminded her parents: 'next time I write will be under Italy's balmy skies'.

At the end of March, she joined a group of friends for a month-long trip – chaperoned by the requisite nun, of course. Joe's secretary wrote to her before she left, sending her the Rome address of a friend of the family, Count Enrico Pietro Galeazzi, a wealthy architect who had close Vatican connections in his capacity as Rome director of the Knights of Columbus, an American Catholic fraternity: 'Your father would like to have you see him when you arrive in Italy as he thinks he will be able to help you a great deal.'[31] Kick knew that this was an order, not a request. The nuns also hoped to arrange an audience with the Pope.

They first went to Venice, which Kick adored. They stayed at the Hotel Gabrielli Sandwirth, and she wrote excitedly to her parents, 'Venice is too wonderful to give you all a good idea of how we are doing here.' She described how they had taken the train with its impressive view of the snow-capped Alps, before passing through Milan and Verona. Her first view of Venice was in pouring rain, but she was unperturbed and the girls and chaperone nun travelled to the hotel on the Grand Canal in two gondolas. She thought it hilarious to be chaperoned by a nun: 'it is the funniest thing to be with a nun in a hotel'.

They visited many churches, and the Accademia which had 'a great many lovely pictures in it'. They took the boat out to the islands of Murano ('the most lovely glass and Mosaics I have ever seen'),[32] Burano ('lace works') and Torcello ('noted for old cathedral of ninth century'). She was having the time of her life: 'we walked for a while after dinner and it was the most perfect night'.[33]

Kick laughed when a friend was ticked off at mass at San Marco. When her friend was taking communion the priest told her that 'her lips were too red'. 'So that's that,' she quipped. In the evening the girls took a moonlit gondola ride: 'Never have I seen such a night – we have all decided to come back here on our honeymoon.'[34] A gondolier sang Venetian melodies to the girls, and the nun joined in, to 'help him along ... she thought the gondola was tipping over every other minute'.

The trip brought out her romantic side: 'We sleep and are awoken by the sound of singing gondoliers.' She loved San Marco and the Doge's Palace ('Perfectly marvelous'), and a trip to the Lido was a great success despite a scrum to get on to the crowded ferry. She complained, however, about the lascivious Italian men. 'It is not very funny here as all the men talk to the girls on the street,' she wrote to her parents. 'We had about 6 in a cavalcade following us all over Venice today.'[35] She sent a postcard to Eunice, Jean and Pat (the other sister, four years Kick's junior): 'no cars at all here. The gondolas are marvelous. All the men walk along the street singing.'[36]

To the boys she wrote: 'Suppose you are tearing Palm Beach apart.' She joked: 'When I made the very crude remark that Venice reminded me of Palm Beach I was all but thrown in the Grand Canal.' She told her brothers that she had fallen in love with Italy.[37]

But it wasn't all gondolas and art galleries and fine dining. Among the gallant Venetians chasing Kick and her friends along the streets of the city were ominous-looking young men wearing black shirts. Kick was ticked off by the nun for not finishing her pea soup: 'the nun proceeded to tell me that since the country was at war I must eat everything.'[38] Italy was at war with Ethiopia (known at the time as Abyssinia). Young Italian veterans, returning from the front, strutted down the streets proudly wearing, stitched on to their military caps, the names of the towns they had attacked. Kick was swept up in the fervour, and attended a Fascist demonstration in the Palais des Doges, in honour of a Dominican priest who had been killed in Ethiopia: 'His brother spoke. – Never seen such a collection of uniforms – very thrilling.'[39] She bought herself a Fascist hat, 'which will certainly make a big hit', reassuring her mother that there was 'Really no sign of war here at all except of course the [League of Nations] sanctions have closed down a great deal of the glass and lace works'.

She may have felt little sense of the war in Venice, but when the party moved on to Florence on 2 April she got caught up in a Fascist parade: 'Just saw a parade celebrating victory of Gondar which was taken tonight. Shall be very Fascist by the time I get home.'[40]

Florence was not what she had expected but she loved it, and described the lovely *pensione* overlooking the Arno, where Dante had supposedly once lived. They visited art galleries and museums and attended lectures on Italian art.

The party reached Rome on 7 April. Kick was entranced. They were staying in a Sacred Heart convent, where another party from Switzerland was staying, as well as a group of English girls – 'and are they English!' she exclaimed.[41] She did the tourist sights, the Colosseum and an old Roman church, and then 'It certainly was a thrill to see St Peters.' After morning mass in the Sacred Heart church, she took a horse and buggy to ride around the Roman parks.[42]

On her father's orders, she made an effort to contact her man at the Vatican, Count Galeazzi, but failed to understand his maid. It was Galeazzi who was intending to arrange a private audience with the Pope. It was Holy Week, the most important week in the calendar of the Catholic Church.

Kick was desperate for a glimpse of the Pope, who was saying mass on Holy Thursday in the Sistine Chapel, so she went along with the other girls and they sat outside on camp stools: 'What a crowd we were all nearly squashed to death.'[43]

In the afternoon of Maundy Thursday, the girls attended Tenebrae at St Peter's. This is a special service in the Roman Church in which psalms and prayers are read to a gradual extinguishing of candles. The final candle, hidden beneath the altar, ends the service, leaving the church in complete darkness. At St Peter's three 'wonderful' relics were being shown: 'Veronica's veil, part of the true cross and the spear that pierced our Lord's heart'. Kick was extremely moved by the experience – 'Never have seen so many American priests all together at once,' she reported to her father.[44]

That evening Galeazzi called at the Convent to see her: 'He is one of the most charming men I have ever met.' He arranged for her to have three tickets for the Pope's mass on Good Friday at the Sistine Chapel. She was thrilled by the honour. The girls dressed themselves carefully in black and a car was sent to fetch them. At St Peter's they went through the 'magnificent' Pacelli apartments and then through to the Sistine Chapel, where 'the Mass was most impressive'. The girls were special guests of Cardinal Eugenio Pacelli (Secretary of State in the Vatican). Kick felt proud of her father's Vatican connections.

The next morning on the way to the Capitoline Hill, they were caught up in a demonstration: 'a policeman told us that Mussolini would probably appear from his office in response to cheering and yelling'. Kick was thrilled that she got to see Il Duce. 'Lo and behold we had only been there about an hour … Il Duce came out with a big stride and an even bigger grin.' Kick was the only girl who had brought along her camera, and in the crowd she was pushed and shoved as she tried to take his picture. 'He is magnificent and one cannot help liking him after seeing the patriotism of the Italians.' She had seen both the Pope and Mussolini on the same day.

Kick was happy in Rome. She enjoyed the Vatican museum, where she shopped for Vatican stamps to send home to Bobby. She had expected rationed food but found it delicious: 'Am still getting very fat and spaghetti is helping plenty.' She loved the way the Italian priests blessed everything, and was amused when the girls were sipping sodas in a café and a priest came in to bless the soda fountain. 'It seems they bless every store, restaurant etc in Italy on Holy Saturday.'

Galeazzi duly arranged the private audience with the Pope. Kick was thrilled: 'The Holy Father spoke a few words to us in French and gave holy cards.' Galeazzi singled Kick out for special attention. Later he took her and a few friends to the ruins of Tivoli, outside Rome. The nuns insisted that the girls had a chaperone since they were 'going out with a man'. Kick was furious and told the nuns that he was 'old enough to be her father'. But they insisted that this was how things were done in Rome.[45]

They left Rome for Naples, and visited a small volcano, where she collected pieces of lava for little Bobby. She shopped for leather handbags, and they drove along the Amalfi coast – 'never have I seen such blue water' – but the road twisted and turned so much that the girls 'were saying our prayers continuously'.[46] In the Bay of Naples she saw a troop ship 'bound for Abyssinia'.[47] They visited Pompeii, lunched at a former Franciscan monastery and then boarded the train for Rome, where they made a final trip to St Peter's. They climbed the Scala Sancta (the staircase said to have been ascended in Jerusalem by Jesus and brought to Rome by St Helena), saw the city by night for the last time, and then went home to pack for Paris. Kick loved the Forum Mussolini ('tremendous') and was sorry to be leaving as there were parades planned for the following day, and Il Duce would be making a speech.

She saw Galeazzi and made her farewells. He gave her a parting gift – his Fascist brooch. 'All the girls are very jealous,' she told her father.[48]

10

Travels with my Mother: Russia and England

I haven't seen any beautiful Kennedy faces for seven months – long, long time that.

Kick Kennedy

Latvia, May 1936.

Kick Kennedy and her mother Rose eyed the tiny, old-fashioned plane with suspicion. As it trundled towards them, they got the impression that its fuselage and wings were lashed together by ropes. To her horror, Rose spotted her luggage being wheeled across the tarmac and realized that, indeed, this was their plane.

During his time in Europe, Joe Jr had toured Russia and had regaled the family with tales that had inspired the intrepid Rose to see it for herself. She asked Kick to accompany her and they flew by commercial jet to Latvia from Paris on the first leg of the journey. Now the small Russian plane would take them on to Moscow. There were only four seats and they were the only passengers. As they strapped themselves in, Rose began reciting Hail Marys silently to herself, thinking of the children she had left behind, whom she was convinced would soon be motherless.

There was a 'convulsive shudder' and the tiny plane was airborne. In the absence of technology, the pilot flew by visual landmarks, tipping the wings so that he could navigate. Rose recalled 'an endless expanse of dark, dense, impenetrable forest, which for variety was sometimes obscured by fog or low-hovering clouds'. It was a terrifying journey. As the landscape loomed up towards them, the pilot would suddenly pull out the choke and rise, 'leaving our stomach's Kick's and mine, back on the latest cloud'.[1]

Suddenly the plane experienced severe turbulence. The pilot, to their shock, after several 'near misses', took his eyes off the terrain and gave over the controls to his co-pilot in order to turn around to smile and wave to Kick and Rose. Rose later recalled that 'After some hours we landed safely. Neither Kick nor I had become airsick. Probably because our normal reflexes were paralysed'.[2]

Kick, homesick for her mother, had been looking forward to the trip, writing to Bobby: 'Mother shall be here in three days and can't wait to see her. I haven't seen any beautiful Kennedy faces for seven months – long, long time that'.[3] She treated herself to a new smart suit and hat, desperate to show her beloved mother that some Parisian chic had rubbed off on her. They had met at the Ritz. Rose recalled the first moment she saw her daughter: 'She looked so pretty and sophisticated, but the moment she saw me she dissolved in tears of happiness as if she were still a little girl. I will never forget what I felt when I saw her. I realized so clearly how lucky I was to have this wonderfully effervescent, adorably loving and extremely pretty child as my daughter and friend'.[4]

Rose was especially moved by her time with Kick because it reminded her of the time she had travelled with her sister Agnes: 'Traveling with Kathleen was such a joy'.[5] She told Kick all the family news, notably that Jack was 'completely recovered'.

Once in Moscow, the American Ambassador William Bullitt, 'a perfect host', met them. Kick and her mother saw the Bólshoi Ballet and, when they took the train to Leningrad, the Hermitage. Rose, always an indefatigable tourist, ensured that they saw 'everything there was to see' in Moscow and Leningrad. They visited schools, hospitals, churches, Lenin's tomb in Red Square and the famous Moscow subway 'where every station is a work of art in marble and mosaic'.[6]

Bullitt advised Kick and Rose to exercise caution and discretion when they used the telephone, as the operator was a spy.[7] Each time they left the Embassy they were followed by a little car. They soon realized that they were under constant surveillance. Rose, with her usual curiosity and love of history, put numerous questions to the guides but was asked to desist, as the guides were being monitored and could get into trouble if the wrong thing was said.

Bill Bullitt told Rose and Kick that one day he had taken himself for a long, relaxing swim in the Black Sea. He swam out deeply, then floated on his back admiring the azure sky. He was enjoying the sense of freedom, of not being followed, until he heard gurgling and splashing from another swimmer. He turned to see the familiar face of one of his NKVD followers, who was pretending to look the other way.

Despite this ominous atmosphere, Rose came to see why Communism was accepted: 'The masses really were better off in a good many ways than they had been under the Czarist system.' She spoke to several of the guides who told her that they much preferred the new system and had better lives, education, facilities, childcare and work opportunities, paid for by the state. One attractive guide amazed her by telling her and Kick that people could now read 'any book in the whole library' that they wanted to, something the Western world took for granted. Rose and Kick were acutely aware that the libraries were purged of books 'critical of communism'. Rose was, of course, dismayed by 'the official doctrine of atheism'.

The Kennedys always believed that experience was better than classroom knowledge. It was an education for Kick to have been to both Italy and the Soviet Union in 1936 during these critical times. She was falling in love with Europe. Travel was opening the world to her in a new and unexpected way. Rose asked her if she wanted to come back home early, but Kick decided that she preferred to stay and do some more travel in Europe. 'Well, darling, I miss you and wish you were along,' Rose wrote from RMS *Queen Mary*, 'but I am so glad that you decided to stay. You are a great joy to us both.'[8] Rose advised Kick to get lots of work done in her final months at the Convent. Kick, on the contrary, was ready to have some fun.

She was still determined to attend the Cambridge May Ball with Derek. While her mother headed home on the *Queen Mary*, she crossed the English Channel with her Noroton friend Ellie Hoguet en route to the university town of Cambridge. They planned to stay for four days and to attend two college balls. She went shopping and bought a beautiful white taffeta evening coat.[9]

They were staying in a vicarage in Cambridge in rather humble circumstances, sleeping on the floor on airbeds. 'None of the rooms had any furniture but a bed.' Kick said she felt as if she were 'rolling all night'.[10] The next morning, Derek was rowing on the Cam in the 'Bump' races, and Kick went along to support him.

Later, she dressed for the Trinity May Ball. Cambridge in summer is one of the loveliest places on earth and the Trinity Ball a highlight of the academic year. Exams were over, and the ball marked the end of the academic year. Strictly white tie and tails for the boys and long dresses for the girls, the event began at nine and the guests were encouraged to wine, dine and dance until dawn. Then, in the early hours of light, they would gather for a survivors' photograph, still in their evening wear. Those who were still awake would punt down to Grantchester where breakfast was served in the Orchard tea garden.

A marquee had been erected on the banks of the Cam, lit with hundreds of lanterns. Kick had dressed carefully in silk chiffon. Derek was her partner for the evening, but many men were captivated by her and asked her to dance. Her friend Ellie was disheartened by the sheer number of Englishmen who fell for her, noting that forty men swarmed around her like bees at a honey pot.[11] They were drawn to her openness and warmth and lack of pretension. The dowdy, prim English girls were simply no match for her, and Kick was incredulous at their drabness. 'There is something wrong with the English Girls,' she told her mother. 'Hardly any pretty evening dresses or girls.' She thought it amusing 'to be walking around in evening clothes in broad daylight.'[12] Her lovely chiffon dress 'took rather a beating'.

Kick thought her time at Cambridge was 'marvelous'. From then she went on to Suffolk with a schoolfriend. She was delighted that there had been no rain in England. Kick was asked if she would go back for another weekend the following year. She was a hit in England – a foretaste of things to come. She was determined to return. She told her mother: 'Tell Jack that he has to come to Cambridge next year.'[13]

Her time at Neuilly was now over and she was to return to Noroton, but it had been the most thrilling success, and her year in Europe had made a deep impression, one that would never leave her. Eunice Kennedy remarked that for her father experience was the most important thing in life for building character, whereas for her mother it was religion.[14] Kick chose experience.

* * *

Kick's European adventure had given her a certain polish and sophistication, though she was still only sixteen. She had visited the best museums, galleries, churches and buildings of Europe and had acquired a new confidence. She had seen the Pope and Mussolini in Rome, attended the Bolshoi Ballet in Russia and the May Ball in Cambridge. Home in America seemed dull in comparison, though it was always a joy to return to Hyannis Port for the lengthy summer vacation. It had been a very long time since she had seen Jack, who had spent most of 1936 resting and building up his strength. He had been recuperating in Arizona and appeared to be making a good recovery before heading to Harvard in September, after a short stint at Princeton.

Now that she was older, and had been away for a year, Kick was becoming aware of the strangeness of her parents' marriage. Rose took solace in her faith. She would go alone to St Xavier's daily mass and, when she was troubled, take long solitary walks along the beach front. She even had her own little summer house (called 'the White House') to retreat to when she wanted to be alone.

Joe, meanwhile, continued to indulge his sexual appetite. Kick's friends felt uneasy about her father's unwanted advances. Some of them refused to watch movies in the basement cinema because he would touch them and pinch them. In the evenings, he would insist on a kiss on the lips.[15] Kick's close friend Charlotte McDonnell was surprised to discover that Kick's parents led separate lives, and that when they came to New York City they always stayed in separate hotels, Mrs Kennedy at the Plaza, Mr Kennedy at the Waldorf.

One day, Charlotte went to meet Kick at the Waldorf and mistakenly entered Joe's suite. He was in the shower and called out that she should leave her coat on the chair and meet Kick and Jack across the hall. He then appeared in just a towel and told the young people: 'Will Hays came in and saw your coat and turned around and walked away, thinking I had a girl in the bedroom.' Joe was clearly delighted by this and Jack and Kick thought it delicious that the man in question was responsible for the Hays Code, banning sexual references from Hollywood movies. Charlotte, on the other hand, was shocked. Her own father would never have behaved like this in front of her friends.[16]

That summer of 1936, Jack invited more of his 'surprises' to Hyannis Port, Cam Newberry, Charles Wilson and Herb Merrick. They all fell in love with Kick, who was the female version of her best brother, bubbly, witty, fun-loving.

Kick's American female friends noticed a new ease in the tomboyish, sporty girl and were amazed by her success and popularity. Kick was not a conventional beauty, especially compared to her sisters, but men continued to flock around her. Kick's girlfriends wondered privately about the secret to her success. Was it her wealth, her clothes, her connections, her warmth? Later on, her many English girlfriends would have the same thoughts and were equally intrigued by her allure.

Her close friend Nancy came the closest to an explanation when she observed that it was her 'aloofness' that set her apart.[17] Kick sensed intuitively that men liked a girl who was hard to get. What Nancy was getting at was Kick's unique ability to be simultaneously warm and cool, friendly but distant, sexy but never promiscuous. Women liked her and rarely felt threatened by her charm, while men adored her and were drawn to her natural sexiness and vivacity. One of Jack's friends, Tom Egerton, recalled, 'I think she probably had more sex appeal than any girl I've ever met in my life. She wasn't especially pretty, but she just had this appeal.'[18] Another devoted Englishman trying to put his finger on her elusive charm said that she had the most 'sex appeal of any woman he had ever known. Not because she was beautiful, but because she was so kind.'[19]

As the sister of red-blooded brothers and a sexually promiscuous father, she was no innocent, and yet she exuded a kind of purity. She was not a vulnerable or needy girl; she was very happy in her own skin. She had that Kennedy streak of independence and spirit that was extremely appealing to the opposite sex. The more aloofness she exhibited, the more her suitors were drawn to her. Jack had this too.

One element of this coolness was her Catholic prudery. The strict religious education she had been given taught her that fornication, masturbation and birth control were sins. While in Europe, she had been genuinely alarmed by the voracious Italian men and had also warned her sisters about Frenchmen: 'Don't eye the Frenchmen or they will be hot on your trail.'[20]

Her extreme self-possession had a darker side: an inability to give fully of herself. This caused her a degree of anguish. Many years later, she confided to a close male friend that she was afraid that she didn't have it in her to be truly intimate with a man. This prudishness was coupled with an extraordinary warmth and charisma. It was a heady and intoxicating mix.

It seemed also that Kick was saving herself for someone special, that she had a sense of destiny. She was happy to date American men, but always at a distance.

11

Politics and Europe Revisited

love from a daughter who needs more sense.

Kick Kennedy

The stage set looked like a 'Sleepy Time Down South' location from a movie about the days of slavery. The bandstand was a replica of a Southern mansion with large white columns and a backdrop painted with weeping willows and slave quarters. The band played on the veranda of the mansion. A few steps down led to the dance floor, which was also used for floor-shows. This was the Cotton Club, which in 1936 relocated to new premises in Times Square on Broadway. It was one of the most sophisticated jazz nightclubs, presenting top-rate black performers for an all-white audience. Waiters in red tuxedos served champagne to Manhattan's caviar-and-martini crowd, along with delicious suppers of venison steak and Chinese chop suey.

The club had an illicit feel. Rumours abounded about associations with the Mob. It opened at nine for dining and light music, then at midnight the entertainment would begin with the first floorshow. It closed at 3 a.m.

Sitting at one of the tables, set out in a horseshoe design, was the sixteen-year-old convent girl Kathleen Kennedy with her brother Jack and his friend Lem Billings. Jack had recovered his health, had begun at Harvard. He had lost his virginity to a white prostitute in Harlem for 3 dollars. Like his father, he had acquired a taste for showgirls and waitresses. Jack was making up for lost time. He made no secret of his libertinism. In part, it may well have been a reaction to his mother's frigidity, her strict piety and emotional coldness, but it was also, given all the health problems he had to endure, a way of feeling alive. Jack Kennedy lived for the moment.

In the fall of 1936, Kick headed back to 'the old fire-trap' of Noroton to finish her Convent education. She was unhappy to be going back and saw Jack and Lem whenever she could. It was like old times, the three of them being together. Jack had promised to take Kick to the Cotton Club. But when Joe discovered that his precious daughter had gone there he was livid.

It wasn't only that he disapproved of Kick's and Jack's duplicity, but he was also worried about the family's public image. Joe was back on the campaign train with Roosevelt. In September of that year, his campaign book, *I'm for Roosevelt*, was published. Joe let his feelings be known and Kick wrote him a contrite letter: 'love from a daughter who needs more sense'. In October, Joe gave a series of nationally broadcast radio speeches, at his own expense, urging voters to back Roosevelt. He sent Kick a telegram asking her to remember to tune in to his latest broadcast. That month he opened up an account for her at Saks.

Kick, to her amusement, had heard rumours that Jack's Harvard friend Torbert Macdonald kept her photograph on his bureau. Jack had met Torby on the Cape by accident, but at Harvard they became firm friends. As with Lem Billings, it was a friendship that lasted all his life. Lem and Torby adored Kick, but she kept them at a distance, treating them as she did her brothers.

Nineteen-thirty-six was an important year for the Kennedy family for two reasons. The first was Roosevelt's remarkable landslide victory in the November elections; he won 523 of the 531 electoral votes.[1] Joe was delighted. Then the same month, Cardinal Pacelli, the Vatican Secretary of State, made a visit to America and wished to meet with Roosevelt. Pacelli was widely considered to be the second most powerful priest in the world. Two and a half years later he would be crowned Pope Pius XII. Pacelli was accompanied on this trip by Enrico Galeazzi, the man who had so dazzled Kick when she met him in Rome, and who had organized for her party a private audience with the Pope.

Galeazzi called on Joe at his office in the Rockefeller Plaza, noting the blue carpet, 'of the same colour as the eyes of this man'. They would become firm friends. Galeazzi said that Joe 'could be as gentle and kind as a gallant knight or as violent and cross as a general at war'.[2]

On a sunny November day, Rose and Joe travelled in a private train with Cardinal Pacelli as he rode to the Hyde Park home of President Roosevelt. Rose felt exalted, thinking herself 'in the presence of a mortal very close to God'. On the way back, Pacelli stopped at the Kennedys' Bronxville home to take tea and meet the children. They were finally achieving their dream of becoming one of America's prominent Catholic families.

Now that Joe was turning into a powerful political figure, with huge press interest in him and his family, Rose spoke to the children about the importance of humility and 'public service'. She would tell them that great wealth brought responsibility. And she would (mis)quote from St Luke: 'To whom much has been given, much will be required.'[3]

In January 1937, Joe and the family were invited to the President's second inauguration, but young Joe and Jack were unable to attend, due to mid-term examinations. The children were invited to a private luncheon in the White House ballroom. A month later, Joe was asked to head up a new federal agency, the United States Maritime Commission. It was not the job that he wanted, but he accepted and leased Marwood again, writing to a friend to say how much he was looking forward to 'nice cool mint juleps and Boston lobster'.[4] Joe was biding his time.

That spring, he wrote a loving letter to Kick at Noroton. He knew how much she disliked it, but felt that she was making a go of it. Jack had told his father how much the nuns liked Kick, and Joe was gratified and encouraging: 'I think that is really a great tribute to you, knowing how you felt about going back to the convent, to have made as big a success as you have of it.'[5]

Kick met a handsome shipping heir called Peter Grace. She was seventeen and he was twenty-three when her closest friend Charlotte McDonnell introduced them. She took Kick to a dinner at her friend Michael Grace's home. That evening his elder brother Peter, a Yale graduate, turned up. He was instantly dazzled by Kick. When his brother offered him a challenge he took it up in order to impress. Michael, knowing that his brother was a hockey player and not a footballer, challenged Peter to tackle a huge football player who was one of the guests. Peter, still in his business suit, tackled the man and broke his leg. With utter insouciance, Peter, without breaking a sweat, walked away with the words: 'If you don't want your friend hurt, don't bring him around here.'

Kick, as he fully expected, was impressed. He had a hunch that she liked tough men. He became her first serious boyfriend. She liked to remind him of their first meeting: 'pretty tough guy, aren't you?'[6]

Peter Grace was similar to her brothers. He had Irish Catholic roots, was educated at an Ivy League college, was a first-rate sportsman and was wealthy. Peter was captivated by Kick. He liked the fact that she was a good convent girl, and wanted to marry her, even though she was only seventeen. When he picked her up for dates he noticed that her father was away on business but her sharp-eyed mother would sit and talk to him while he waited for Kick to get ready.[7]

In June 1937, Kick finally graduated from Noroton. Joe sent her a congratulatory telegram: 'You have proved to me very definitely that you are made of fine stuff and I am more than proud of you.' She was free at last. She enrolled at Parsons School of Fine and Applied Art in New York to learn design and decorating. But, for the summer, it was back to Europe.

Rose, young Joe and Kick boarded the SS *Washington* for their European tour, planning, vaguely, to meet up with Jack later in the summer.

Jack's trip was on a low budget, as Lem was short of money. Lem was impressed by Jack's ability to slum it.[8] Kick had given her brother a present of a leather-bound diary entitled 'My Trip'. Lem observed that this European tour was a seminal moment in Jack's life. 'He had been studying French and European history at Harvard, and now he wanted to see it all himself.'[9]

They travelled to France, Italy, Germany, Holland and England. Jack was disappointed that they were forbidden entry to Spain on account of the civil war. Lem observed a new seriousness in Jack as he encountered Europe in those pre-war years, showing advanced powers of 'observation and judgment'.[10] 'He was the same irrepressible, girl-obsessed millionaire's son from Bronxville, yet also a different Jack, for the intellect that he normally kept so well concealed was at last engaged. Harvard had begun to bite.'[11]

Jack kept detailed notes in the diary that Kick had given him, and sent letters home to his father about the European situation. Though no fans of Fascism, both young men were impressed by Italy, as had been Kick the year before. 'Italy was cleaner and the people looked more prosperous than we had anticipated,' recalled Lem. 'I had a feeling when I was in Italy that Mussolini had done a lot of good for Italy.'[12]

In Germany, Lem noticed that Jack insisted on picking up every hitch-hiker. He was puzzled about this until he realized Jack's strategy. Most of the hikers were students, who had good English, which meant that the two Americans learnt a lot about the situation in Germany. Jack and Lem loathed Germany and the Germans. Jack noted in his diary: 'Hitler seems popular here, as Mussolini was in Italy. Although propaganda seems to be his strongest point.'[13] He found the Germans arrogant and insufferable, virulently nationalistic and anti-American. The nicest German they met, he said, was a dog called Dunker, which they bought for Jack's current girlfriend. They missed seeing Hitler speak at Nuremberg by just a few days, something they always regretted.

Kick and Joe Jr took in tours of Ireland, home of their ancestors, and of Scotland. In Ireland they stayed for two weeks. 'Loved every part of it from Killarney upwards,' Kick told her father.[14] Killarney, in County Kerry, is one of the most beautiful parts of south-western Ireland. Lush and green, it boasts lakes, waterfalls, woodland, beaches and moors. She thought the scenery 'gorgeous', and sent her father a postcard of Dinis Island, with its spectacular hills and lake. One of the most memorable sights was the fifteenth-century Ross Castle, on the edge of the waters of Lough Leane. Kick could never have anticipated that one day she would have her very own Irish castle. She wrote excitedly to her father, in Washington, that she was 'amidst many Kennedys'.[15]

She visited her Neuilly Irish friends in the small seaside resort of Portrush in County Antrim, in Northern Ireland: 'It was cold but a lot of fun.'[16] Rose and Joe had spent their lives trying to escape their Irish roots, but Kick loved the Irish: 'they really are awfully nice, but there is quite a marked difference between a Northern and Southern Irishman. Prefer the Southerners.' She told Joe Sr that she had 'kissed the Blarney Stone, which was quite a feat'. Kissing the stone, which is supposed to give you the gift of the gab, involves climbing to the top of Blarney Castle, near Cork, and stretching backwards over the edge of a parapet. Kick achieved it, while Joe Jr, pessimistically, told her how easy it was to fall to your death below.

From Ireland it was on to Scotland. They were staying at the grand country house of their father's friend and business associate Sir James Calder, with whom relations were now less strained than they had been. They went trout fishing and met some Scottish friends of the Calders, and Kick went shopping to buy tweeds and sweaters. An English MP took a shine to Kick, and asked her to go out with him when she got back to London.[17] Joe went shooting every day, and walked across the moors wearing only one shoe, as his other foot had blisters. Sir James gave Kick a small rifle to shoot rabbits: 'I shall try my luck today.'

Back in London, Kick arranged less glamorous lodgings, a cheap boarding house in Talbot Square, off Hyde Park. She met up with Jack, now back from Germany, and they went shopping before heading off on a train to Southampton to meet Rose. Kick and Rose left for home and Jack made his way back to London and Lem. On the journey, he consumed a 'liberal dose of chocolates and tomato juice'. He suddenly became very ill, covered in hives. He saw no fewer than four doctors, who were puzzled by his hives and low blood count. Lem said that Jack was terribly sick, but as usual he did not complain. Lem joked to Jack that if he ever wrote his life story he would call it 'John F. Kennedy, a Medical History'.[18] Suddenly the hives disappeared and off they went, exploring England.

At the end of August, the boys went home and were met by Kick in New York. They proudly handed over the brace of grouse they had shot in Scotland for her to look after while they went through customs. When they met up afterwards, she told them that the birds had smelt so bad that she had thrown them off the dock. Jack and Lem were furious.

This trip to Great Britain was memorable for Jack and Kick. It was when they truly fell in love with England. Both romantic by nature, they adored the lush scenery, the stately homes and castles and, above all, the people. They intuitively understood the understated British humour. Both being gifted with 'Irish Blarney', they appreciated wit and irony. They had a very British sensibility: never cry, don't show your emotions, make light of troubles and always keep a sense of humour. Kick and Jack were drawn to emotional coolness, but also to loyalty and kindness. A friend was a friend for life.

Lem said that Jack would do anything to hide his emotions, but at the same time he was extremely warm: 'I never knew anyone with stronger feelings of loyalty.'[19] The journalist Joe Alsop thought that there was something 'intrinsically English' about Jack: 'He was terribly old-fashioned, almost like, sort of English grandee kind of snobbishness. It was a kind of snobbery of style ... he was snobbish about courage, and he was snobbish about experience ... He wanted experience to be intense ... to my way of thinking he wasn't really like an American.'[20]

71

Jack's love of reading, especially history, and his intellectual curiosity endeared him to the English people he met. His travels in Europe, much as the situation was deteriorating politically, moved him deeply. Like Kick, he also relished being in countries (France, Italy and Southern Ireland) where Roman Catholicism was the main faith. Throughout the great European road trip, he never missed church on Sunday.

When he returned to Harvard, Jack took as one of his courses 'The History of European Art'. He had become a Europhile. He saw England as 'the political anchor of Europe, the guarantor of peace between arrogant Germans, complacent French, noisy Latins and Communist Russians'.[21] This was not a position that his father would share. Jack wrote in the diary given to him by his sister: 'Isn't the chance of war less as Britain gets stronger?' Lem noted that after their European tour there was a new seriousness to his friend.

Jack and Kick were to get to know England more thoroughly than they ever could have anticipated. Rose had a plan. She was just as ambitious as Joe, and now they wanted payback from Roosevelt for Joe's support. In her memoirs, Rose made the point that Joe wanted a diplomatic role, but he was bad at languages. What else could he do?

12

The Ambassador

You tempt all the Gods of the world by diving into the Court of St James's as an expert … if you don't realize that soon enough, you are going to be hurt as you were never hurt in your life.

Boake Carter, friend of Joe Kennedy[1]

In the fall of 1937, Joe Kennedy entered the Oval Office with Jimmy Roosevelt, the son of the President and one of his closest friends.

'Joe, would you mind taking your pants down?'

Joe looked at the President, incredulous. 'We couldn't believe our ears,' recalled the President's son, who had arranged the meeting.

'Did you just say what I think you said?' asked Kennedy.

The President replied, 'Yes, indeed.'

James Roosevelt recalled that 'Joe Kennedy undid his suspenders and dropped his pants and stood there in his shorts, looking silly and embarrassed.' The President told Kennedy, 'Someone who saw you in a bathing suit once told me something I now know to be true. Joe, just look at your legs. You are just about the most bow-legged man I have ever seen. Don't you know that the ambassador to the Court of St James's has to go through an induction ceremony in which he wears knee britches and silk stockings? Can you imagine how he'll look? When photos of our new ambassador appear all over the world, we'll be a laughing stock. You're just not right for the job, Joe.'[2]

Having been chairman of the SEC and later of the Maritime Commission, Joe had been angling for the position of Secretary of the Treasury. When it was made clear by FDR that he was not in the running, he set his mind on Ambassador to the Court of St James's, egged on by Rose. Kennedy, as an Irish-American, had no great love for England, but with Hitler's rise and Mussolini's march through Ethiopia it was now one of the most important diplomatic posts in the world.

Roosevelt was initially sceptical in the extreme about the idea of Joe as Ambassador to Great Britain. When his son Jimmy told him the position that Joe was angling for as a reward for his loyalty, the President was so flabbergasted that 'he laughed so hard he almost toppled from his wheel-chair'.[3] On reflection, though, he saw the value of getting Joe out of the way abroad. The story goes that the President had already made up his mind to give Joe the post when he summoned him to the Oval Office, but couldn't resist the opportunity to tease him about his bow-legs. Joe responded that he would obtain special permission to wear trousers. Within hours he had secured that special permission. The story may well be apocryphal, symbolic of Joe's refusal to take no for an answer and of his ability to charm his way to whatever he wanted.

The post was his. From now on in the family he was to be known as and given the title of 'the Ambassador'. He was the first ever Irish-Catholic Ambassador to Great Britain. Colleagues and friends were amazed by the appointment. Why was he appointed to a diplomatic role when he was so noted for his lack of tact and diplomacy, the blunt, plain-speaking Irish Bostonian with the dubious reputation? There were many friends who strongly advised Joe not to take the job. He didn't have the skills, he would be Roosevelt's puppet, and he would no longer be able to speak his mind freely. He was all wrong for the role, and it would be a disaster.

Joe simply would not listen. He told everyone that he was joining an elite and distinguished line of men. No fewer than five US Presidents had held the post. And, above all, he felt that it would benefit his children for their father to be Ambassador to the Court of St James's.

In the meantime, Roosevelt, who did not trust Joe Kennedy for a single second, made arrangements for him to be watched hourly, 'and the first time he opens his mouth and criticizes me, I will fire him'.[4]

* * *

It was agreed that Kick would drop out of Parsons and help her mother in her new role as Ambassador's wife. She would also make her 'debut' in London. Rose took elocution lessons and made preparations to relocate her large family. They knew enough about English life to understand that they needed some American modern conveniences. There was a lot to do before the move in February 1938.

Rose had ensured that her daughters would each have a fabulous trousseau. The girls had shopped in Paris for outfits that would equip them for the English Season. Tweeds for racing, tea dresses, fur coats for when it turned cold, and evening dresses of silk chiffon. Kick was always stylishly dressed, and she soon began to dress like an upper-class British girl, with cardigans and pearls. She loved hats, and wore outlandish creations that suited her quirky face. She sometimes wore pink camellias in her hair.

In October, Kick made another 'Spiritual Bouquet' to her parents: 100 masses, 100 communions, 100 rosaries, 25 acts. She was still seeing Peter Grace, who was as smitten as ever but nervous about the prospect of Kick's relocation. England seemed a long way away. Kick, on the other hand, didn't appear to be too heartbroken about leaving him or America.

There was enormous excitement on both sides of the Atlantic about the arrival of the Kennedy family at the Court of St James's. They had planned to arrive together in February, but Rose had had an emergency appendectomy, so she and the children embarked a few weeks later than planned. The Ambassador would be waiting there to greet them. Eunice, at Noroton, wrote to her mother about her shock at hearing of her operation: 'I am sure you will be up and even running around dear old England in no time.'[5]

13

At the Court of St James's

I guess I'm off to find my Destiny.

Kick Kennedy

Kick Kennedy was a celebrity even before she set foot on English soil. She arrived with her mother and four siblings on 17 March 1938 on the SS *Washington*. The rest of the family were coming on a later boat. The family faced an army of journalists greedy to catch an image and interview with this most photogenic of families. Joe teased Kick about the press that she had already received.

She was shocked to discover, on her arrival, that a report had reached England that she and Peter Grace were to be engaged. Kathleen was charming to the English reporters: 'Really, I don't know very much about it. I can't think how that started. It's so silly, but he's awful nice. I like him a lot, but I do not know anything about him at all.'[1]

Rose later recalled that 'everyone was interested' in Kick being married into the Grace family.[2] This was the start of huge media interest in Kick and her love life. The English press were enchanted by Kick, who had just reached her eighteenth birthday and was so pretty and smiley. 'Kathleen, aged 18, is in love,' screamed the *Daily Express*. As Deborah Mitford recalled, 'when they arrived it caused a sensation in London because no diplomat had ever arrived with nine children before.'[3]

Rose was beside herself with excitement; it was the culmination of her dreams, but she advised the children to just 'act natural'.[4] Accompanying the family were their governess Elizabeth Dunn and their new nurse Luella Parsons. The crossing had been stormy, and Rose had been made anxious by news of Hitler's annexation of Austria, the Anschluss.[5]

Rose, poised, slim and impeccably dressed, was also a hit with the Brits, who described her as 'vivacious as a screen-star, as wise as a dowager'. Likewise Joe's down-to-earth honesty and brusqueness endeared him to everyone. 'You can't expect me to develop into a statesman overnight,' he remarked.[6] But everyone agreed that it was the nine handsome children that were Joe and Rose's greatest assets. *Life* magazine reported that Great Britain 'got eleven Ambassadors for the price of one'. The family was 'big enough to man a full-sized cricket team'.[7] England had taken them all to its heart.

Rose's father, Honey Fitz, teased Joe about the photo coverage of his grandchildren. Joe, ever sensitive when it came to his father-in-law, replied stonily: 'We are not sending any pictures to any paper ... If you have an attractive daughter and attractive grandchildren, you can't get mad if their pictures appear in the papers.'[8] In fact, the Ambassador, canny as ever, knew how to take advantage of the favourable publicity. He also hired a speech-writer, a public relations man and an RKO publicist named Jack Kennedy who was nicknamed 'London Jack'. The faithful Eddie Moore joined the Ambassador to head up the London team.[9]

Rose recalled that she felt that once they were in England they became 'public property', and had become 'adopted' by the British people: 'Wherever we went, we were greeted with smiles and waves and bright looks – a spontaneous outpouring of human warmth that I shall never forget.'[10]

Debo Mitford later wrote of the immense impact that the family made: 'nothing like the Kennedy family had been seen before in the rarefied atmosphere of London diplomatic circles. For the next seventeen months they enlivened the scene.'[11] Teddy and Bobby sailed their boats in Hyde Park, rode their bikes around the city and took photographs of the Guards at Buckingham Palace. The press greedily noted every detail, treating the family like celebrities or royalty. When Kick delivered homemade biscuits to the Great Ormond Street Hospital for Children or rode a horse on Rotten Row in Hyde Park, the press recorded it.[12] The high-society magazine

Queen predicted that she would be the star of the Season, the most exciting debutante.

The ambassadorial residence at 14 Prince's Gate was impressive, even by Kennedy standards. It was a six-storey, fifty-two-room mansion on the edge of Hyde Park and within walking distance of the Embassy. It had a huge ballroom with Aubusson carpets. One of the first-floor rooms was a copy of a chamber in Versailles. Rose chose a beautiful first-floor room for her own study. The house had twenty-one bedrooms, though thirteen of them were for live-in servants, which Rose thought excessive. She took over some of the servants' bedrooms for the children, for her nannies and as guest rooms.

Despite its grandeur, the house had fallen into disrepair. Joe Kennedy spent a quarter of a million dollars of his own money on refurbishment.[13] Rose thought that the rooms were too bare, so several works of art were loaned by William Randolph Hearst from his castle in Wales. The house had its own lift, much to the delight of twelve-year-old Bobby and six-year-old Teddy who pretended to be bell boys, to the amusement of the staff.

Joe had prepared Prince's Gate for the arrival of the family.[14] He had imported an American freezer from New York and consumables such as coffee, clam chowder, candy, Nivea Creme and cough medicine. Rose brought her own American cook, Margaret Ambrose, who supplied the family with their much loved home dishes of creamed chicken, strawberry shortcake and Boston cream pie.[15]

Though not a drinker himself (apart from the odd tumbler of Haig & Haig whisky), Joe ordered 2,000 bottles of champagne for his cellars. He intended to throw memorable parties.[16] Once again, his time in Hollywood had proved useful for his understanding of the power of image. For him, the Court of St James's was merely another stage set.

As Ambassador, Joe was invited to all of the most important events, and was automatically made a member of the most exclusive British clubs. Rose and Joe initiated a succession of dinners, luncheons and tea parties to entertain their many guests. (The tea-party idea was later a major feature of Jack's presidential campaign.) The newspapers noted that Kathleen helped her parents to entertain. At one of their Thursday entertainments, tea was served from a buffet covered with a yellow damask cloth and decorated with a large bowl of sweet peas. The press made much of the Kennedy women's clothes. Rose was 'charming in a long skirted dress of light sky blue crepe', Kick wore 'a smart frock of black with white stars'.[17] Rosemary, who could not be trusted at such events, was rarely mentioned.

Joe and Rose were invited to stay at Windsor Castle with the King and Queen and their two small daughters, Elizabeth and Margaret (Edward VIII had abdicated in order to marry the now divorced Mrs Simpson, and had been succeeded by his brother Bertie as George VI). Rose later remembered this as one of the 'most fabulous, fascinating events of her life'. She decided that she would model her own behaviour on that of the Queen: 'She has a very pleasant voice, a beautiful English complexion, great dignity and charm; is simple in manners, stands very erect and holds herself well and is every inch a Queen ... I lay in bed thinking I must be dreaming, that I, Rose Kennedy, a simple, young matron from Boston, am really here at Windsor Castle the guest of the queen and two little princesses.'[18]

Rose later ranked the weekend as the fifth best of her life. Her daughter Kathleen would also describe an English country-house weekend as 'the best thing that ever happened to me', when she was invited as a house-guest to Cliveden, the seat of Lord and Lady Astor.[19] A few days after her parents' visit to Windsor Castle, Kick joined the Astors for Easter weekend. It was there that she was introduced to a smart set of aristocratic young people who would embrace the wholesome American girl with the dazzling smile.

14

'I Get a Kick Out of You'

Very chummy and much gaiety. Dukes running around like mad freshmen.

Kick Kennedy

Kick had arrived in time for the English Season – that dizzying round of balls, dinners, teas, races and regattas that began with the Royal Academy Summer Exhibition and the First Spring Meeting at Newmarket, and ended with the royal garden party at Buckingham Palace. The Season was the time when society families left their country estates and headed to Mayfair for three months of socializing. It was a huge industry dedicated to the marriage market: getting the right sort of people to marry the right sort of people. As Debo Mitford observed: 'Dance bands, dressmakers, milliners, hairdressers, caterers, hotels, restaurants, florists, hire car firms and photographers all benefited from the trade whipped up by the frenzy of the Season.'[1]

Many of the men had titles, others were impoverished noblemen or second sons looking for the right kind of American heiress from the land of plenty. From late Victorian times such transatlantic transactions became the norm. Wealthy American girls were known as 'dollar princesses' who found themselves mixing in the upper echelons of the British aristocracy. Winston Churchill's mother, Jenny Jerome, the daughter of a Wall Street speculator, married the Duke of Marlborough's younger son, Lord Randolph, in 1874. A generation later the 9th Duke of Marlborough married the eighteen-year-old Consuelo Vanderbilt, a beautiful, rich American from one of New York's most famous families, for a $2.5 million marriage settlement.

One of the most famous American expatriates was Nancy Astor. She first came to England as a divorced woman with a small child, and then met and married the son of Viscount Astor. Her wit was legendary, which endeared her to English society. When one woman asked whether Nancy had come to England to 'get our husbands' she retorted: 'If you knew the trouble I had getting rid of mine.'

From the moment Nancy set eyes on Kick Kennedy, she sensed a kindred spirit. Lady Astor had given a dance at her London home in St James's Square for the King and Queen, to which the Kennedys and Kick were invited. The evening was a great success, and the Kennedys were awed by the opulence and extravagance with which the Astors entertained their guests. Great clusters of laburnum blossoms and lilac cut from Cliveden adorned the golden ballroom in which the King and Queen danced. The rest of the house was full of flowers: vases of arum lilies, bright red and delicate pink carnations, and sweet-smelling stock covered every available surface. Lovingly placed on the oval dining-room table were Lord Astor's gold racing trophies as well as valuable gold plate.

The women were dressed in their finery with diamond tiaras and glittering jewels. Kick wore a gown of pink and white, and dazzled everyone with her wit and warmth. Nancy invited her to Cliveden. It was Kick's introduction to an English stately home. Lady Astor became 'Aunt Nancy'.

Cliveden was a huge Italianate, Baroque mansion nestling on the edge of the Thames. It stood within 400 acres of beautiful woods and formal gardens. Kick later admitted to Nancy that she had been 'scared to death' at the prospect of spending the weekend there.[2] It was Nancy who asked Lady Jean Ogilvy, daughter of the Earl of Airlie, to take Kick under her wing and teach her the ropes. Jean was to become one of her closest friends. Jean took her role seriously, though it soon became clear that Kick did not require looking after. She was amazed when Kick, eschewing formality, telephoned and invited her to the Embassy to listen to American jazz on her prized Victrola.[3]

Jean was also close to her cousin Billy Hartington, the eldest son of the Duke of Devonshire. His younger brother, Andrew, first set eyes on Kick on the staircase of Cliveden that April weekend. 'It was her vitality that overwhelmed us,' he later recalled. 'I had never met anyone with such vitality before.'[4] That weekend, Kick met another of Andrew Cavendish's cousins, David Ormsby Gore, the second son of Lord Harlech, who was to become a close friend of Jack Kennedy. Like Andrew, David was one of the second-sons club – the 'spare and not the heir'. Though he was bookish and intellectual, David was a rebel as an undergraduate at Oxford, where he refused to do much academic work, drank heavily and spent hours listening to jazz.

Andrew's and David's mothers were Cecils, members of an illustrious Tory family descended from William Cecil, Lord Burghley, chief minister to Queen Elizabeth I. Burghley's son, Robert Cecil, followed him in the role of Secretary of State and King James I rewarded him with the title Earl of Salisbury and the wealth to build a magnificent seat, Hatfield House, which remained the Cecil family home. The Cecils were known to be great talkers. This was an attribute extremely attractive to the Kennedy children, who were such superb raconteurs themselves. That weekend, Kick heard about but did not meet Andrew's elder brother, Billy, who, not caring much for Cliveden or parties, had declined the invitation.

A weekend house party at Cliveden would be intimidating to any eighteen-year-old girl, and especially for an American unused to English country-house ways. Each guest would be assigned a maid who would unpack the suitcase and lay out clothes and toiletries. After supper, beds would be turned down and toothpaste would be squeezed on to toothbrushes, hairbrushes laid out and fires lit. Dinner would be a formal affair, tables set with gleaming silver and sparkling crystal, the food served by liveried footmen.

Kick took it all in her stride and charmed the redoubtable Nancy. What Nancy realized was that Kick was not a typical debutante. Most of the English debs were shy and silent, would speak only when spoken to and rarely ventured a strong opinion. In this kind of stilted and repressed company, Kick shone. She had been raised in a noisy, spirited and clever family, had opinions of her own, but voiced them in such a warm and witty manner that she rarely caused offence.

The weekend was a tremendous success, but it didn't turn her head. The Astor crowd was agape when she nicknamed the formidable Duke of

Marlborough 'Dukie-Wookie'. She wrote to Lem of her weekend: 'Very chummy and much gaiety. Dukes running around like mad freshmen.' Lem, still in love with Kick, had made a marriage proposal, which she had gracefully declined – 'Come on, Lem, you're not the marrying kind' – but she continued a correspondence with him.[5] To Nancy Astor she wrote with gratitude for turning everything around for her. 'All the loneliness I had for America has disappeared because now England seems so very jolly,' she wrote in her thank-you letter.[6]

Kick was soon invited to another country weekend, this time at the Cecil family seat, Hatfield House in Hertfordshire, the magnificent Jacobean mansion built on the site of the old Hatfield Palace where Elizabeth I had spent her childhood. The Marble Hall holds the *Rainbow Portrait* of Elizabeth and her gloves and silk stockings were treasured items. If ever Kick were to feel thousands of miles away from home it would be in this historic house. Robert Cecil, Andrew Cavendish's cousin, was the tall, charming heir to Hatfield. His coming-of-age party the year before had lasted for five days.

Robert invited his Etonian and Oxford friends for a country weekend party. Kick was also asked to attend. She was put into the Oliver Cromwell room ('rather ironic', she noted in her diary). She observed that several Catholic girls had been invited to the house party, including Clarissa Churchill, Lady Lovat, Veronica Fraser, Virginia Brand and Sybil Cavendish. 'Rather funny as they hate them so much,' Kick wrote, knowing of the Cecils' long-standing contempt for Roman Catholics.[7]

The young people played tennis and rounders and were taken through the famous maze. One of the guests got drunk at dinner and squirted Kick with a water siphon. When she went to bed early she discovered that some-one had sneaked in to arrange an apple-pie bed. This was a practical joke in which the sheet was doubled back to prevent anyone from stretching out full length. Anthony Eden helped her to straighten out the sheets.[8] Tony was the brilliant younger son of Sir William Eden, and had recently resigned as Foreign Secretary in protest at Prime Minister Neville Chamberlain's policy of appeasement. Kick appreciated his kindness.

The next morning, she discovered that Robert Cecil had hidden all her left shoes in the maze. Robert and his friends were trying to teach her a gentle lesson in English mores: her habit of kicking off her shoes when in company was not quite the done thing. In her diary, she notes that it was his grandmother's idea. It was a churlish prank to play, given the potential for embarrassment and humiliation. If she were ever to feel like a gauche American Catholic arriviste, an outsider, this would do the trick.

But they were not reckoning on a Kennedy. Kick was not the sort of girl to sit quietly in her room. She dressed as normal and came down to dinner wearing one black and one white shoe: 'all very tricky as I had on black & white dress', she reported in her diary.[9] Throughout the weekend she wore two right shoes which meant that she found it difficult to walk properly. One of the girls, Lord Lovat's daughter Veronica Fraser, drawled: 'Why are you limping, Kick?' 'Oh,' Kick replied with insouciance, 'Robert broke my leg before dinner.'[10]

Everyone in the room roared with laughter, and she was instantly accepted. Veronica was amazed at her sangfroid: 'what a terrific sport', she thought.[11] With this one brilliant move, she had become accepted into British upper-class society. Kick couldn't seem to put a foot wrong, even in the wrong shoe.

15

The Debutante

My train not fastened on – only put on at last minute. Walked by
very quickly.

Kick Kennedy's diary

The three women posed for the cameras outside the American Embassy.
Rose Kennedy was in the middle, flanked by her two pretty daughters,
Rosemary and Kick. Rose was so glamorous and beautiful that she looked
more like another sister than a mother. As usual, the press could not get
enough of the Kennedy girls. A Movietone News crew filmed them preparing for their presentation at the Court of St James's. Joe Kennedy's eldest
daughters were 'coming out'.

Rose was in her element in England, and she had finally won the social
acceptance that she had always sought. One of her most important duties
was to choose the American debutantes to be presented at court. The
Boston Globe duly reported: 'American debutantes of 1938 cannot stick
three white feathers in their hair and drop three curtsies before the Queen
of England without the sanction of Rose Fitzgerald Kennedy.'[1] She must
have been more than a little surprised to discover later on that Joe was
limiting her power by insisting that all American girls presented at court
must have parents living in England. If she felt annoyed with Joe's new
sanction, she did not say so. Besides, it just meant that the spotlight shone
more brightly on her own daughters.

In early May, Kick wrote to Lem Billings to tell him that she was to be presented at court: 'Wish you could be here for it. I so often think of you when I meet a guy who thinks he's absolutely the tops and is just a big ham. What laughs you and Jack would get. Very few of them can take any kidding at all.'[2]

Kick and Rosemary had spent weeks being prepared for court. They practised their curtsey over and over again, mainly for Rosemary's benefit. Many debs attended the Vacani School of Dance near Harrods for the same reason. It wasn't simply a matter of mastering the deep curtsey and keeping one's back perfectly straight, it was mastering it wearing a full-length gown without tripping on the long train of the dress while wearing a headdress of ostrich feathers. Lem was endlessly amused by Kick's tales of the absurd manners and traditions of England.[3]

Rose was determined that everything should run smoothly. Her girls would be the best-dressed debs on the big day. For the court presentation, Rose had been advised to choose a British fashion designer who would understand the particular requirements, such as the correct length of the train. The dress code was extremely strict. Trains on gowns were required to be no longer than 2 yards from the shoulder, veils no longer than 45 inches. Rose went to Molyneux, the foremost designer in London, and chose for herself an exquisite gown of white lace, embroidered with tiny gold and silver beads. Twenty-two years later, she would wear this dress for Jack's inauguration as President.

Rosemary also wore a Molyneux gown of white tulle with silver thread. Kick's gown was from Lelong in Paris. It was white, trimmed with silver croquettes. Their veils were made of the finest net, and they wore the requisite three ostrich feathers in their hair, the insignia of the Prince of Wales. No jewellery was permitted for the young women, who carried simple bouquets of roses and lily of the valley.

Kick's diary entry records the preparations for the day, the hairdressers, the press photographers and the early supper. Once at Buckingham Palace, she waited in a room with diplomatic staff; her father took up his place 'in front of Throne'.[4] There was a last-minute glitch when she realized that her train was not properly fastened on.

Kick entered the great Throne Room, a magnificent red, white and gold ballroom. The King and Queen sat on gold thrones on a dais. The girls were 'called' by the Lord Chamberlain and each was drilled to walk slowly until she reached a gold crown embroidered in the carpet; there, careful not to step on her train, she would make her curtsey, smiling before stepping to the right, never turning her back on the Queen.

Rosemary made a slight stumble when she curtseyed to the Queen, but it was barely noticed. The evening was a huge success. The *Evening Standard* singled out Rosemary, who 'looked particularly well in her picture dress of white tulle embroidered with silver'.[5] The May issue of *Queen* singled out Kick: 'I was impressed by her approximation to the best type of our own English girls of the same age. She had none of that rather sophisticated air and ultra self confidence which is sometimes associated with youthful Americans.'[6]

On 2 June, a few weeks after she had been presented at court, Kick had her coming-out ball at Prince's Gate. Rosemary was coming out too, but all eyes were on Kick. Dinner was for eighty, and then a ball for 300 guests. Jean Ogilvy helped Kick arrange the all-important seating plan. 'Quite a sweat as there is so many petty jealousies in London,' Kick remarked in her diary.[7] Each table had eight places, and one of the guests on her table was pretty Debo Mitford, the youngest of the Mitford girls, the gaggle of daughters of the eccentric Lord Redesdale. On her right was Prince Frederick of Prussia and on her left Eric Duncannon, the Earl of Bessborough's son. Lord Duncannon, Kick's age exactly, was a handsome, charming man, whose perfect French earned him the nickname 'Le Dauphin'. Nancy Mitford called him the 'Angelic Eric Duncannon'.[8]

The ballroom was festooned with pink and purple flowers. Entertainment was laid on by Harry Richman (famous for *Puttin' on the Ritz*), together with Ambrose and his Band. Kick danced with many noblemen: the Duke of Kent, Viscount Newport and Prince Frederick.[9] She was twirled around the dance floor to 'Got a Date with an Angel' and 'By Myself'.[10] Rosemary danced with just one man who had been hired for the occasion. She danced beautifully, but there were rumours in London that the eldest Kennedy daughter, though lovely, was 'slow'.[11]

Debo Mitford, Jean Ogilvy's cousin, recalled in her memoirs only three debut parties in that Season of 1938, and the outstanding one was Kick's. She described the scintillating company at her table and the wonderful Ambrose band and Harry Richman: 'but it was the Kennedys themselves who lit up the evening'.[12]

In her diary, Kick recorded that the party went on until 3 a.m. To Lem she wrote: 'Our brawl went off very well … tried to get everyone to cut in but it was the most terrific effort. They all acted as if it was absolutely the lowest thing in life to tap someone on the shoulder … but otherwise every-thing was wonderbar.'[13]

Once again, she had demonstrated her ability to circumvent English propriety without seeming vulgar. This lack of concern for social niceties was very much part of Kick's particular charm. She would chew gum and walk around barefoot or hold pyjama parties for her friends at the Embassy. One of her most endearing qualities was her manner of telling jokes or funny stories. She would get halfway through and then burst into uncon-trollable laughter before reaching the punch line, a trait inherited from her grandfather John Fitzgerald.[14] Everyone around her would be laughing with her, not at her.

She would regale her friends with a joke about an American who tells an Englishman that his favourite breakfast is 'a roll in bed with Honey'. The Englishman retells the joke at White's: 'I've heard a frightfully funny story from an American. I asked him, what's your favourite breakfast? And do you know what he said to me … a roll in bed with strawb'ry jaaahm.'[15] It was Kick's attempt at an upper-class English accent that was so delicious and enthralling. She had a taste for a bawdy joke and somehow seemed to get away with behaviour that would not be tolerated by anyone else.

Jean Ogilvy remembered a formal dinner party where Kick threw a bread roll down the table at a guest, and before long everyone was throwing food. By the end of the evening Kick was standing on the table hurling bread rolls: 'If someone else had done that, it might have been rude or shocking … But she had this way about her that made it seem an absolute liberation.'[16] Friends realized that what she was doing was stripping away stuffy and suffocating English reserve. Her friends giggled when she nick-named the King and Queen 'George and Lizzie'.

The more she was teased ('Do speak English again, Kick'), the more she laughed with that dazzling Kennedy smile. Her self-deprecating sense of humour and her sense of irony were just so English. Kick intuited that once won over, the English would be friends for life.

Rose fussed and fretted over being accepted, whether finger bowls were required, should she wear tweeds for a country-house weekend. Her voice ('like a duck with laryngitis') was mocked among Kick's friends.[17] She began to speak with a slight English accent, and it was whispered that Mrs

Kennedy was giving herself airs and graces. If Kick, by contrast, didn't understand rules of protocol, she simply asked one of her English girl-friends: 'Okay, so what do I do *now*?'[18] She sensed that the way in to English high society was not to ape the English or to conform but to set herself apart, to be utterly and completely herself. The British upper classes loved the way she played up to her Americanness rather than copy the British and adopt a phoney English accent. At the same time, she poked fun at all the things her aristocratic friends thought sacred. Her strategy worked perfectly, and, to everyone's astonishment, she rose to the top of English society. She was voted England's most important debutante of 1938.

Debo, a great beauty herself, recalled that 1938 was a vintage year for beautiful girls, but, for her, one girl stood out:

Two 'Sylvias' (Lloyd Thomas and Muir), Ursula (Jane) Kenyon-Slaney, tall, blonde and willowy; June Capel, unbeatable for looks and charm; Gina Wernher, of unmistakable Russian descent, with high cheek-bones and slanting eyes; Pat Douglas, striking, with veritable violet eyes; Sally Norton, whose perfect figure in Victor Stiebel was made for jealousy; Clarissa Churchill, with more than a whiff of Garbo in a dress by Maggy Rouff of Paris. Pamela Digby – whose famous career was to culminate in the American Ambassadorship to Paris – was rather fat, fast and the butt of many teases; and there was Kathleen (Kick) Kennedy, sister of John F. Kennedy, not strictly a beauty but by far the most popular of all.[19]

16

Lords a-Leaping

We weren't always listening, but Kick was, you see. That was her
great charm and fascination to all those boys – part of it.

Lady Lloyd

In America, Kick's friends bewailed the fact that every man whom she met
fell in love with her, and now the same thing was happening in stuffy, class-
conscious England. This time, however, it wasn't Harvard and Princeton
friends of her brothers, but English noblemen. They simply couldn't get
enough of her.

Debo Mitford later recalled: 'Vital, intelligent and outgoing, Kick was
able to talk to anyone with ease and her shining niceness somehow ruled
out any jealousy. Suitors appeared instantly but I noticed from the start that
none of the girls was annoyed by her success and I never heard a catty
remark made behind her back.'[1]

The young aristocratic men she met, raised by nannies and sent to
boarding school at an early age, found her warmth irresistible. And they
came a-courting: Anthony Loughborough (grandson of the Earl of
Rosslyn), William Douglas-Home, son of the Earl of Home, Jakie Astor
(Nancy's youngest son), Robert Cecil and Hugh Fraser. They were titled,
rich and handsome, most of them Old Etonians.

The men found her so different from the English aristocratic girls they
met. It was not simply that she was funny and friendly and charming, and

exuded sex appeal, but that she was interested in politics and conversation. This was a girl raised to have an opinion about the world: it was meat and drink to her. Kick's friend, Lady Jean Ogilvy, eldest daughter of a grand Scottish aristocrat, the Earl of Airlie, recalled that she was always interested in the men's talk, especially as they endlessly discussed the deepening political crisis in Europe: 'We weren't always listening, but Kick was, you see. That was her great charm and fascination to all those boys – part of it.'[2]

William Douglas-Home was a handsome, rakish figure, with the voice of a 'constipated Bishop'. Home, who would later base a character in one of his plays on Kick, was smitten. He came to visit her in Prince's Gate and was served a drink by a man in white tie and tails. 'Could I have a small one?' he asked, assuming that he was addressing the butler. 'You could if you poured it' was the reply from the man who introduced himself as Kick's father. Joseph, as ever, was keeping a keen eye on the men who were paying court to his daughter. Douglas-Home described Kick as 'the merriest girl you ever met. She had the same witty conversation that Jack had.'[3] One night at Hever Castle in Kent, Kick agreed to marry Douglas-Home, but the next morning she had forgotten all about it. She asked him to drive her to meet another suitor.

Kick's London scrapbooks were filled with messages from her suitors: 'Your devoted lover, Prince Ahmed Husain, Oxford'; 'Darling Kick, when – oh when?'; 'You'll always mean everything to me.' Kick enjoyed the attention, but she kept them all at a distance, which only made her more alluring. She had the same ability as Jack to focus all her attention on the person she was speaking to, as though they were the only person in the world.

Debo remembered meeting Kick time and again in the 'heady atmosphere of that summer'.[4] Together they would go to the Pathé cinema in Piccadilly, 'a one-hour programme that included news, a Walt Disney film and an inferior imitation'.[5]

Kick's diary for 1938–9 reads like a roll call of the rich and famous. She listed the people she had met: Lord and Lady Bessborough, Lord Ogilvie, Lady Colefax (an English Elsa Maxwell, she noted wryly), Duff and Diana Cooper, the Earl of Portsmouth and so on. In May, she attended a house party at Blenheim Palace, where she sipped punch and wrote up the historical details in her diary: 'Beautiful palace belonging to the Duke of Marlborough in Oxfordshire ... Built by Vanbrugh 1705–24 Façade 400 ft. long. Park 2700 acres'.[6] After dinner a group of drunken Oxford undergraduates arrived, including Jakie Astor, Hugh Fraser and Robert Cecil. They were so inebriated that they began flinging champagne bottles around the room and broke a statue.[7] The next morning they went to watch cricket at Ditchley. Then at Sunday lunch they were joined by a 'walking minister', a preacher who was 'walking around the countryside collecting his flock (a very curious sight with staff in hand)'.[8]

Kick went to Oxford for Eights Week, a four-day regatta of bumps races on the River Isis. There was a reception in honour of her father, and she won the admiration of the undergraduates by her keen interest in their (male) debates. The Rhodes Scholars, she noted, were mainly from the Middle West of America.[9]

On 23 May she attended Lady Astor's dance given in honour of the King and Queen: 'Everyone had decorations on but no knee breeches.' The guests all wore white gloves, and she noticed Charles Lindbergh talking to the Queen on the sofa.[10] She went on to another coming-out dinner and danced the 'Big Apple' until the early hours.

Two days later, she lunched at St James's Palace with Pat Britten of the Grenadier Guards, and was highly amused to be encouraged to take snuff from a horse's hoof. The next day she was invited to a dinner given by Lady Violet Astor. It went on and on and on. When her parents went to the Opera House to see Joe's favourite, Toscanini, Kick slipped off to the theatre, and then on to a club to hear Harry Richman 'who sings Thanks for the Memory perfectly'.[11]

She was unimpressed by the Cambridge Footlights, but ran into the celebrated Oxford don Maurice Bowra, who recognized her from press photographs. At Oxford she spotted the infamous Bullingdon boys, dressed in their dining club's blue tailcoats. Then it was on to Glyndebourne, the private opera house in Sussex, with its 'most lovely gardens'.[12] They saw Mozart's *Don Giovanni*. Next was Wimbledon, dominated by American players. Rose's parents had come to London from Boston, and Josie attended Wimbledon, seated in the Royal Box with Queen Mary, George V's widow.

On 1 June Kick went to Epsom for Derby Day, taking Lord Derby's private train. She loved the races, even though the rain fell. Later that day she returned to London for the Court Ball. She wore a white lace gown with a shocking-pink bodice. She noticed 'all the women beautifully bejeweled'. She giggled to see her father (the only man not in breeches) trying so hard to 'force a smile out of old Queen Mary'. Band leader Ambrose played at the ball, and the highlight of the evening was when a crooner arrived and started singing. Ambrose had asked the Lord Chamberlain if he was allowed to bring a crooner. He agreed, thinking a 'crooner' was a musical instrument.[13] Kick noted in her diary that the Duke of Kent danced the 'Big Apple for all he's worth', and that Duff Cooper, First Lord of the Admiralty, was hopping about with a shoe on his head.[14] Kick's Convent days were well and truly over.

Royal Ascot in mid-June was for many the social highlight of the Season. Special trains were put on to convey people to the racecourse, and if you were a deb you took your place in the Royal Enclosure. Kick stayed at Cliveden for Ascot week: 'House chock full'.[15] On the first day of the races she was amused to see the finery: 'Everyone dressed up like stuffed turkeys'.

For Gold Cup Day at Ascot, the women were dressed in beautiful soft pastels of blue, lavender and dusky pinks. Rose Kennedy caused something of a sensation by wearing a gorgeous black organdie Patou dress and hat. She wrote in her diary that she was determined to 'stand out'. Her strategy worked. The *Evening Standard* described the Queen's and the Princess Royal's dresses, but the only photograph was of Mrs Kennedy.[16] When the King and Queen arrived in their carriage, Joe exclaimed, 'Well, if that's not just like Hollywood.'[17]

During the Season there were balls on Mondays, Tuesdays, Wednesdays and Thursdays, with occasional dinners on Fridays in the country. Debo Mitford recalled how humiliating it was for the less popular girls, who had no dance partners. They would hide in the powder room or fill in pretend names on their dance cards. Kick also noted in her diary that the 'card system is beastly'.[18] She was acquiring English phrases. She never had a problem with dance partners.

All through June, Kick attended party after party. Receptions would take place before the balls, often in hotels or in a private house. As well as the 'Big Apple' the young people danced 'The Lambeth Walk'. It was the era of the big bands: Joe Loss, Carroll Gibbons, Roy Fox, Nat Gonella, Ambrose (Kick's favourite), the great Harry Roy and Benny Goodman, 'the King of Swing'. They danced to the songs of Cole Porter, Noël Coward and Irving Berlin.

Debo Mitford recalled that Robert Cecil and Hugh Fraser were the most energetic dancers: 'coats off, pouring with sweat, stumping and thumping with no real steps, just enjoying themselves madly. Muv [Lady Redesdale] said, "If young men all go on like this there will be a war."[19] By the summer of 1938, war was indeed a distinct possibility, but everyone seemed to ignore it. They were all living for the moment.

Debo remembered that Kick was always beautifully dressed, shopping in Paris for her clothes. Debo herself was on a strict budget, but her friend spent a small fortune on dresses, hats and shoes. Kick wore her trademark single pearls and white gloves, her hair perfectly coiffed. Like her mother, she was slim as a pencil and kept a close eye on her weight. But if she looked like an American princess, she did not play up to the role. Friends noted that she would often be seen patiently walking her sister Rosemary in Hyde Park, relieving the maid.[20]

17

'A Merry Girl'

Grace is wildly in love with you and is heading for England this summer in order to clinch the romance – so watch it, Kick.

Lem Billings

Kick's new English friends noticed that she talked incessantly about her brother Jack, who was shortly to arrive from Harvard for the summer. Jack, she told them, was obsessed by everything British, from history to literature to politicians. He was fascinated by Winston Churchill and had read everything he had published, including his edited speeches. Churchill's *Great Contemporaries* was one of his favourite books. In Churchill's *Marlborough* Jack read about the great British families that he was now about to meet in the flesh: the Cavendishes, the Marlboroughs and the Cecils.

Jack was amazed by Kick's popularity and by the way she had risen inexorably to the top of this exclusive set. She dragged him along to every party and dinner, proudly introducing him. Her friends were charmed by this tall, skinny, handsome young man who looked as if he were Kick's twin; they were so similar in face and manners, finishing one another's sentences, talking non-stop about anything and everything. They made a fascinating double act. Kick's friends noted the peculiar closeness between her and Jack. She threw a party at Prince's Gate to introduce him to her friends. She took him around the room, whispering into his ear; then the two of them would descend into fits of laughter.[1]

Jean Ogilvy thought him 'very much a boy, all long skinny arms and legs, but very, very attractive'. Nobody knew how ill he had been just a few months before arriving in England. He exuded health and vitality, moving with a 'careless grace … not arrogant, but simply confident'.[2]

Young Joe had arrived in England at the same time as Jack, so the family was reunited for American Independence Day. The English press went wild when young Joe, with his movie-star good looks, and Jack arrived to join the family. That July, *Vogue* magazine lauded the Kennedys as a family who had 'swept like a conquering horde upon London, which has lowered its defences and admitted itself stormed'. The magazine devoted pages and pages to the photogenic Kennedys.[3]

The press kept up their fascination with the American Ambassador, 'whose whole family is taking to London life with the ease of the proverbial ducks to the pond'. One member stood out: 'But it is Kathleen especially who is about everywhere, at all the parties, alert, observant, a merry girl who when she talks to you makes you feel as if you were seeing it all for the first time, too.'[4]

Kick was thrilled to have her good-looking elder brothers in London. Young Joe and Kick got up early most mornings to ride together, cantering down Rotten Row. Though young Joe was extremely handsome, he was not as popular as Jack. He was too irascible, like his father, and espoused similarly isolationist views about the increasingly worrying European situation. British men found him brash and quick-tempered, and the women thought he was sexually aggressive.[5]

Jack shared Kick's great vitality and wit, and her friends were drawn to his keen intelligence and sense of irony. He teased his sister over her plethora of aristocratic suitors, and laughed at the idea of his rather ordinary-looking sister being the belle of England, but after meeting some English girls he quipped that 'she had no competition'.[6] He seemed bemused by the shy, silent English debs. One of his dates was mute all night until she finally broke the silence to describe the brook at the end of her father's garden.[7] Not the kind of girl to interest Jack Kennedy.

Kick's diary for July shows that she and Jack were constantly together. She took Jack and Joe to meet the Bessboroughs, and then to a dinner dance at Lady Astor's noting, 'no hard drink as usual for an Astor party'.[8]

William Douglas-Home thought that Joe carried heavily the weight of being the eldest Kennedy child. He considered that Jack was intellectual in a bright, quick way, but that Joe was 'much more serious and had … gravitas about him'.[9]

Jack was a keen dancer (one of Kick's nicknames for him was 'Twinkletoes'), and he took his sister to nightclubs. One of the most popular was the 400 in Leicester Square. Debo Mitford recalled that members could buy a bottle of spirits there, write their name and date on it, and on the next visit the bottle would be waiting for them.[10] Kick was beginning to spread her wings, and deceive her parents. For the first time in her life, she was meeting friends who were not Catholic, and who wanted to have fun. She was liberated, and she was resisting Rose's attempts to restrict her movements. She and her brothers drank alcohol, something that her parents frowned upon.

Nevertheless, Kick did have some Catholic friends. One of them was a recently converted Catholic, Evelyn Waugh, the celebrated comic novelist and chronicler of the crazy antics of the 'Bright Young People'. Waugh was charmed by Kick. They met at a dinner, and Waugh asked her what was the size of her 'dot'. Kick had no idea what he meant and assumed he meant the size of her belly button; she responded that she didn't think hers was larger than any one else's. Waugh replied that hers must be ample, as her father was in finance. She finally realized, to her great amusement, that he was referring to her dowry.[11]

Kick's best friend was the beautiful and willowy Sylvia 'Sissy' Lloyd Thomas. She had lustrous dark hair, hazel eyes and translucent skin. Sissy's father, Hugh Lloyd Thomas, was a former private secretary to the Duke of Windsor, and he had died in February 1938, in a steeplechase accident. Sissy came to the Embassy to stay with Kick in the months following the tragedy. Unlike most of Kick's friends, Sissy was a Roman Catholic, and the girls had a special bond. They were like sisters. Unlike many of her other friends, Sissy recognized the more serious side to Kick. The girls often attended mass together. It was important to both of the girls that they should marry Catholic suitors. But Sissy was deeply in love with the handsome young aristocrat David Ormsby Gore, who was extremely anti-Catholic. The girls chatted endlessly about their suitors.

That summer Lem wrote to Kick to warn her that Peter Grace was determined to hold on to her. 'Grace is wildly in love with you,' he told her, 'and is heading for England this summer in order to clinch the romance – so watch it, Kick.'[12] Peter had made plans to visit England in July. He sailed on the *Queen Mary* and arrived on the 25th of that month, full of excitement and anticipation at the thought of Kick 'always bubbling over and that wonderful smile'. At the Embassy the butler opened the door and Peter announced himself, adding that Kathleen was expecting him. When the butler informed him that she was in Sussex at the races, Peter was distraught.

Peter knew that she was expecting him and that this was a rejection of the highest order, given how far he had travelled in order to see her. He turned right around and took the next boat back to New York. Kick was indeed at the races, and she had a new suitor.

18

Billy

> She was a young girl, extremely attractive around all these dukes
> and princes. She was getting around in the highest circles in
> England.
>
> Peter Grace

Buckingham Palace, 17 July 1938.

It was a perfect English summer's day. The scene was the King and Queen's annual garden party, which was the official close of the London Season. Black clouds were gathering over Europe in 1938, but few would have noticed them on this sun-filled day.

Kick Kennedy was one of the Queen's guests at the garden party, along with her parents, her brothers Jack and Joe and her sister Rosemary. She was not impressed by the event: 'Very hot and very dull procedure'.[1]

She was looking out for a young man she had met in recent weeks. His name was Billy Hartington. Kick had been introduced to him by Sissy's boyfriend, David Ormsby Gore. David and Billy were cousins and had been brought up so closely that they were more like brothers. David Ormsby Gore (lifelong friend to the Kennedy family) was a brilliant young man, fond of reading, politics and jazz. He knew that, ever since being introduced to Andrew Cavendish, Kick had been curious to meet the elder brother, the Marquess of Hartington.[2]

On 13 July, Kick noted in her diary that she had attended a garden party at the Tower of London at which Queen Mary came up the River Thames on a barge. That evening Billy Hartington, in the company of his aunt, Adele Cavendish (sister of Fred Astaire, married to Billy's uncle Charlie), picked her up to take her to dinner with the Duke and Duchess of Kent. After dinner she went with the Mountbattens (Lord Louis, who would be the last Viceroy of India, and his wife Edwina) to their penthouse flat and danced the night away.[3]

Billy was instantly smitten. Kick thought he would be yet another of the effete, bashful English noblemen she had met in London, and nothing like the masculine ideal represented by her athletic American brothers and Peter Grace. But this tall handsome young man stirred her interest. He was quite different to his brother Andrew. As the eldest son of the Duke of Devonshire, he took his position and his responsibilities seriously.

The Cavendishes were one of the first families in the land. Billy's ancestor Sir William Cavendish, who married Bess of Hardwick (the earldom of Devonshire was bestowed on their son), was an English courtier and MP closely connected to Henry VIII. It was William who oversaw the dissolution of the monasteries at the end of the 1530s. The family seat was the magnificent Chatsworth in Derbyshire, and the family also owned Lismore Castle in Ireland, Hardwick House, also in Derbyshire, Bolton Abbey Hall in Yorkshire and Compton Place by the sea at Eastbourne in Sussex. Their splendid London residence overlooking Hyde Park, Devonshire House, was sold directly after the First World War, in order to pay death duties, but they still had a townhouse in Belgravia.

The Cavendishes were known for three things: wealth, politics and being supremely anti-Catholic. The 4th Earl was one of the 'Immortal Seven' who issued a secret invitation to William of Orange to depose the Catholic King James II and set up the Revolution Settlement of 1689 to guarantee the sovereignty of Parliament over a constitutional monarchy and restrict the royal succession to those who professed the Protestant faith. He was created Duke of Devonshire six years later. Billy's grandfather died in 1938 and his father Edward succeeded him as the 10th Duke.

Born in December 1917, Billy Hartington had been educated at Eton and was now an undergraduate at Trinity College, Cambridge. Like so many of his ancestors, he wanted a political career. At the Buckingham Palace garden party, where Rose later recalled Kick looking at her loveliest, he invited her to be his guest at 'Glorious Goodwood', one of the highlights of the British flat-racing season, held on the estate of the Duke of Richmond. She would stay with him at his family estate in Eastbourne. Kick, knowing that Goodwood fell on the same day as Peter Grace's arrival, agreed to be Billy's guest. The house party contained many of her new friends, including Debo Mitford, Robert Cecil, Tom Egerton, Irene (Rene) Haig, Zara Mainwaring and Jakie Astor. Rene Haig was irked that Billy had asked Kick along, as until then she had been Billy's favourite.[4]

On 25 July, the day Peter docked, she left with Jack for Compton Place, 'to spend Goodwood with the Devonshires'. Her diary noted Peter's arrival in England, but said nothing more about him. Despite his pain and humiliation, Peter later refused to criticize Kick: 'I don't blame her. She was a young girl, extremely attractive around all these dukes and princes. She was getting around in the highest circles in England.' She had got swept up with the 'highfalutin people of England … I sort of figured she was caught up on that glamour, and you can't fight that.'[5] Kick might have been swept up by the glamour of the English aristocracy, but she always retained a healthy scepticism towards the upper crust.

A picture of Billy and Kick at Goodwood was published in *Queen* magazine, Kick wearing a printed tea gown and jaunty hat and Billy in suit and trilby. She liked Compton Place ('not a big house', she observed). Goodwood was 'Quite smart but not like Ascot'.[6] When Jack became President of the United States, he reminded Debo of the outing to Goodwood as being an especially memorable occasion.[7]

Goodwood was Kick's first meeting with Billy's parents, and if she felt daunted, she didn't show it. The meeting was extremely difficult for Eddie, Billy's father, who was known for being extremely anti-Catholic, but he was impeccably mannered and Kick was amused by his eccentricities.

Eddie was a true English eccentric who wore paper collars, a threadbare suit and no overcoat whatever the weather. He smoked Turkish cigarettes that he lit with a tinder cord, occasionally burning holes in his suits. He would have been a dentist if his life had turned out differently. He loved fly-tying and spent hours trying to judge which flies were the most attractive to salmon. 'He made an odd sight, a white apron over his well-worn, blue velvet smoking jacket, leaning across a table covered with all the ingredients for fly-tying … Once the flies were ready, he lay in the bath imagining he was a salmon while Edward, the butler, pretending to be a fishing rod, jerked them over his submerged head.'[8]

Eddie was MP for Derbyshire West for fifteen years, until 1938, when his father the 9th Duke died, and he was elevated to the House of Lords. He was driven to meetings in the 'Yellow Peril', his 1914 Humber. Debo Mitford recalled that Eddie was not much good at small talk, and was often silent: 'Coming from a family that never drew breath, I found this silence intimidating.'

Both Kick and Debo adored Billy's mother, the Duchess. She came from the illustrious Cecil family, but she was no social snob and everyone who knew her loved her. Her nickname was 'Moucher', and Debo wrote that she was 'quite unconscious of the effect her goodness, beauty and ready understanding had on all around her'.[9] Her pride and joy was her first-born son, Billy. She doted on him and they were exceptionally close. If she felt alarmed by Billy's infatuation with Kick Kennedy, she did not show it.

The Duke of Devonshire had recently published an anti-Catholic pamphlet in which he railed against Catholic girls marrying into the British aristocracy. Kick was potentially the embodiment of the very type he had warned against. But she managed to charm even him. After the weekend, he wrote to Lady Astor and gave his first impression: 'She is very sharp, very witty, and so sweet in every way. The Irish blood is evident, of course, and she is no great beauty, but her smile and her chatty enthusiasm are her salvation. I doubt, of course, she'd be any sort of match for our Billy even if we managed to lure her out from under the papal shadow.'[10]

In the meantime, Rose and Joe had arranged a summer holiday in the South of France. For the first time in her life, Kick rebelled against her mother. She stayed with Billy, saying that she would meet them later on. Debo recalled that Rose, 'a forceful character of whom all the children were in awe', was not pleased. She 'wondered what reception Kick would get when she eventually joined her family'.[11] Kick's rebellion was a taste of things to come.

19

The Riviera

On the pleasant shore of the French Riviera, about half way between
Marseilles and the Italian border, stands a large, proud, rose-colored
hotel. Deferential palms cool its flushed façade, and before it
stretches a short dazzling beach. Lately it has become a summer
resort of notable and fashionable people.

F. Scott Fitzgerald, *Tender is the Night* (1934)

The Hôtel du Cap, huge, white and shimmering in the heat, perched on a
dense, tree-covered cliff above the sparkling sapphire-blue Mediterranean
Sea. The hotel was a Napoleon III chateau, located on the southern tip of
the Cap d'Antibes in 22 acres of pine and tropical gardens. Candy-striped
cabanas were located among the rocks down below the hotel, where guests
would descend 150 steps down a mile-long esplanade to reach the boulders
along the sea.

Its famous restaurant, the Eden Roc Pavilion, was built below the hotel
and overlooked the swimming pool. Guests would feast on 'flame-red
lobsters, pink shrimp, orange salmon, purple sea urchins, midnight blue
mussels, silvery fishes, primrose langoustines, and pearly-gray oysters'.[1]
Ice-sculptures of leaping dolphins, reclining mermaids and majestic swans
adorned the tables alongside fluted goblets and ornate silver. It was a riot
of 'shimmering Technicolor'.

As one of the most famous hotels along the Côte d'Azur, immortalized by Scott Fitzgerald as the Hôtel des Etrangers in his great Riviera novel *Tender is the Night*, it was where the 'beautiful people' gathered. Dressed in the silks and linens of Lanvin, Molyneux and Schiaparelli, they exchanged gossip, sipped cocktails and observed one another.

A thirteen-year-old girl, chubby and plain, played on the rocks below under the watchful eye of her English governess. She stared enviously as the large group of young people gathered at their cabana, close to her own. She had never seen anything quite like them. The boys were so virile and handsome, the girls so pretty and sporty. She made enquiries and discovered that they were the children of Joe and Rose Kennedy, here for the entire summer. The girl, Maria, thought them 'wonderful' and remarked, 'I would have gladly given up my right arm, the left, and any remaining limb, to be one of them. They looked, and were, so American. All had smiles that never ended, with such perfect teeth each of them could have advertised toothpaste.'[2]

Maria Sieber was the shy, awkward only child of one of the most famous and beautiful screen sirens of the Golden Age of Hollywood, Marlene Dietrich. Maria, known by her mother as 'the Child', had been raised in Hollywood seclusion by the doting but controlling Dietrich. Surrounded by bodyguards and nannies and tutors, she barely knew any other children. She became her mother's dresser, accompanying her to the studios and ensuring that her every wish was met. From an early age, she was aware that her parents' marital arrangements were unconventional. Though they would be married for half a century, they mainly lived apart and took lovers. In the early years, Dietrich made some attempt at pretence, but once Maria became a teenager, her mother was open about her many male and female lovers.

Maria lived in the shadow of her magnetic, beautiful and talented mother, but she inspired great love and affection in almost everyone she met. Many of Dietrich's friends and lovers pitied the timid girl, who was so obedient, never answered back and, despite her privileged upbringing, never displayed a spark of petulance or spoilt behaviour. She made friends with her bodyguards and the staff, always careful to ensure that she hid her friendships from her jealous mother, who demanded complete and all-encompassing devotion.

Now, in Antibes, she was captivated by the Kennedy family, who looked so jolly and were so much fun. Maria was delighted when the younger Kennedys ran up to her mother on the beach asking for her autograph.

Maria would always remember this Riviera holiday, and its special 'summer light ... Stark, intense, hot and white, making all color come into its own'. She recalled that during that 'first summer in Antibes, Dietrich forsook her beiges and blacks, wore flowing beach robes in Schiaparelli's invention "shocking pink" and looked divine'.[3]

No one was more impressed than Rose Kennedy: 'Marlene is gracious, animated, pleasant to meet, seems to be taking a holiday with her hair thrown to the winds and no worry about make-up.'[4] Rose might not have been so pleased with Dietrich had she realized that her husband Joe would soon embark upon a passionate affair with her.

Young Joe and Kick arrived from London on 3 August. Kick found Cannes oppressively hot and was happier at Cap d'Antibes, where Rose had rented a private villa called Le Domaine de Beaumont for two months. She found household help, ordered in supplies of fresh milk and cream, arranged for tours of the region and encouraged the children to keep journals. She was desperate for skinny Jack to put on weight, while ensuring that the other children did not. The children obsessed about their weight, driving her to distraction: 'Almost go mad listening to discussion of diets, as Jack is fattening, Joe Jr. is slimming, Pat is on or off, and Rosemary (who has gained about eight pounds) and Kathleen and Eunice are all trying to lose'.[5]

The Ambassador, despite the growing crisis over Hitler's sabre-rattling, joined the family later in August. He recalled the 'blue Mediterranean and the sun-drenched sands, the casualness of people in a holiday mood, luncheons, teas, dinners and golf'.[6] It didn't feel a million miles away from Hyannis Port, and the family was together.

That summer, Dietrich had broken one of her own rules, never to allow herself a suntan. With no film scheduled, she 'embraced the process of acquiring a tan', wearing for the first time a bathing suit with a new-fangled built-in bra that showcased her amazing cleavage and her long legs: 'the first ever exposure of Dietrich's body to summer was born, and the admiring glances were legion'.[7]

No one was more admiring of Dietrich than the man described by her daughter as 'the sexy Irish politician on the cliffs below'. He was always drawn to Hollywood movie stars, and there was none more queenly than Dietrich. They flirted together openly, and the families spent time together. Maria was invited to the Kennedy villa for lunch. She was terrified and changed her sundress four times, desperate to look not like an 'aristocratic European' but like a 'normal child coming to lunch'. The problem was that she just didn't have the first idea of how to behave like a normal child. The dining table was very long, and she sat with the younger children listening 'while the older ones discussed topics and issues proposed by their father, while Mrs. Kennedy supervised the serving of lunch by her staff and the table manners of her youngest'.

As usual, Joe took control at the dinner table, asking the children questions about politics and the economy. Maria observed that 'most of the questions were directed at the bigger boys, but the younger children, boys and girls, were expected to listen and contribute if and when they had something to add. He drew them out, prodded them to back up their arguments, and filled in the blanks.'[8] For someone who was constantly criticized by her own parents, she was amazed by the warmth and solidarity exemplified by the Kennedy family: 'Never once was a critical comment made without corroborating evaluation. No sarcasms.'[9] She, who was so used to Hollywood movie stars of the first rank – Judy Garland, Clark Gable, Mae West, Greta Garbo – was enraptured by their particular brand of magic: 'No one "starred", and yet, all had a star-like quality.'[10]

Maria never forgot the Kennedy children. She remembered young Joe as 'the heir, broad and chunky, a handsome football player with an Irish grin and kind eyes'. She adored and fell in love with Jack, 'the glamour boy, the charmer of the wicked grin and the "come hither" look – every maiden's dream. My secret hero'. Eunice she thought a little daunting: 'opinionated, not to be crossed, the sharp mind of an intellectual achiever'. Pat was closest to her in age, but 'not gawky, nor fat, with not a pimple in sight'. Bobby was the 'fixer' in the family, 'the one who knew everything, and never minded being asked to share his information'. Jean was 'a quiet, gentle girl, who picked up forgotten tennis rackets and wet towels'. And 'Teddy on his chubby legs, [was] always running, always eager to show you love, trying to keep up with his long-legged siblings'.

Maria loved them all. She remembered Kick as 'a lovely girl who assumed the role of the official eldest daughter, even though she wasn't and seemed to have matured too soon because of it'. Quiet but intelligent and highly observant, Maria noticed how Kick felt the pressure of Rosemary's incapacitation. She saw the difficulty for her of being not the eldest daughter but having to assume the role. Maria loved and was drawn to Rosemary, 'the damaged child amidst these effervescent and quick-witted children'. Rosemary became her special friend. 'Perhaps being two misfits, we felt comfortable in each other's company.' The two girls would sit in the shade, 'watching the calm sea, holding hands'.[11]

Maria liked Rose Kennedy, who was so kind. She felt bad when she realized that her mother and the Ambassador had begun an affair. He was, she recalled, 'a regular visitor to our beach cabana', and he made sure that everyone knew as much.[12] To save embarrassment, Maria stopped visiting the children: 'I didn't want any one of his family to feel uncomfortable.' As usual, Rose turned a blind eye. Maria felt a sense of kinship with the children, whom she felt sure knew what was really going on. She overheard a woman whispering that Joe Kennedy was Gloria Swanson's lover, and surmised that 'maybe they [the children] were as used to their father disappearing as I was my mother'.[13]

The former King Edward VIII and Wallis Simpson were now living in exile in France as the Duke and Duchess of Windsor. The Kennedys, much to the chagrin of the King and Queen, accepted an invitation to dine with them. They went sailing together.

On 14 August, Kick and Jack left the Riviera for a ten-day stay in Austria's equivalent of Monte Carlo, the Wörthersee, a lake in the southern state of Carinthia. Their host had a house on the lake's edge. One night they went out to a bar. A member of the party was an Austrian Jew called Rudi. Another was an Englishman called Peter, who became engaged in a fist-fight. The climate in Austria since the Anschluss in March was such that it would have been all too easy for a bar-room brawl to turn into a racial attack: Kick noted that Rudi was 'scared to death as Nazis would probably have killed him'. It was a grim reminder of the tense situation. With more than a touch of understatement, Kick wrote that 'everyone says that Austria has lost its sense of gayness and carefreeness'.[14] After ten days, they returned to the South of France. In Cannes, Kick went swimming and almost drowned: 'I was left by all my younger brothers and sisters for 45 minutes while they aquaplaned.'[15]

At the beginning of September Kick was invited by another friend, Jane Kenyon-Slaney, to stay with her in Scotland for her twentieth-birthday celebrations. She knew that she would be meeting up with Billy, who was also there for the grouse season. Janey, a beautiful, tall and elegant blonde, became one of Kick's closest friends. She was a granddaughter of the Duke of Abercorn, and Kick loved her aristocratic drawl ('It's soooo extraordinary').[16]

Everyone was aware of the deeply worrying political crisis as Hitler prepared to annex the Sudetenland. Billy, whose sense of honour and duty was deeply ingrained, believed that Britain would fight alongside the French to protect Czechoslovakia.

They were all waiting for Hitler's speech at Nuremberg on 12 September. For many Americans, it would be the first time they had ever heard him speak (this was the first world crisis to be played out in real time on the radio). Though Hitler screeched and screamed and railed against the Czech government, he did not, as had been expected, declare war. But it was only a matter of time. When Rose boarded the sleeper train to Paris, she remarked in her diary that the coming months would be 'an accumulation of meeting and seeing men who are shaping the world's destiny'.[17] She had a 'heartbreaking' conversation with a Frenchwoman she encountered along the way, who said: 'My grandfather was killed in the war in 1870 against the Germans. My husband and brother were killed in the war in 1914, and my cousin was blinded. And now they are asking me to send my son to war in 1938. I cannot, I will not.'[18]

Kick, meanwhile, was on her way to Scotland, but stayed first in Leicestershire with the Duke and Duchess of Rutland at Belvoir, 'a lovely castle, high above the trees'. She loved the interiors: 'everything in the house is full of historical interest'. She found the Duchess very pretty, and noted that she had been one of the four trainbearers at the Coronation. The Duke, though, was 'rather sour and very pompous. He wears a white tie at dinner which is a sure sign.'[19] She was moved by her meeting with the Duke's mother, whom she thought a great beauty and very talented. She heard the story of how the Dowager Duchess had lost her eldest son when he was only nine. After he died of a sudden illness, she locked herself in her room for six weeks and when she emerged she had sculpted a beautiful model of his small body: 'It was practically a miracle as she had never done any before.'[20] She went on to become a distinguished sculptor and painter.

Kick, looking slim and tanned from her time on the Riviera, was desperate to be reunited with Billy. On 19 September, she arrived at Cortachy Castle in Angus, north-east Scotland.

20

Peace for our Time

All you can hear or talk about at this point is the future war which is bound to come. Am so damn sick of it.

Kick Kennedy

Kick loved the beauty of the Scottish heather as she took walks around the grounds of Cortachy Castle. The castle, a cream house overlooking the River South Esk, dated back to the sixteenth century but had been given Gothic turrets in the nineteenth. It was said to be haunted by the ghost of a drummer boy, who would play his drum late into the night. Kick was more excited to be reunited with Billy than troubled by ghosts.

Jane's father, Lord Airlie, who was the Queen's Lord Chamberlain, was dressed in a kilt. Kick found him 'terribly Scotch'. He took the party to meet his mother, the Dowager Lady Airlie, who lived in a different castle which was 'also supposed to be haunted'. The dowager was 'very sweet' and they ate roast potatoes.[1] Back at Cortachy, the men went shooting every day, complaining that the grouse were not plentiful, and in the evening the party gathered around the gramophone and chatted into the night.

Kick was amused when one of the guests let off the fire hydrant and Jakie Astor spilt whisky all over the floor. But despite the high jinks, everyone was troubled by the news abroad and gathered around the radio to hear the newsflashes about the Czech crisis. 'The international situation grows increasingly worse,' Kick noted in her diary. She wrote to Lem Billings: 'All you can hear or talk about at this point is the future war which is bound to come. Am so damn sick of it.'[2]

Kick left for racing at Hamilton Park with Billy, and then went on to Balado, near Kinross, to stay with a Scottish girl called Frances Dawson: 'It was not much fun as the crisis is at its height and it was touch & go for war.'[3] She listened to Chamberlain's radio address saying that he had done every-thing he could. Rose was in Scotland, too, and she listened to the Prime Minister's speech, 'urging people to keep calm, to cooperate quietly and with confidence, and not to give up the last shred of hope'. The next day Rose wrote in her diary: 'Today, individual, brooding silence was general, as were unsmiling, unemotional faces. Everyone unutterably shocked and depressed, feeling from the Prime Minister's broadcast that his hopes for peace are shattered and that war is inevitable.'[4]

The world was waiting to hear what Hitler would say on 26 September. Down in London, the Ambassador wrote to Arthur Krock: 'I have a few minutes before Hitler speaks … I'm feeling very blue myself today because I am starting to think about sending Rose and the children back to America and stay here alone, for how long God only knows. Maybe never see them again.'[5] Her father might have been making plans to send the children home, but Kick was determined to stay in Britain.

Hitler's speech from the Sportpalast in Berlin could leave no one in any doubt about his intentions. 'Shouting and shrieking in the worst state of excitement I've ever seen him in,' said one observer, 'he stated … that he would have his Sudetenland by October 1 – next Saturday … If [Czech President Edvard] Beneš doesn't hand it over to him, he will go to war.'[6]

Kick attended the Perth races on 28 September (the press reported that she had gone hatless). While she was there, the news came through that Chamberlain was making his final attempt to intercede with Hitler and taking a flight to Munich. Hitler had requested a conference with Chamberlain, Mussolini and the French Prime Minister, Edouard Daladier. The relief was enormous. Kick wrote in her diary: 'when the news came through that he was going to Munich, I have never seen such happiness'.

The next day, Kick left for London on the overnight train. She arrived in the morning 'to find Peace and everyone deliriously happy'. That night she went to the theatre with Billy and then on to the Café de Paris. It was the night of Chamberlain's return: 'so imagine the excitement'.[7] Nevertheless, she found it terrifying that trenches had been dug in front of the houses in preparation for fortification against air raids.

When the Prime Minister returned from Munich he was hailed as a hero. Chamberlain, Daladier and Mussolini had signed an agreement with Hitler, giving over the Sudetenland to Germany. Hitler and Chamberlain also signed a declaration that their two peoples desired never to go to war with one another again. Hitler told his Foreign Minister Joachim von Ribbentrop that the 'scrap of paper is of no significance whatsoever',[8] but Chamberlain waved the note to the crowds who had gathered outside 10 Downing Street and made his 'peace for our time' speech. He read from the declaration he had signed and added, 'my good friends, for the second time in our history, a British Prime Minister has returned from Germany bringing peace with honour. I believe it is peace for our time. We thank you from the bottom of our hearts. Go home and get a nice quiet sleep.'

Joseph Kennedy, always in favour of appeasement, was ecstatic. In his *Diplomatic Memoir* he recalled that 'the tone of the crowds had changed. They were cheering and laughing and waving at every passerby.' Smiling as he entered the Embassy he said, 'Well, boys, the war is off.'[9] President Roosevelt, though no fan of Chamberlain's, sent a congratulatory telegram.

Not everyone was happy. Duff Cooper, First Lord of the Admiralty, immediately resigned in angry protest: 'What do these words [of the Munich agreement] mean? ... Do they mean that [Hitler] will get away with this, as he has got away with everything else, without fighting, by well-timed bluff, bluster and blackmail?'[10] Winston Churchill, in the political wilderness and adamant against appeasement, denounced the Munich agreement in the House of Commons in powerful words:

> We have suffered a total and unmitigated defeat ... you will find that in a period of time which may be measured by years, but may be measured by months, Czechoslovakia will be engulfed in the Nazi régime. We are in the presence of a disaster of the first magnitude ... we have sustained a defeat without a war, the consequences of which will travel far with us along our road ... we have passed an awful milestone in our history, when the whole equilibrium of Europe has been deranged ... And do not suppose that this is the end. This is only the beginning of the reckoning. This is only the first sip, the first fore-

taste of a bitter cup which will be proffered to us year by year unless by a supreme recovery of moral health and martial vigour, we arise again and take our stand for freedom as in the olden time.[11]

Rose was present in the House and she was impressed by Churchill's oratorical skills, even though Nancy Astor heckled him: 'fascinating, delightful and easy to follow', she commented in her diary.[12] On 3 October, she took Kick to the final session of Parliament, where Churchill reiterated his warning: 'England has been offered a choice between war and shame. She has chosen shame, and will get war.'

Joe Kennedy definitely saw Munich as his triumph too and was given an opportunity to express his views in a speech he gave before the Navy League on Trafalgar Day on 19 October. Everyone was expecting a tribute to the great British spirit, which wasn't quite what happened. Rose, ever the politician's daughter, warned her husband that his speech was controversial and could be damaging: 'Have you thought how this would sound back home?' He didn't listen and went ahead. His message was that democracies and dictatorships 'have to live together in the same world, whether we like it or not'. At no point did the Ambassador speak of his own personal abhorrence of Hitler, which was an egregious mistake. The President was furious that Kennedy had implied publicly that America was pro-appeasement. He openly reprimanded him in a radio address. The American press attacked him vociferously. American citizens wrote to him denouncing him: 'It is unbelievable the way you have misrepresented your country … by suggesting that the United States of America should submit itself to Nazism! Shame, Shame, Shame!'[13]

For Joe Kennedy, it was the beginning of the end.

The Ambassador, terrified that war was imminent, had cabled Washington to find out 'what ships could be made available for the hordes of American citizens clamoring to get home'.[14] In the meantime he had his three youngest daughters fitted for gas masks at their school in Roehampton. He told Rose that none of the children wanted to go home to America, except for Teddy who wanted to have his tonsils out back home, so that he could 'drink all the coco-cola he wishes and all the ice cream'.[15] It was dawning on Joe that in coming to London he had made the biggest mistake of his life: 'I am still trying to think of the fellow who suggested my name as Ambassador to Great Britain. Shooting would be too good for him.'[16]

21

Chatsworth

Cavendo tutus: Safe through Caution.

Devonshire family motto

Billy chose his moment carefully to showcase the peculiar magic of Chatsworth. They went together on an early-October day, when the grounds were at their loveliest. Chatsworth nestles in a valley in the picturesque Peak District. The honey-coloured Palladian mansion sits on the east bank of the River Derwent. Below, a steep wooded hill and expansive parklands lead down to the Wye and Derwent valleys.

Billy's family had lived there since 1549, and each generation had improved the house and gardens. A sculpture gallery displayed the 6th Duke's collection of marble statues, the magnificent library held a valuable collection of early printed books, and there were wonderful paintings by Rembrandt, Van Dyck, Poussin, Reynolds and dozens of others. Old Master drawings were a particular speciality: the collection was the finest in the world other than that of the Queen at Windsor.[1] Then there were the collections of gold and silver plate, the exquisite porcelain, the gems and jewels.

Kick would have been shown the Mary Queen of Scots apartments, where the Catholic queen had once been held against her will as a prisoner of Elizabeth I, and the beautiful rosewood rosary beads made for Henry VIII and Catherine of Aragon. She saw portraits of Billy's ancestors, and heard about their long-standing links with religion and politics. She also learnt about the extraordinary Cavendish women: from beautiful Bess of Hardwick in the sixteenth century to the infamous Georgiana Duchess of Devonshire in the eighteenth century, who went canvassing in the streets for the Whig party and turned the drawing rooms of Chatsworth into a salon and a hub of political power. Portraits of Bess and Georgiana lined the walls. Georgiana, like Kick, was not a conventional beauty, but she had vitality and charisma and her passion was politics. She was a perfect role model for the Kennedy girl reared at a dinner table where politics were part of everyday conversation, and where the concept of public service was continually stressed.

The vast gardens of 105 acres included an Elizabethan Garden and lawns landscaped by the great eighteenth-century designer 'Capability' Brown. There was an Arboretum and a Pinetum. Billy and Kick walked for hours around the grounds in the October sunshine. The house glowed a deep, burning ochre in the low sunlight. She particularly loved the Willow Tree Fountain, an imitation tree, made of lead, which squirted water at unsuspecting guests.[2]

Kick knew what was at stake. Billy was showing her all that she would own and be part of if they were to think of a life together. Back at Churchdale Hall, the house near by where Billy and Andrew were brought up ('a small house but very comfortable'), she talked with Billy 'for hours every night'.[3] He told her that the family was planning to move into the great house at Christmas. He would take rooms at Chatsworth and planned to spend time working in the archives for his undergraduate thesis.

As her diary faithfully recorded, Kick spent much of her time that winter either with Billy or thinking about him. She sneaked into a church service in his old school, Eton: 'the most impressive thing in the world with all those boys singing for all their worth'. She undertook some charity volunteering work at a nursery school in the east end of London, though she struggled with the cockney accent: 'Have great difficulty in understanding anything they say. Imagine they have same with me.'[4] The very next morning, 'after getting away from our most industrious seat of learning' (the day nursery!), she set off for Newmarket with Janey. They missed two trains but arrived in time for the fourth race and then went over to Cambridge, where they had tea in Billy's rooms. He ordered them a taxi to the station, which bemused her since outside the College there were three cars belonging to his guests with the chauffeurs sitting idle. They missed the train, returned to College and ended up being driven back to London by one of the chauffeurs.

As the romance progressed, Kick and Billy's circle expressed their surprise at the union. They seemed like the strangest of couples. Billy was so tall and refined, so very English. Kick was a bundle of energy, lively and petite – so very Boston Irish. Billy was known to be languid and took things slowly. His mother told a story about how he once declined a cup of coffee because he couldn't be bothered to drink it.[5] Perhaps he inherited his lethargy from the 5th Duke of Devonshire, who once refused to get out of bed when a footman informed him that Chatsworth was on fire. 'It's your job to put it out,' he drawled and went back to sleep. Billy was punctilious about matters sartorial, and was always formally dressed in exquisite tweed and linen suits with a tie, even when he was at a picnic.[6] He was so fastidious that once, when forced to share a bedroom with his untidy brother Andrew, he drew a chalk line down the middle of the room to keep the disorder at bay. Kick was messy and had a habit of throwing her clothes in a heap on the floor for someone else to pick up and tidy away.

The Kennedy brothers, Joe and Jack, were puzzled by their sister's interest in Billy Hartington. He just didn't seem to be the right sort of man. He was such a contrast to Kick, who was so lively and so full of energy. He didn't appear to share the Kennedy sense of humour. Though he had a dry wit, Billy had a tendency to take himself seriously, which was largely due to his deep sense of duty and responsibility as the heir to Chatsworth. He was an intellectual, and it was a long-standing joke between Jack and Kick that though so clever she was no intellectual.

But Kick saw much in Billy to love and admire. Though earnest and thoughtful, he had not the slightest arrogance. He had a self-deprecating sense of humour, which she relished. His love of history and politics and his gentleness and kindness offered exactly the combination to attract her. She liked Billy precisely because he was a true gentleman and didn't push too hard. Her parents' marriage gave out such conflicting signs: she knew that her father was a philanderer and that her mother turned a blind eye. Kick, though sexually charismatic, was shy. But she also took a dim view of male promiscuity, intensified by the behaviour of her father and brothers. At a London dinner party a married man's affair was gossiped about. 'That's what all men do,' she said. 'You know that women can never trust them.'[7]

Other friends recalled that Kick disliked being touched. She particularly frowned on the sort of man who was known in social circles as NSIT (Not Safe in Taxis).

As for Billy, he was simply mesmerized by Kick, by her energy, her spirit, her dazzling smile and her funniness. Their friends remarked that in her company he seemed more confident and sure of himself. Billy had always worried that women were attracted to him because of his wealth and status, whereas Kick teased him about his aristocratic pedigree: 'Being a duke is something of a joke, isn't it? It's like being a cartoon character, no?' Billy would laugh out loud, and then catch himself and say, 'Well, no, not quite a joke.'

His sisters, Anne and Elizabeth Cavendish, who were devoted to Kick, thought that her teasing irreverence was just what he needed to stop taking himself so seriously. He needed to be laughed at a little: she was Elizabeth Bennet to his Darcy. She would call him at Chatsworth and when the butler answered the phone she would say: 'Hello, is the King perchance in his castle today?'

Billy's cousin Fiona Gore said: 'It was wonderful to see. Here was this lively American girl who through some odd circumstance had become the toast of the town, and she was paying all this attention to Billy. It gave him such confidence. She swept him off his oh-so-steady feet.'[8] For Debo Mitford, the 'pale English beauties' who fell at Billy's feet were no match for Kick's 'high spirits, funny American turn of phrase, so like her brother Jack's, and extreme good nature ... she was loved by everyone who knew her.'[9] She described Billy as 'a charmer of great intelligence. He had a great presence ... and he was loved by everybody ... He and Kick were about the two most popular people you could imagine.'[10]

Billy himself compared Kick to a plant whose roots had been pinched tightly to force luxuriant growth and bloom.[11] Once he had met her, there was no other girl for him. She was irresistible. As she was falling in love with the England that he embodied, he was falling in love with her as the incarnation of American confidence and hope. She allowed him to begin to believe in himself.

As the months went on Kick began to feel deeply for Billy. She started collecting newspaper clippings about him, pasting them into her London scrapbook. Again and again her diary records long talks into the night. Billy loved conversation and he was delighted that Kick was passionate

Leabharlanna Fhine Gall

about politics. But she kept the news of her romance from Rose, knowing that her mother would regard the religious difference as an absolute impediment.

Rose was determined that Kick should take some courses at King's College in London, but they were interested only in girls who wanted to pursue full-time degrees. Joe, meanwhile, was coming under increasing criticism from both the English press and President Roosevelt in Washington. In the weeks following the Munich pact, the President told Kennedy to urge Chamberlain to open discussions with Hitler on the Jewish refugee problem. Kennedy had no intention of doing so, believing that the priority was 'securing a viable, long-term peace agreement with the dictators, one that would include but not be centered on the rescue of the Jews'.[12]

The events of *Kristallnacht* (the Night of Broken Glass) on 9/10 November, in full public view, showed the lengths to which Hitler was prepared to go in his persecution of the Jews. *The Times* protested: 'No foreign propagandist bent upon blackening Germany before the world could outdo the tale of burnings and beatings, of blackguardly assaults on defenceless and innocent people, which disgraced that country yesterday.' The brutal excesses horrified the Ambassador: 'I am hopeful that something can be worked out, but this last drive on the Jews has really made the most ardent hopers for peace very sick at heart.'[13] No one was a more 'ardent hoper for peace' than he was, but his isolationist views and his vehement anti-war stance were becoming untenable.

Joe Jr wrote in his diary that his father was 'tired of his work. He claims that he would give it up in a minute if it wasn't for the benefits that Jack and I are getting out of it and the things Eunice will get when she comes out next Spring.'[14] Joe Sr saw the success that Kick had had that year and was determined that the same should happen with Eunice. What he and Rose still did not know was the extent to which Kick was leading a secret life with Billy. She was dining with him at Claridge's, the Savoy and her favourite nightclub, the Café de Paris. At the Savoy, she observed tartly: 'All Billy's relatives sitting about getting an eyeful.'

Kick was one of the few young people to be invited to a reception at Buckingham Palace in November in honour of King Carol of Romania and his son Prince Michael. Kick described King Carol as 'rather fat but very gallant'. Prince Michael was 'good-looking with dimples'. Rumours began to circulate about a romance between the Ambassador's daughter and Prince Michael. For Kick, this was a good cover for her increasingly serious relationship with Billy.

The family (except for Jack) was united for Thanksgiving. Then on 9 December Kick was invited to dine with the Devonshires in their London home to celebrate Billy's coming of age. This was a modest affair: his official party at Chatsworth had been postponed because of the death of his grandfather the previous May. Kick was given the place of honour on Billy's right-hand side: 'Rather frightening with the Dowager Duchess and Lord and Lady Harlech giving me dirty looks'. She was glad to escape with Billy to Quaglino's. Then they went on to the 400 Club where they encountered two of the Devonshires' footmen 'singing filthy songs'.[15]

On 10 December, Joe Kennedy returned to America. For the Christmas vacation he was planning an extended break in Palm Beach with his friends and Jack, who arrived with Lem Billings and Rip Horton in tow. Jack had taken a semester off from Harvard to serve as Joe's secretary in London, and would be returning to England after Christmas.

After a racing day at Sandown, Kick and her friends were involved in a tragic car accident when a cyclist was hit by David Ormsby Gore's car. The boy, a fifteen-year-old farmhand called Peter Baldock, died three days later. Kick was in another car with Billy and did not witness the accident. She later recorded that David was exonerated, since Baldock had no light on his bicycle. The accident did not seem to stop the party mood: there were 'Mad games on lawn' the next day.

Her relationship with Billy was growing ever deeper. At a party she sat downstairs with him and they talked intimately throughout the evening. She broke a dinner date with another man to go out with Billy and then discovered that one of her friends had told her date, who was upset by her duplicity.

Her mother now knew that she was seeing Billy, but believed that he was just another of her many suitors. Rose had attended a lunch in which she sat next to Billy's father, the Duke of Devonshire, noting in her diary: 'father of Billy Hartingare, one of Kathleen's beaux of the moment'.[16]

A week before Christmas, snow fell. Kick went Christmas shopping with Billy and then they headed to Ciro's for dinner. There they found Billy's father having dinner with his mistress, Lady Dufferin. The head waiter came to warn Billy. Kick wrote: 'it seemed so funny for father & son to be

Family: Joe Jr, Jack, Rosemary, Kick, Eunice, Pat, Bobby and baby Jean.

Kick on her sled, with Mrs Moore.

Studio portrait, aged seven.

Family summers on Cape Cod: swimming in Nantucket Sound (*above*);
the house by the sea in Hyannis Port (*below*).

The growing family in front of the Hyannis Port house, arranged as always in descending order of age (Joe Jr, Jack, Rosemary, Kick, Eunice, Pat, Bobby, Jean).

With Joseph P. Kennedy and Rose Fitzgerald Kennedy.

Sporty Kick: diving and tennis at Palm Beach.

At Palm Beach: in
a rickshaw with
Rosemary and,
right, the house on
Ocean Boulevard.

Life on the beach: with Jack, above, and with friends, below.

London: the Ambassador's residence at Prince's Gate, overlooking Hyde Park.

The Vatican: the family, with Switzers in attendance, dressed for their audience with the Pope (Rosemary, Kick, Jack, Joe Jr, Rose Fitzgerald Kennedy, Joseph P. Kennedy, Bobby, Eunice, Jean, Pat).

in the same place like that but it didn't phase Billy at all'.[17] The Duke came up to them and asked them if they had seen Billy's brother Andrew. Presumably because he was only eighteen, the Duke did not want Andrew to see him with his mistress.

Two days later Kick and her family departed for skiing in St Moritz.

22

St Moritz and Rome

Pray for me.

The Pope to the Kennedys

St Moritz was the winter playground for the rich and famous. Rose and eight of her children set off for Switzerland, stopping over in Paris. 'Whole carriage filled with Kennedys,' Kick wrote in her diary. The faithful Moores were also in attendance, though Eddie got into a quarrel with a porter, which Kick found hilarious, as the men were arguing in different languages. The family finally arrived at their luxurious hotel, Suvretta House, on Christmas Eve just in time to go to Midnight Mass in the small chapel near by.[1] The McDonnells were also joining the party.

Suvretta House stood among the beautiful mountains of the Ober-Engadine, with stunning views of Lakes Champfer and Silvaplana. The sense of peace and calm was interrupted by family mishaps: Bobby sprained his ankle, Joe Jr hurt his arm tackling one of the steepest slopes at high speed, and Teddy wrenched his knee. As ever, the press couldn't get enough of the photogenic Kennedy children on the slopes; they were the epitome of health and wholesomeness. On Boxing Day, Rose had a press call with ten photographers. Two days later, she received a telegram from her husband informing her that she had been chosen by the Associated Press as 'Outstanding woman of the year for selling the world the American family'. The Kennedy family's place in 'American cultural lore' was assured by several jokes about them in Cole Porter's new Broadway musical, *Leave It to Me*. The main character and his wife were loosely based on Joe and Rose. At one point in the play, the social-climbing wife asks her husband why she can't have nine children 'the way the Kennedys do'. The audience roared when her husband replied, 'Because I'm tired.' Jack had made a point of attending the opening night and told Rose: 'It's pretty funny and jokes about us get by far the biggest laughs, whatever that signifies.'[2] Kick, who adored the music of Cole Porter, was tickled.

On New Year's Eve, Rose and the children attended a dinner and a party. Kick noted in her diary that she and Joe Jr skived off mass.[3] As the children moved into adulthood, Rose no longer had the control over her brood that she had once had. Skipping mass was one way to rebel.

In the new year of 1939, Rose wrote to the President, thanking him for the opportunity he had given them. There were rumours circulating in the press that the Kennedys were going home, but Rose squashed them, showing herself the politician's daughter that she was in her response to the press: 'We like England and we just love the English. I've had some of the happiest times of my life in England. All the children like it too.'[4] None more than her daughter Kick, who was finally off the leash and having the time of her life.

Back in London, Rose began attending art lectures at the Wallace Collection: 'it won't be long before Papa will be paying for every picture in Christie's', Kick joked.[5] Joe Jr had joined the family in London and was teaching Kick to play bridge, which she found 'quite a struggle'. Rose, worn down by the 'fogs and gray skies and chill of the English winter', had left in early 1939 for one of her adventures, a quick shopping trip to Paris and then on to Cannes, Italy, Greece, Turkey, Palestine and Egypt.[6] To accompany her she had invited a woman called Marie Bruce, whom she had met at a lunch. Marie was recently widowed and was surprised that Rose had asked her along. She later recalled Rose's sensitivity and kindness: 'She is very perceptive to people's unhappiness and reacts to it, tries to help.' Marie thought that Joe Jr had inherited this quality, a 'humanity' that was 'astonishing'.[7] Marie Bruce would become extremely close to the family and would, in later times, be a surrogate mother for Kick.

As soon as Kick arrived back in England on 14 January she went off to dine with Billy. She continued to see him throughout January and February, their assignations rendered easier by her mother's absence. Kick was painfully aware that her father's conduct was drawing unfavourable comments from her English friends. In February, she wrote to Joe who was taking a long break in Palm Beach: 'People feel you rather let them down over here & caused a great deal of unnecessary jitters in America by your statement about "war is inevitable".'[8] She was torn between her adoration of her father and her deep loyalty to the English. She had always seen him as politically infallible, as someone whose opinions were always right and prescient. But now the Ambassador was becoming a liability to his children.

On Valentine's Day, Kick and Billy attended the wedding of his friend Derek Parker Bowles and Ann de Trafford, the eldest daughter of a millionaire racehorse owner. Billy would later be godfather to their first-born son, Andrew Parker Bowles. Rose wrote to tell her husband that 'Kick goes out with Billy', but she was still not taking the relationship seriously; as far as she was concerned, he was still just one of her many suitors. In the meantime, Kick was excited to hear the news that her beloved Jack was coming back to England.

Upon arrival, Jack wrote to the ever-faithful Lem: 'Met the King this morning at Court Levee. It takes place in the morning and you wear tails. The King stands and you go up and bow. Met Queen Mary and was at tea with Princess Elizabeth, with whom I made a great deal of time.' He also joked, 'Thursday night I'm going to Court in my new silk breeches which are cut to my crotch tightly and in which I look mighty attractive.'[9] He may have been his usual teasing self with Lem, but he was deeply concerned about the political situation in Europe. He spent hours with Kick's friends, debating the fallout of the Munich agreement. Billy and his circle were appalled by what they saw as Britain's betrayal of Czechoslovakia and Chamberlain's cowardice in not standing up to Hitler. One of Jack's heroes was Raymond Asquith, son of the then Prime Minister, who had died nobly in the trenches of the First World War. Jack argued that Asquith, a true soldier and gentleman, symbolized a Great Britain long gone, and that the British were now 'decadent'. Billy disagreed. He would never forget this conversation. Strikingly, Jack and Billy decided to make Munich a subject of their undergraduate studies.[10] Both young men had fathers they deeply admired; but both fathers had shown support for Chamberlain and the Munich agreement. This shared disparity drew them together.

Billy and Kick were inseparable that spring. Kick's London diary records the dances, the dinners, the races, and always Billy's name was top of the list, though she rarely allowed herself to write deeply about her feelings for him. Teasing him was the way to his heart. When he took her to a Spanish restaurant she threatened to steal an ashtray as a souvenir ('good old American custom'), but 'needless to say it embarrassed the Marquis no end'.[11] The most intimate times were when they talked deep into the night: 'long chat with Billy about life'.[12]

They had been spending time in the Café de Paris and the 400 Club, often in the company of Debo Mitford and Billy's younger brother Andrew. Billy and Andrew had a rather strained relationship. Andrew was still jealous that Kick had chosen Billy above him, but things got easier when Andrew began courting Debo, who shared Kick's gift of liveliness and spirit. Like Kick, Debo was one of a large brood, where teasing and jokes were very much the fabric of family life. Debo's eldest sister, the writer Nancy Mitford, teased her mercilessly: one of her nicknames for Debo was 'Nine' (supposedly Debo's mental age). This was the sort of joke that Kick loved.

Kick was intrigued by the Mitford sisters. Debo had had a difficult time in recent years. Her closest sister, Decca, a fully paid-up member of the Communist Party, had run away from home with her cousin Esmond Romilly (Winston Churchill's nephew and some said his illegitimate son). They had married and eloped to Spain, but then returned to Rotherhithe in south-east London. Two other sisters, Diana and Unity, were self-proclaimed Fascists. Diana, the exceptionally beautiful one, had left her wealthy and devoted husband Bryan Guinness to become the mistress of Oswald Mosley, the leader of the British Union of Fascists. They had married in Joseph Goebbels's drawing room, in the presence of Hitler, in 1936. Unity was obsessed with Hitler and stalked him in Berlin for months on end, before becoming a close friend. She was living in Germany, and had courted huge controversy because of her relationship with Hitler.

Unity and Diana fascinated Kick. Kick was conscious of how much Lady Redesdale, the girls' mother, monitored Debo's movements, insisting that she be chaperoned. Kick observed wryly: 'What about Unity I ask myself.'[13]

The Cavendish brothers and their lively, outspoken girlfriends became a close foursome. Kick experimented with alcohol, without the knowledge of her abstemious parents. The Cavendish boys had discovered a ruse to get free drinks at the expense of their father. The Duke would ask the waiters to label his drinks bottle with the name of a fish beginning with H (for Hartington, his own courtesy title until the previous May), so his sons would ask the waiters if there was a bottle belonging to 'Mr Hake or Herring or Halibut'.[14]

In early March, Kick was summoned to Rome to attend the coronation of the new Pope. Rose was still travelling in Egypt when she heard the news that Pope Pius XI had died. As the white smoke snaked out of the chimney of the Sistine Chapel heralding that a new Pope had been chosen, Rose heard that it was to be her friend Cardinal Eugenio Pacelli. A message arrived that Joe was to represent the United States at the inauguration. Rose, in a state of great excitement, headed for Italy, where the rest of the family were gathering. The children came in a private railway car, with the exception of Joe Jr, who was witnessing the last days of the civil war in Spain.

On 12 March it was a beautiful sunny morning in Rome. At 6 a.m. four cars arrived to take the family to St Peter's. The girls were dressed modestly, with veils covering their heads. The family headed into the basilica and were seated opposite the new Pope's throne, where mass would be said. The Ambassador noticed Mussolini's son-in-law (and Foreign Minister) Count Ciano marching through the church 'giving [the] Fascist salute and bowing and smiling' and 'was convinced he was a swell-headed Muggo' (the latter presumably being a slang term for a follower of Mussolini).[15] Ciano was angry that his seat was occupied by a Kennedy child. After mass, they went outside and saw the Pope crowned in front of the enormous crowd.

The following day the family had a private audience with the new pontiff. They were photographed outside the Vatican. Rose wore a long black dress and veil. Kick was in a beautiful knee-length black dress with a long black veil. She wore her trademark single strand of pearls. The boys were in suits.

The children were carrying medals to be blessed by the Pope for their numerous friends. They came in and each genuflected and kissed the Pope's ring. The Pope chatted to the family and reminded Teddy of when he had met him in Bronxville and Teddy had played with his cross. He gave the little boy some rosary beads, then walked over to a table and reached for a white box containing another string of beads, which he gave to Rose. He gave rosary beads in white casings to all of the children and they all knelt before him while he blessed them and said, 'Pray for me.' They were so overawed that they forgot to ask the Pope to bless their medals, so they sent someone back to have them blessed.

Afterwards, they went to the Sistine Chapel and saw the works of Michelangelo and Raphael. They were shown the special room where all the Cardinals were locked up for the election of the Pope. Joe noted in his diary, 'we then had our pictures taken and went home to lunch after the most thrilling day of our lives'.[16]

Later in the afternoon, the family went for tea at Castel Gandolfo, the Pope's private summer residence 20 miles outside Rome, perched above Lake Albano. Visitors were rarely allowed in its hallowed walls, so it was yet another honour for the Kennedys. They walked around the formal gardens and parterres. Inside the house, the Ambassador was amused to find a tray with Gordon's gin and Canadian Club whisky. Jack Kennedy got up to kiss a Cardinal's ring, while a photographer snapped away. He joked that his Protestant girlfriend's father would be mad if he ever saw the picture.[17] If Kick were thinking at this moment about her own Protestant boyfriend, Lord Hartington, she would have been very aware of the gulf that separated them.

Kick wrote a long article for the League of Catholic Women, an American organization that would give great support to the work of the Red Cross during the war. Entitled 'Impressions of the Coronation of Pope Pius XII', this was Kick's first piece of published journalism. She revealed herself to be an extremely able writer: 'All here is movement and color ... As the procession advances down the aisle the singing of the Sistine Chapel is drowned in the crescendo of cheering. There is but one thought and that is for the pale and wan figure, who, with slow, gentle movement, lifts his hand in the sign of the Cross.'[18] Kick was beginning to establish herself as a key figure in American Catholic circles. She was the daughter of His Excellency the American Ambassador to the Court of St James's. She had a lot to live up to. And now she was taking her first steps as a journalist.

While they were in Rome, German troops crossed the Czech border and marched into Prague. The shock reverberated around Europe. Hitler had flagrantly broken the Munich agreement, and Chamberlain's trust had proved misplaced. War now seemed inevitable.

23

The Gathering Storm

These Catholic girls are a menace!

Lord Richard Cavendish

Kick was embarrassed by her father's increasingly erratic behaviour. She threw a supper party at Prince's Gate for her circle. Billy and David Ormsby Gore were guests of honour, and Jack had returned from travelling in Europe. When supper was over, Joe invited the party to his screening room, where he had a surprise film set up for the young people. To Kick's mortification, Joe showed a film of the Great War, of young men being blown up in trench warfare. The Ambassador jumped up in front of the screen with the horrific images behind him and yelled: 'That's what you'll look like if you go to war with Germany.'[1]

Kick whispered to Billy, 'You mustn't pay any attention to him. He just doesn't understand the English as I do.' She knew that Billy had already volunteered for the Coldstream Guards. They were the oldest regiment in continuous active service in the British Army, dating back to the time of Oliver Cromwell. For Billy, it was a matter of honour and duty to volunteer, even though the government was shortly to introduce conscription. Most of Billy's friends had followed suit.

The young men were incensed by the Ambassador's outburst. And the women were also infuriated. Kick's friend Katharine Ormsby Gore had spent time in Vienna after the Nazis' takeover and had personal experience of their atrocities. A kindly Jewish doctor in the same apartment block had set her broken foot, and one morning she awoke to find he had 'disappeared' in the middle of the night, the door blowing in the wind. She insisted on repeating her story to anyone who would listen: 'I was a terrible bore on the subject.'[2] During Joe Kennedy's outburst, Jack refused to comment or take sides. He was biding his time, taking everything in.

In May 1939, the Ambassador wrote a letter to the editor of the *Saturday Evening Post* in which he declared that 'the best interests of the United States are served by peace in Europe and not by war … I have nine children and I have young friends, and I regard them all as my hostages for my devotion to the interests of the United States, first, last and always.'[3] The Ambassador's problem was that he just couldn't see beyond his family. He was a fiercely protective father, and all he could think of was his own sons being led like lambs to the slaughter. Many years later, Jack's wife, Jackie, cut to the quick of her father-in-law's psychology. 'Why Papa, you're all black and white', she told him.[4] Joe knew that the war would destroy much that he had built for his family with his own determination and energy, and he was right. But he was wrong about England being finished, and there was no one more vocal about England's true grit than Kick.

Billy's action in volunteering for the war was focusing Kick's mind on their future together. In their numerous long talks into the night, he told her about his new rooms in Chatsworth and the undergraduate thesis he was writing on the Whig oligarchy in the eighteenth century and the part his own ancestors had played in the history of his nation. He had been reading the letters of Georgiana, Duchess of Devonshire.[5]

At a time when everything was changing so rapidly, Billy felt that the new world had much to teach the old world and a Cavendish–Kennedy alliance would be symbolic of Anglo-American amity. Their children would, he imagined, one day be part of a new and better international future. He was deadly serious about marrying Kick, but for now the subject of religious differences was carefully avoided. David Ormsby Gore's romance with the Catholic Sissy Lloyd Thomas was the talk of London, leading Lord Richard Cavendish, a great-uncle of Billy's, to proclaim that 'These Catholic girls are a menace!'[6]

The King and Queen were to undertake a PR visit to America and, before they left in early May, Rose and Joe threw a dinner party for them at Prince's Gate. This was Rose's finest hour, and she was determined that it would be perfect. Eschewing the conventional French cuisine so beloved by the English upper class, she ordered shad roe from Baltimore, ham from Virginia and pickled peaches from Georgia, all flown in especially. As a final American touch she put American strawberry shortcake on the menu. Orchids and strawberries were imported from Paris.

Much to everyone's amusement, all of the Kennedy children attended the supper, the six younger ones on a small table in the dining room. It was a huge success. The Kennedys had triumphed again, and it was mainly due to Rose and the children. Rose wore a turquoise satin dress, while the Queen was in an exquisite pink satin gown.[7] After dinner, they watched the movie about a much loved schoolmaster, *Goodbye, Mr Chips*. Rose noticed that the Queen had a little weep.[8]

Later that week, Rose and Joe went to Lady Astor's dinner at her London townhouse, where they met the Duke of Devonshire, Billy's father, who told her that he was going to make a tour of Africa. After dinner, Kick and her friends arrived for the dancing. Rose left at 1.30, leaving Kick still dancing with Billy.

Kick made the most of her freedom when her mother returned to America in May. In Rose's absence, Kick took over as sister Eunice's chaperone while she prepared for her Season. The sisters introduced an innovation at an Embassy tea party by having the tea and cakes at intimate tables, rather than at the customary single long one.

On 9 June, Kick gave her first public speech. It was at the American Women's Club, and she proved herself to be an able substitute for her parents. Her words were witty and self-deprecating: 'I rather wish that my Father were here to "deputize" for me. He always has things to talk about – at least nine familiar – subjects'. Urging people to open their purses, she joked: 'You're going to have fun – and pay for it!'

Rose and Joe were back in time for Eunice's debut party. Described as a 'small dance', it was a far cry from Kick's debut the previous year, but still a great success. Billy was Kick's guest and he spent the whole dinner telling Rose how wonderful her daughter was. They danced the 'Big Apple', the Duchess of Northumberland singling out Jack Kennedy. Rose was a little shocked by the 'Big Apple', which had its origins in an African-American ring dance. But Eunice was thrilled with the event: 'I had achieved the aim of every young girl – that of being presented at the Court of St James's – the world's greatest empire – The Empire upon which the sun never sets.'[9]

This was Kick's sentiment, too, but it certainly wasn't the Ambassador's, who believed that England was all washed up, and that it would certainly lose if it went to war with Germany. Nancy Astor was preparing Cliveden as a military hospital. The world was inching closer and closer to war, and yet the parties went on.

The Kennedys had given a Fourth of July garden party at Prince's Gate, and that evening the family attended a ball, where Joe was alarmed to discover the gossip that Kick had been seen at the 400 Club. He took her aside, and reprimanded her. Rose also had her say, noting in her diary her spirited daughter's defence, in which Kick changed the subject from moral standards to money: 'When I told her about the high standard we had in the United States she immediately rejoined with the sentence "but that in having this high standard of living for a few people, we have trodden a lot of others under foot in this country and in other countries".'[10] Kick Kennedy was never one for toeing the party line.

24

The Last Hurrah

In this brilliant scene at Blenheim, I sensed the end of an era.
Duchess of Marlborough[1]

The middle-aged man sat at a table in the corner of the spectacular ball-room. One of the guests, a young man, threw a contemptuous glance at the 'warmonger' Winston Churchill deep in conversation with Anthony Eden: 'Oh look at that poor old has-been. My father says he's still a potential trouble-maker, but he won't get any public life now.'[2] Young Jack Kennedy thought otherwise. He revered Churchill, was an avid reader of his books and often went to Westminster to hear his speeches. Jack was thrilled to see Churchill in person and in intimate surroundings.

It was the last, great party before the war, and it took place on 7 July 1939 in one of England's most magnificent stately homes, Blenheim Palace in Oxfordshire. Jack and Kick were invited to celebrate the eighteenth birthday of the Duke of Marlborough's daughter, Sarah, but the thrill for the family was that seventeen-year-old Eunice had also been invited for the weekend celebrations.[3] She left a long, detailed account of Blenheim: 'There is something very English about the way it retires from the rest of the world behind a grey stone wall and a gateway which alone gives indication of its character. It is no ordinary country house; it is a national monument.'[4] Jack told Lem it was nearly as big as Versailles.

A thousand guests danced in the golden palace lit by hundreds of lamps; outside, the terrace and lake were floodlit in colours of blue and green, and Japanese lanterns hung in the trees. Don Carlos and his Strolling Players, incongruously dressed in Tyrolean costumes, walked the grounds singing. For many, it was the end of an era. Henry 'Chips' Channon MP wrote in his diary, 'I have seen much, travelled far and am accustomed to splendour, but there has never been anything like tonight.'[5]

Inside, the library had been transformed into a magnificent 'ballroom of flowers', with lilies, pink and white hydrangeas, gloxinias and malmaisons. 'Huge sparkling chandeliers sent sparkling light into every corner of the room.'[6] The ladies wore 'bouffant' gowns, tiaras and jewels. There were footmen in knee breeches and powdered wigs, carrying trays of champagne. The debs draped their fur stoles around the marble statues that lined the palace. In the morning they discovered that thieves had apparently sneaked into the palace and stolen them.

The servants watched as royalty and aristocracy arrived, filing into the banqueting room according to rank. Later in the evening, a ten-course dinner was served. Eunice recalled appetizers, soup, fish, game, greens, dessert, sweets, savoury and side dishes: 'How does the English youth remain so slim?' she joked. Chips Channon wrote of 'the 'rivers of champagne'.

Kick's favourite, Ambrose and his Band, played the latest songs: 'Dancing Cheek to Cheek', 'Night and Day', 'It Had to be You', 'Begin the Beguine', 'Moonlight Serenade'. The guests danced all night, both in the ballroom and on an open-air dance floor built on the terrace overlooking the illuminated lake. At dawn, hotdogs and coffee were served.

The next day there was an experimental 'blackout', and then the guests played hide and seek. Chips Channon wondered whether they would ever see the like again. Jack Kennedy, too, sensed that it was the end of an era. He had befriended Tony Loughborough, the heir to the 5th Earl of Rosslyn. Tony's father had committed suicide when his son was just twelve, and Joe Kennedy had taken him under his wing. Tony fell desperately in love with Kick, although she clearly had eyes for no one but Billy. While their friends were forming serious relationships with the threat of war looming, Jack and Tony formed an alliance they called 'Ross Kennedy', which involved seducing as many women as they could find. Jack wrote to Lem: 'it's really too bad you're not here as it's all darn good fun – never had a better time.'[7]

The partying in the summer of 1939 had an even greater intensity than the Season of 1938, no doubt because everyone knew that war was inevitable. Kick's friends constantly discussed the situation in Europe.[8] That summer, one of her old flames, Jack's Harvard chum the athletic Torbert Macdonald, came to stay. He was still in love with Kick and was keen to impress. He, Jack and Kick attended the athletics meeting at White City in west London where he was sure he would triumph: 'I tried very hard because I was showing off to Kick and everybody … but finished a close third.'[9] He was devastated, and felt that she had lost interest in him. It was difficult for an all-American boy to compete with Lord Hartington.

At the end of July, Kick left London for Spain with young Joe and their friend Hugh Fraser, younger son of the 14th Lord Lovat and a prominent Roman Catholic who had a commission in the army. It was her first taste of the damage war could wreak. She was in a country run mercilessly by General Franco's autocratic military regime with a history of terrible war crimes. She had a worthy guide in Joe, who had been an eyewitness to the siege of Madrid. He had been deeply shocked by the poverty, death and devastation he had witnessed as a result of the civil war. Kick was impressed by the admiration in which her brother was held: 'I remember thinking then, of how brave Joe was when different Spaniards told me of how he, the only American there, used to walk about the streets during the horrible, bloody days of the siege of Madrid.'[10]

Kick met General Moscardó, who had held the fort of Alcázar for three months. She was told the story of how on 23 July 1936 he had picked up the telephone within the Alcázar to hear that Republican forces had kidnapped his sixteen-year-old son, Luis. The boy spoke up proudly, 'Father, if you surrender your command to the enemies of Spain in order to save my life, I shall disown you and never more acknowledge you as my blood!' His father replied, 'Die like a Spaniard, my son!' The story went that enraged Communists then shot Luis in the head.[11] In the Alcázar today, the telephone remains on display. It became clear to Kick that there had been horrible brutalities on both sides during the civil war.

At the beach of San Sebastián, Kick wore a long, modest bathing suit, as now strictly required by law, but Joe got into trouble for going bare-chested. Another family member was also getting into trouble in Fascist Europe. Jack went driving through Nazi Germany in the company of David Ormsby Gore and Torby Macdonald. Ambassador Kennedy had warned the young men to 'stay out of trouble'. He told them that the Germans were tough and paid no attention to laws and rules: 'if anything happened, just back away'.[12] Stopping the car (with British licence plates) to inspect a Nazi monument, they were attacked with stones and bricks by Nazi stormtroopers. Jack told Torby: 'You know, how can we avoid having a world war if this is the way these people feel?'[13] To his father, he wrote from Munich: 'The German people are being whipped into a fierce hatred of the British.'[14]

The boys made their way to France, as Joe and Kick came up from Spain to Cannes to meet the rest of the family for their summer vacation. The residence was the Domaine de Ranguin, which reputedly had the 'finest rose garden on the Riviera'. The family sailed, sunbathed and played golf.

Marlene Dietrich was staying again at the Hôtel du Cap. She called the Ambassador 'Papa Joe' and asked for advice about her career. That summer, she took up with a lesbian cross-dressed heiress who appeared suddenly on a magnificent three-masted schooner, dressed as a pirate. The pirate rowed ashore and lunched at the Eden Roc. Dietrich was enchanted. So for once there was a summer when Joe Kennedy could concentrate more on his family.

Kick's English friend Janey Kenyon-Slaney was her guest at Cannes. Jack had a huge crush on Janey, but she didn't return his affection, causing ever-loyal Kick to complain, 'I can't think why you're not being nicer to Jack.' Torby noted that Rose was keeping Kick 'exiled' in France, away from Billy. She was desperate to return to England for Billy's big delayed birthday party at Chatsworth, but Rose forbade her to attend. Kick did not dare oppose her mother's wishes, but privately she was furious at being left out of the celebrations.

It was a lavish affair involving 2,800 guests over a period of three days. There was a dinner and a ball, and a garden tea party with a circus, showing performing horses and dogs, and live music by Billy's regiment, the Coldstream Guards. As was the tradition, Billy gave presents to the staff and tenants, all 3,000 of them. By the end of the weekend, the Duchess had to put her arm in a sling because she had shaken so many hands. Kick had missed one of the most important days of Billy's life, though she cut out numerous clippings of the great event and pasted them into her scrapbook. She noted that Irene Haig, her rival, was there, looking 'very smart in coat and skirt and new-style felt hat with shovel brim'. Billy was, as always, dressed impeccably in a beautifully cut suit, handsome and poised. His brother Andrew later recalled that the atmosphere of the party 'had something of the Duchess of Richmond's ball before the battle of Waterloo. We sensed it was the closing of an age.'[15]

On the very day of the party, August 15, a story was published in the *Boston Globe* under the headline 'Kennedy Girl May Wed Peer'. A denial was issued, but Billy and Kick had indeed begun talking about marriage. Nevertheless, in France she threw herself into the family holiday. The *Tatler* published a two-page spread about the family in August, with photographs of them linking arms and flashing the Kennedy smile. It was the last holiday they would ever have together as a family in Europe.

Joe and Jack headed back to Germany, where young Joe bumped into Debo's sister Unity, just two weeks before she put a revolver to her head and pulled the trigger. He described her as 'one of the most unusual women I have ever met ... thinks only of the Führer and his work. She looked at me rather funnily when I called him Hitler, as if I was taking his name in vain.' Unity told him that she felt sorry for the Jews, 'but you had to get rid of them'. She said that Hitler greatly admired the British and would do them no harm 'unless they forced his hand'. He ended his notes on Unity: 'She is the most fervent Nazi imaginable, and is probably in love with Hitler.'[16]

On 21 August, on the news from Europe of Germany's imminent invasion of Poland, the Ambassador flew back to England. Once home, Chamberlain informed him that 'I have done everything that I can think of and it seems as if all my work has come to naught.'[17] Back in the South of France, the news that the war was coming ran through the hotel like a 'flash fire'. Guests began to pack up and leave.

Joe called Rose, telling her that they must leave France immediately. The children were summoned from the beach. Kick and Janey were still wearing their tennis clothes and were told to head for the station. Their luggage would follow them later.

On 24 August, the Ambassador issued a press release urging Americans to leave England: 'Accommodations are now available on most vessels. The same may not be true in another day or two.'[18]

The following day, Joe saw Chamberlain, whom he described as 'a broken man'. Arrangements were made for Rose and the children to be evacuated to Wall Hall Abbey in rural Hertfordshire. Gas masks were issued and Anderson air-raid shelters assembled. These were makeshift structures of corrugated iron half buried in the back garden.

Germany invaded Poland on 1 September. Billy Cavendish was ordered to his regiment the next day. The Ambassador was devastated by the invasion. He called the President and told him it was the end of the world, the end of everything.

25

'This Country is at War with Germany'

3 September 1939.

Under a clear blue sky on an early-autumn Sunday, three sombre-looking adults walked together from the American Embassy to Westminster. They were used to the lens of the photographers forever seeking a photograph of the handsome, smiling Kennedys, but there were few smiles today. Young Joe and Jack were wearing suits and ties. Kick was wearing an elegant and demure black dress trimmed with white, her trademark pearls, white gloves and wide-brimmed hat. She looked impeccably English. She had come a long way from the all-American girl in bobbysocks and sweater of two years before. They noticed people in the streets carrying gas masks.

Shortly after eleven o'clock their father, sitting in his office in the Embassy, had listened to Prime Minister Chamberlain speaking on the radio:

I am speaking to you from the cabinet room at 10 Downing Street. This morning the British ambassador in Berlin handed the German government a final note stating that unless we heard from them by 11 o'clock that they were prepared at once to withdraw their troops from Poland, a state of war would exist between us. I have to tell you now that no such undertaking has been received, and that consequently this country is at war with Germany.

As soon as the broadcast had finished, Joe telephoned Chamberlain and was surprised to find that he was immediately put through. The Prime Minister told the Ambassador: 'We did the best we could but it looks as though we have failed.'[1] At 11.20 a.m. Joe issued a Diplomatic Dispatch: 'The Prime Minister has just broadcast that no undertaking having been received from the German Government to withdraw its troops from Poland, Great Britain is in consequence at war with Germany. Kennedy.'[2]

Less than an hour later, Jack, Kick and Joe Jr stood in the Strangers' Gallery in the House of Commons as the Prime Minister made what Rose described as his 'heart-broken, heart-breaking speech'. Chamberlain was crushed by the realization that his policy of appeasement had failed: 'This is a sad day for all of us, and to none is it sadder than to me. Everything I have worked for, everything I have hoped for, everything I have believed in during my public life has crashed into ruins.' Joe Kennedy echoed these words in his diary that night: 'I almost cried. I had participated very closely in this struggle and I saw my hopes crash too.'[3]

But the three young adults were more impressed by backbencher Churchill, who evoked loud cheers with his impassioned oratory: 'Outside, the storms of war may blow and the lands be lashed with the fury of its gales, but in our hearts this Sunday morning there is peace ... our consciences are at rest.' Jack and Kick were spellbound by Churchill's speech: 'This is not a question of fighting for Danzig or fighting for Poland. We are fighting to save the whole world from the pestilence of Nazi tyranny and in defence of what is sacred to man.'[4]

Almost immediately an air-raid siren went off, sending panic through the crowds who had gathered outside the Embassy. The Ambassador rushed out to find Rose, Kick, Joe and Jack returning from Parliament on foot. He told them to go immediately to an air-raid shelter in the basement of the couturier Molyneux. The incongruity was not lost on fashion-conscious Rose: 'I thought later, what an ironic way for a woman to build her war experiences.'[5] Joe walked over to Molyneux's to cheer them up and found them in good shape.[6] Meanwhile, panicky Americans rushed into the Embassy, demanding to know when the next boat was going.

Chamberlain's War Cabinet went into session. That afternoon, Parliament passed the National Service (Armed Forces) Bill which provided that men between the ages of eighteen and forty-one were liable to be called up. At 6 p.m. sharp, families clustered around their wirelesses once more as King George VI broadcast to the British Empire on the BBC, lamenting that – for the second time in the lives of most – they were at war.

That night Kick gathered her English friends to talk about the war. There was a great sense of energy and excitement. Chatsworth was being turned into a boarding school for girls, the paintings, antiques and treasures all carefully packed away. All of Kick's friends were joining up or getting involved in the war effort in some way, the women offering their services in factories or hospitals.

Kick held a farewell dinner at Prince's Gate for the young men about to go to war, and once again her father embarrassed his children by claiming that England would be 'badly thrashed'. For the young men like Billy in uniform, his remarks were offensive. Joe simply did not understand why Billy and his friends felt so strongly about the humiliating Munich pact, and why they would fight to the death. Even Jack misunderstood the British sense of honour and principle. He would later claim that it was 'fear, violent fear' that had motivated the British.[7] He was wrong. Only Kick understood, because she knew through her long talks with Billy of his supreme sense of duty and principle.

Kick, feeling that her destiny was in England, begged to stay. Her father refused. He didn't care that he would be criticized for sending the family back to safety while London was bombed. Rose was secretly relieved that Kick would be removed from her romance with Billy.

The plan was that the Ambassador would stay in England alone with Rosemary, who was doing so well at her Montessori school. Joe, terrified by the thought that his family could be torpedoed on the boat back to America, arranged for them to return in batches. Kick was to return on the *Washington* with her mother, Eunice and Bobby. In the meantime, Kick said her goodbyes to her beloved friends. There was a strong possibility that she might never see Billy Hartington again.

The Kennedys planned their final weekend in London. There was only one outsider present, Tom Egerton, who remembered the occasion vividly: 'They were all so gay and they never stopped talking, chatting away, sometimes even over the top of one another.' But he also remembered Kick's misery.[8]

Later in September Kick wrote an account called 'Lamps in a Blackout', probably intended for publication.[9] The piece is a first-hand narrative of experiencing the blackout in that first month of the so-called 'Phoney War'.

It begins lyrically: 'Blackout, blackout. England must be blacked out, and on the night of September 19, issuing her final defense commands, England lay in dark silence while smiling moon and twinkling stars shone over her like lights of an anticipated victory'.[10] Then it becomes more personal: 'It is an eerie experience walking through a darkened London. You literally feel your way, and with groping finger make sudden contact with a lamp post against which leans a steel helmeted figure with gas mask slung at his side'. She takes the reader with her as she makes her solitary journey around the city's deserted streets:

> You pause to watch the few cars, which with blackened lamps, move through the streets. With but a glimmer you trace their ghostly progress … Gone are the gaily-lit hotels and nightclubs; now in their place are sombre buildings surrounded by sand-bags. You wander through Kensington Garden in search of beauty and solitude and find only trenches and groups of ghostly figures working sound [-detector] machines and searchlights to locate the enemy.[11]

On the first night of the blackout, it was all excitement and mistakes. Little Teddy ripped the curtain and within three minutes air-raid wardens were complaining of 'great streaks of light shining through the window'. Accidents occurred: Jean slipped and sprained her ankle; Joe Jr came home with a very swollen black eye, the result of walking into a lamppost. The next morning they heard news of accidents, people bumping into trees, tripping on the kerb, being hit by cars, broken legs, even deaths. 'Thus, now one hears tap, tap, tap, not of machine guns, but of umbrellas and canes as Londoners feel their way homeward, for it is a perilous task.'

The narrative then zooms into her bedroom, where she lies dreaming of 'peace and the bright lights of New York', only to be awakened from her reverie by a series of 'piercing blasts that shook me from my bed'. She grabs her gas mask, offers her soul to God and runs downstairs to meet the rest of the family. They wait for the servants, help one another with gas masks and run for the air-raid shelter: 'within fifteen minutes the streets were cleared of men, women, children and animals'. She notes the 'unlovely women' in curl-papers and face cream, a woman upset that she had to leave her dog, another who promises to enter a convent if she is spared ('I wonder if she did'). Then after forty minutes, the all-clear sounds and it is back to bed, everyone muttering a prayer of thanks.

Through all the drama, there seems to be no fear. And Kick, in love with England and her English lord, delivers her swansong to London: 'But yet the moon shines through and one can see new beauties in the silent, deserted city of London. It is a new London, a London that looks like Barcelona before the bombs fell.'[12]

26

The Personality Kids

It all seems like a beautiful dream.

Kick Kennedy

The SS *Washington* was packed with Americans returning home to safety. The liner was loaded with 1,756 passengers, beds pushed into every available space.[1] Kick wrote to her father from the liner: 'I can't get excited about landing, but I suppose it will come when we sight that Statue of Liberty.'[2] She made a rare dig at her adored father when she joked, 'Everybody said they didn't think the Germans would torpedo this boat with us on board,' letting him know that she was acutely aware of his public reputation as an appeaser.

Returning home to Bronxville was a shock to the system. The house had not changed, but Kick had: 'it was like returning to a house you lived in as a child and being surprised at how shabby everything suddenly seems'.[3] But she soon adapted to American social life, visiting the World's Fair twice and taking up again with Peter Grace. She went to a polo match with him and to the theatre. Everything was as it always had been, but she now felt detached.

Her friends noticed the change in her. Nancy Tenney was surprised to see her using English expressions and calling people 'Darling'. One weekend when she was staying overnight with Nancy, Kick left her shoes outside the bedroom door, expecting them to be polished.[4] She knew that her friends thought she had changed, but she couldn't get England out of her mind. She wrote to her father, telling him that her life there now seemed 'like a beautiful dream': 'Thanks a lot Daddy for giving me one of the greatest experiences anyone could ever have had. I know it will have great effect on everything I do from here on in.'[5]

Kick tried to get into the prestigious Sarah Lawrence College, but was not accepted, despite the fame of her family, so she decided to attend Finch College on Manhattan's Upper East Side. It was little more than a finishing school: 'It is a junior college and one gets a diploma, which is something,' she wrote to her father. The only thing in its favour was its location.

Kick socialized with her brothers Jack and Joe and, as usual, their male friends flocked around her in what Jack began to call her 'boys club'. Peter Grace, Zeke Coleman, George Mead, Lem Billings, Torby Macdonald: they all loved her company as they frequented the Stork Club and the Persian Room at the Plaza Hotel. The Kennedy trio got a new nickname: the 'personality kids'.[6]

Kick loved big-band music. Ambrose and his Band had been her favourite in London, and now she danced to Benny Goodman, Artie Shaw and the Dorsey Brothers. She was seen on casual dates with Jack's friend George Mead and the press even speculated that she was engaged to Winthrop Rockefeller.[7] Winthrop had been spotted buying her an expensive ski jacket for Christmas, and the gossip columnists went wild at the thought of a Kennedy–Rockefeller union.

At one point, Jack flew into a fury with her for flirting with his friends, and railed at her for her 'insincerity'. 'Gosh Kid, that's too close to a knuckle,' she replied, twirling her hair round her finger, and just carried on.[8] The truth was that her heart was in England and with Billy. Nancy Astor wrote to her to say that the Cavendish brothers were bemoaning her absence. Kick wrote to her friends in London and to her father for news of the expected bombing and invasion, but still nothing was happening as the Phoney War stretched out. The press joked that Hitler was trying to bore the British into peace.

Joe, desperately missing the family and dependent upon family letters and a precious brief weekly phone call, only had one daughter left in England for company. Rose and Joe were celebrating twenty-five years of marriage and he wrote her a loving, affectionate letter: 'to say they have been great years is understatement. They've been the happy years the poets write about. I would like to live every day of them over with you again, but wouldn't want to live one more without you.'[9]

Rose threw herself back into Bronxville life, and began making speeches for women's groups about her life in England. She recalled one day encountering some hostility from a Boston group of predominantly Irish Catholics when she said, 'Now, of course, you're all familiar with Windsor Castle.' She was careful not to make that mistake again.[10]

While Rose raved about her time in London, Joe remained adamant that England was a lost cause. He wrote to the President in September, 'I personally am convinced that, win or lose, England will never be the England that she was and no one can help her to be.'[11] England didn't stand a 'Chinaman's chance'. The President was disgusted by Joe's defeatism, but still wanted him in England out of the way.[12]

Jack was now back at Harvard, and was romantically interested in Kick's friend Charlotte McDonnell. He wrote to his father that it was his 'first taste of a Catholic girl so will be interested to see how it goes'.[13] He was completing his thesis on 'England's Foreign Policy since 1931'; in an interview recorded after his death, Rose suggested that his decision to choose this subject was shaped by his affinity for the British and his exposure to government circles in England's great homes. It was Kick who had facilitated all this, since it was through her friends that Jack had been given access to English high society.

Joe managed to get home for Christmas, and the family, as ever, headed off to Palm Beach. Kick was delighted to see her father and hear the news about London and her friends. He was still refusing to allow her to return to England. He told Jack that going back would undo all of her happy memories. She would have to be content with sending jazz records and presents when he returned to London in the new year.

27

Operation Ariel

Daddy ... Is Billy all right?

Kick Kennedy

In late February 1940, the Ambassador was recalled to London, where he took up residence in a mansion outside Windsor called St Leonard's. The English press were less than enamoured by his extended leave of absence in time of war. He had spent the first two months of the year in Palm Beach recuperating from his recurring stomach ailments. Once back, in letters home, he tried to explain his unpopularity amongst the British: 'The things they say about me from the fact that I've sent my family home because they were afraid, to the fact that I live in the country because I am afraid of being bombed etc etc. All rotten stuff but all the favorite dinner parties at Mayfair go right to work hauling the US Ambassador down. It's for that reason it would be silly for you or the children to come over. It might spoil your pleasant impressions.'[1] What he didn't know was that the British Foreign Office had opened a secret 'Kennedyiana' file to monitor his 'defeatist' views.[2] His isolationism and defeatism were put down to his fear of losing his vast wealth: 'He only thinks of his wealth and how capitalism will suffer if the war should last long.' In reality it was as much his fear for his children that was his motivating sentiment.

Rose, ever the politician, advised moderation: 'Joe, dear, I have a definite idea that it would be a wonderful feat if you could put over the idea that although you are against America's entering the war – still you are encouraging help to England in some way. It seems to me most people in America would be sympathetic to the idea, & it would endear you to the hearts of the British.'[3] As so often, he refused to listen to his wife's sage advice.

The family spent Easter at Palm Beach. Kick was ever more desperate to return to England. She persuaded Jack to intervene on her behalf, so he wrote to his father: 'Kick is very keen to go over – and I wouldn't think the anti-American feeling might hurt her like it might do us – due to her being a girl – especially as it would show that we hadn't merely left England when it got unpleasant.'[4] But still Joe would not relent.

In the first week of May, Kick and Jack and a few friends attended the Maryland Hunt Cup in Baltimore. After the races, they attended the Hunt Ball, Kick beautifully dressed in a flowing gown, and Jack in tails.[5] Her old admirer Zeke Coleman told Kick he was still in love with her and Eunice told her father that he was the 'first boy completely approved of by all the Kennedys'.[6] The only problem was that Kick was in love with someone else, and that someone would soon be fighting the Germans. Kick wanted to do her bit for England and wanted to be back with her friends, helping with the war effort, not dancing at balls in America.

She continued to badger her father, but he was still adamant: 'I am more convinced than ever that the children should not come over here. I quite understand Kathleen's interest, but she can take my word for it that she would have the dullest time she ever had in her life. All the young fellows are being shuttled off to war.'[7] She told him that a vote had been taken at Finch College in a debate about whether or not America should enter the war. Only two had voted in favour, and she was one of them.

Norway fell to Hitler, then Holland and Luxembourg. Kick was told that Billy was heading for the renowned Maginot Line, of which the French were so proud and in which they had invested billions of francs. It was supposed to be an impenetrable fortification against attack from Germany, an intricate system of shelters, barricades, communications systems, obstacles, bunkers, observation posts, supply depots, strong houses and anti-tank barrier systems. Kick believed that he was there, but she had no need to fear, because everyone knew that the Maginot Line was impenetrable ...

In fact, the Coldstream Guards were on the Franco-Belgian border in an area not encompassed by the Maginot Line. In the early-morning darkness of 10 May 1940, the Germans unleashed their Blitzkrieg, artillery and heavy armour on the ground, Stuka dive-bombers terrifying from the air. A German decoy army sat outside the Maginot Line, while a second army cut through Belgium and the Ardennes Forest. French and British troops were caught in the retreat and pushed back. Within five days, the Germans were well into France.

The day before the attack through the Low Countries Chamberlain decided to resign as a result of the disastrous failed attempt by British forces to prevent the fall of Norway. Winston Churchill's hour had come. Ambassador Kennedy was now faced with a very different Prime Minister. As German forces continued to advance, Kick, in a panic made all the worse because she was so far away, wrote to her father: 'At the moment it looks as if the Germans will be in England before you receive this letter. In fact from the reports here they are just about taking over Claridges now. I still keep telling everyone "the British lose the battles but they win the wars".'[8] Despite her jokey bravado, and her digs at her father's defeatism, Kick was worried about her London friends, and especially Billy. She wrote on 21 May, 'I have received some rather gloomy letters from Jane and Billy. Billy's letter was written from the Maginot Line. Daddy, I must know exactly what has happened to them. Is Billy all right?'[9]

She tried to lighten the tone, telling Joe that the Bronxville house was looking beautiful ('all the trees and the flowers are out') and describing Jack's high spirits on a week's vacation from Harvard: 'He really is the funniest boy alive. He had the Irish maid in fits the whole time. Every time he'd talk to her he'd put on a tremendous Irish brogue.' But Billy was very much on her mind. He was in serious fighting in France and by 24 May his unit had retreated to Dunkirk. For the Allied forces, surrounded on all sides by the Germans, it seemed that they would perish or be captured. It was, in Churchill's words, a 'colossal military disaster'. On 26 May the War Office made the final decision to evacuate the troops across the English Channel.

Billy's fellow soldiers were among the thousands evacuated from the beaches between 27 May and 4 June. By the ninth day of the evacuation, more than 300,000 soldiers had been rescued by a hastily assembled fleet of over 800 boats: British destroyers, fishing boats, ferries and lifeboats. What had seemed a disaster had turned into a triumph. That, at least, was how Churchill spun it. Hailing the rescue as a 'miracle of deliverance', he made his greatest speech: 'We shall fight on the beaches, we shall fight on the landing grounds, we shall fight in the fields and in the streets, we shall fight in the hills; we shall never surrender.'[10] Joe, by contrast, wrote to Rose to say that 'the jig is up' and that 'the finish may come quite quickly'.[11] As far as France was concerned, he was right. Paris fell on 14 June. But he was totally out of tune with the spirit of Britain.

The Cavendish family was in despair when they heard about Dunkirk because there had been no news of Billy. News eventually reached the Duke that Billy had been left in Flanders, since he could speak French. Yet every time the Duke wrote to his son, the letters came back unopened. During a weekend spent at Cliveden, the Duke tried to hide his concern from Nancy Astor and her guests, but his sad face fooled nobody. It was now a fortnight since Dunkirk and still nothing from Billy.[12] The Duke and Duchess returned to Churchdale Hall in Derbyshire, their residence during the war. Another week of waiting passed.

Then on 18 June Jean Ogilvy, who was in London, was amazed to see Billy walking through the door of her mews house. He told her that he had got out of France by hiring a small car and driving all the way to Saint-Nazaire on the Atlantic coast, from where more Allied forces were evacuated in an operation called Ariel, which began on 15 June. Billy was lucky to escape. The Luftwaffe attacked the evacuation ships the day after he got out. A converted Cunard liner, the *Lancastria*, was sunk with thousands of troops and civilians on board. It was the worst ever loss of life on a British ship. Churchill ordered a news blackout.

Though Billy looked well, Jean soon realized that he was deeply troubled by the retreat. He felt that the British had acted dishonourably: 'We ran away!'[13] He believed that they should have fought to the death. Some of his family members believed that Billy never got over Dunkirk.

Kick, now in Hyannis Port for the summer, was overjoyed when she heard that Billy was safe. She was maid of honour at the wedding of her old Noroton friend Anne McDonnell in Long Island, where she married Henry Ford II. Henry had converted to Catholicism in order to wed her. It was heralded as 'the wedding of the century'. Marriage was much on Kick's mind; so many of her London friends were marrying quickly because of the war.

It was a glorious summer on the Cape, and the family threw themselves into their usual sports and games. Jack graduated from Harvard and in July published his thesis, *Why England Slept*, to wide acclaim. His praise of Churchill as a hero strayed far from the Kennedy line.

Young Joe wrote to his father on 12 June: 'The country has gone through the most amazing change of public opinion ... There is a feeling around here that we are going to have to get in before very long.'[14] He planned to join the navy or the air force. Back in Cape Cod, the other children found their own ways of helping the war effort: Jean was attending the Red Cross and making bandages, while Kick knitted a scarf for Billy.[15]

A summer visitor remembered a huge pile of Jack's book on the floor. 'They're going like hot cakes,' the young author said. At dinner – a vast spread – that evening they all argued about the Federal Reserve System and then watched a movie. Their visitor looked back on the day: 'a sailing race, an aggregate of twenty-three sets of tennis, a debate on the forces involved in the Spanish Revolution ... a paper contributed by the girls listing the qualities that should be present in an ideal husband, the daily game of touch football, and, finally, a local war that broke out after the movie over the issue – would Ingrid Bergman go to fat'. There was, he sensed, a 'feeling shared by everybody that anything was possible and the only recognized problem was that there would never be enough time'. The Kennedys were, he recalled, 'the most heightened group of people, much less one family. I thought to myself – that's the best I've seen.'[16]

28

The Fourth Hostage

It would be difficult for an impartial observer to decide today whether the British are the bravest or merely the most stupid people in the world.

New Yorker, 29 June 1940

The Luftwaffe launched its first attack on Britain on 10 July 1940, bombing the south coast. On 13 August, German bombers attacked airfields, factories and the London docks. On the 25th, a bomb fell 300 yards from the Ambassador's weekend residence near Windsor. The Foreign Secretary, Lord Halifax, wrote in his diary: 'everyone is no doubt inclined to think a judgment on Joe for feeling he was likely to be safer there than in London'.[1]

Then on 7 September 1940 the air-raid sirens wailed as more than 300 bombers filled the skies over London. This was the beginning of fifty-seven consecutive nights of bombing. The British public pulled together and got involved with the war effort. Many civilians became members of the Home Guard, the ARP (Air Raid Precautions service) and the AFS (Auxiliary Fire Service). The Boy Scout Association guided fire engines, the boys becoming known as the 'Blitz Scouts'. And women were playing their part. Kick's friends were all joining in. Sally Norton and Osla Benning had jobs in an aeroplane factory.[2] Debo Mitford worked in a canteen for servicemen at St Pancras station. Her sister Nancy had a (short-lived) job driving for the

ARP, before helping out with evacuees and then getting war work at a first-aid post. 'I enjoyed the war very much, I'm ashamed to say,' she later recalled. 'Everyone was in a very good temper. Nice and jolly.'[3] As the Battle of Britain raged on, there was a sense of purpose, of excitement. For aristocratic women like Kick's friends, it was a time of great liberation, both social and sexual.

There was certainly plenty of glitz in the Blitz. Without the need for chaperones, the girls worked by day and played at night. The West End was full of live music, crooners, cocktails and big bands. The most popular nightclub was the Café de Paris in Piccadilly, whose doors had stayed open not least because, being subterranean, it acted like an air-raid shelter, of a kind much preferable to an Anderson in the bottom of your garden. Wartime London was a place of danger, but also of excitement and reckless passion. Proximity to death meant feeling intensely alive, and illicit sex abounded. Making love was a way of defying death.[4]

Kick was feeling isolated and bored in school, and heard the news that many of her friends, swept up in war panic, were getting engaged. Sissy Lloyd Thomas was now married to David Ormsby Gore, with Billy as best man. She wished she could have been there. Janey Kenyon-Slaney was engaged to Peter Lindsay and Debo Mitford to Billy's younger brother, Andrew. She also heard that Billy was back with her old rival, Irene Haig.[5] But she was still writing to him, telling him that she was desperate to come to England but being prevented by her father.

In September, Kick holidayed in Montana for a month with her old friend Nancy Tenney. Two other friends, newlyweds Francis and Cynthia McAdoo, went too. They stayed at the Flying Ranch at Wise River. The Old West was an eye-opener for Kick, full of handsome cowboys. She walked around with her hair in curlers, laughing and joking as if she didn't have a care in the world. But, despite her laughter, she was plotting to return to England. That October, she arranged a lunch and fashion show in aid of the Allied Relief Fund, an organization dedicated to providing aid for British sailors disabled in the war.[6]

Back in England, Joe knew that he was perceived as a loose cannon and a troublemaker. Aware that the President was sidelining him by communicating directly with Churchill, and hating being ignored, he became more and more angry and frustrated. He wrote to Rose on the last day of September to tell her that he intended to come home, 'either for consultation or to resign – that is entirely dependent on Mr. Roosevelt. Frankly, I don't care which.'[7] Rose herself saw exactly what was going on in Washington: 'They think the Pres[ident] does not want you home before the election due to your explosive–defeatist point of view, as you might so easily throw a bomb which would explode sufficiently to upset his chances.'[8] She meant his chances of winning a third term in the upcoming election.

Rose was right. But the President was wary of alienating Joe altogether and finally recalled him for 'consultation' in October. He told the Ambassador not to talk to the press and to come straight to the White House. Joe made his goodbyes in London, knowing that he would not be returning, and anxious to protect his reputation. He saw his old friend Neville Chamberlain, who was seriously ill and dying from cancer. Joe noted in his diary: 'Clasped my hand in his two and said, "This is Goodbye, we will never see each other again." Terrible Feeling.'[9]

Joe Kennedy left London on 22 October 1940. He had been Ambassador for two and a half years. He was met by the family – Kick and the rest of the girls – at La Guardia Airport. Wearing beautiful fur coats, they smothered him in kisses before he was besieged by the press. 'I have nothing to say until I have seen the President,' he announced.

His trusted friends and advisers asked him whether he still had the President's support, and Rose urged him to remember that for the sake of the family he should support the President. She calmly reminded him that he had been the first Catholic to be US Ambassador to Britain and the American representative for the Pope's coronation at Rome. The President ensured that Rose was invited to the White House. It was her job to keep her husband calm. Roosevelt asked for Joe's support by way of a public radio announcement supporting his re-election for an unprecedented third term. He knew the benefit of having Joe declare that he was not intent on sending America's sons to fight England's war. Joe also had the Catholic vote.

Joe vented his spleen, told FDR of his anger and humiliation, and finally agreed, with bad grace, to give the radio address. What Joe wanted above all was to keep America (and his sons) out of the war, and he trusted that the President wanted this too. He urged rearmament 'because it is the only way America can stay out of the war'. The speech he gave ended on a highly emotional note:

My wife and I have given nine hostages to fortune. Our children and your children are more important than anything else in the world. The kind of America that they and their children will inherit is of grave concern to us all. In light of these considerations, I believe that Franklin D. Roosevelt should be re-elected President of the United States.[10]

The President, hugely relieved, gave a speech in Boston, saying how pleased he was to 'welcome back to the shores of America that Boston boy, beloved by all Boston and a lot of other places, my Ambassador in the court of St James's, Joe Kennedy'. Kick sent a telegram to her father: 'The Pres[ident] really went to town for you tonight in Boston amidst terrific cheers from the crowd … It's great to be famous – Goodnight from your fourth hostage.'[11]

Joe simply couldn't enjoy his victory. When FDR was re-elected President in November, he headed for Washington and told him that he was resigning. Nothing could shake his pessimism. He was simply unable to see that the war was not going the way that Hitler intended. The RAF were holding off the Luftwaffe. London had not been cowed. But Joe would not accept that he was wrong. It was the end of the world for him. It was also the end of his career.

29

Billy and Sally

Sometimes I feel that almost anything is better than an existence
that is neither one thing or the other.

Kick Kennedy

8 March 1941.

A tall, dark, handsome man was running across Leicester Square heading for the Café de Paris. He was late and he couldn't find a taxi. He was a
famous face in wartime Britain. He was Ken 'Snakehips' Johnson.

Snakehips was just twenty-six and at the height of his career, a dancer,
singer and bandmaster. He had been training to be a doctor at Edinburgh
University but left to become a singer. He had earned the nickname
'Snakehips' because of his silky, sensuous dancing style. He had his own
band, the West Indian Orchestra, and they had secured a residency at the
Café de Paris.

Captain Billy Cavendish was in London on leave. He had been seeing a
lot of Kick's friend Sally Norton. Sally spoke fluent German and had been
recruited to the signals-decoding operation at Bletchley Park, where she
was assigned to Hut 4, the German naval section. She remembered taking
the oath of silence and signing the Official Secrets Act. She pretended to
her friends that she was keeping records of those due to be given war
honours.

Sally's position gave her a newfound confidence and independence; she no longer needed a chaperone to date men. She recalled dancing all night and then taking the milk train back to Bletchley Park at five in the morning, still wearing her evening clothes.[1] At the first opportunity, she and her friend, the beautiful Osla Benning, who was dating Prince Philip of Greece, would dash up to London to meet their boyfriends. Billy Cavendish was stationed at Elstree and met up with Sally in London, returning to their old haunts, the Café de Paris, the 400 and the Mirabelle. They usually began the evening with cocktails at the Ritz before heading off to dinner and then a nightclub.

Mr Gibbs, the head porter of Claridge's, would inform Sally that Lord Hartington was in town and would meet her later that evening. On the night of 8 March, Sally and Billy had dinner and then set off for the Café de Paris to see Snakehips. As they left the Ritz they heard the wailing of sirens and as they got to the Mirabelle 'the guns and bombs sounded'.[2]

When they arrived at the Café de Paris, they saw a scene of carnage and devastation, people being carried out on stretchers. The unthinkable had happened to the 'safest' nightclub in London. The band were ten minutes into a rendition of 'Oh Johnny' when two bombs burst through the roof, down a shaft on to the ballroom. One rescue worker tripped over a girl's head and saw her torso still sitting in a chair. Some perished as the powerful blast sucked the air out of their lungs, a deadly phenomenon which caused the victim to display no outward signs of injury, but instead left them statue-like, frozen in the pose they'd been in at the moment of impact.

Thirty-four people were killed, including bandleader Snakehips. Some reports claimed that his head had been blown from his shoulders. He died with a flower still in his lapel. Eighty more were injured. One man was carried out on a stretcher: 'At least I didn't have to pay for dinner,' he said to the crowd. Billy Cavendish, arriving with Sally Norton, went inside to investigate and was horrified by what he witnessed. 'Well, then, let's go on to the 400,' said Sally.[3] All evening Hitler's bombs rained on London. Sally noted the events in her diary, recording that every time a bomb rocked the room, its velocity propelled her across the dance floor, but they carried on dancing. The bombs continued until 4. a.m. They finally saw their opportunity and ran to Claridge's. To their astonishment Billy and Sally found a party there in full swing. Sally's mother was among the guests. When the all-clear finally sounded they went for a walk. 'It was horribly beautiful,

London at that moment. The sky was a brilliant red. As the All Clear faded out there was a complete and utter silence, except for the crackling of fires in the distance.'[4]

With death so near, many were quick to wed. Two days after a massive raid, on 14 April 1941, Deborah Mitford married Billy's brother Andrew at St Bartholomew the Great in Smithfield. Debo wrote to Kick to tell her all about the day.

Kick took out a subscription to the *Transatlantic Daily Mail* to keep up with world news. She pasted into her scrapbook articles about the 'Lend-Lease' agreement (material aid provided by America 'for the government of any country whose defense the President deems vital to the defense of the United States'). She wrote letters applying for nursing courses run by the American Red Cross. She told an English friend that she was just killing time while she planned her return to England.

In May, FDR declared a 'state of unlimited national emergency' in response to Nazi Germany's threat of world domination. He urged Americans to consider entering the war before waiting to be attacked. Kick and her family gathered round the radio to hear the President's speech delivered from the White House. It was an impassioned speech in which Roosevelt declared that 'The Nazi world does not recognize any God except Hitler' and that 'It is unmistakably apparent to all of us that, unless the advance of Hitlerism is forcibly checked now, the Western Hemisphere will be within range of the Nazi weapons of destruction'. He went on to speak movingly about Britain's courage: 'In June, 1940, Britain stood alone, faced by the same machine of terror which had overwhelmed her allies. Our Government rushed arms to meet her desperate needs ... And now – after a year – Britain still fights gallantly.'[5]

Kick wrote to her English friend Janey Lindsay, explaining her response to the broadcast: 'After the President's speech last night everyone feels that we are in the war although there has been no official declaration ... All possible aid to you for the survival of the British Empire is the only way in which our economic, political and moral life will be safe for the future.' She ended her letter, 'We do live in upsetting times ... But sometimes I feel that almost anything is better than an existence that is neither one thing or the other.'[6]

* * *

By June 1941, Joe Jr had enlisted in a special unit of the US Naval Air Corps, and by the end of the summer Jack too was in uniform, as an officer in Naval Intelligence. Kick had enrolled at Florida Commercial College, still plotting to return to England. She was worried that she had not heard from Billy for many months. She knew that he was getting closer to Sally Norton, and she feared that he had lost interest.

The family gathered for the usual Hyannis summer of touch football, sailing, riding and movies. They were glad to be together, the only blight being Rosemary's increasingly erratic behaviour. She was becoming aggressive and lashing out at her siblings. On one occasion, she attacked her grandfather.

As the summer on the Cape drew to a close, the Kennedys dispersed to their schools and jobs. Kick pondered on her inability to connect fully with men. In a letter to Janey Lindsay she talked about how all her English friends were getting married but remarked that there were 'still no signs of marriage' in her own family: 'Sometimes I feel that I am never going to take that on. No one I have ever met ever made me completely forget myself and one cannot get married with that attitude.'[7]

She turned her mind to her career. Her father told her that she had to 'get a job and earn a living'. She was a good writer, a good listener, had plenty of intellectual curiosity and a way of getting people to open up to her. People instantly trusted her. Her friend Page Huidekoper was now working as a journalist on the *Washington Times-Herald*. Kick managed to get an interview on the paper with the editor, Frank Waldrop.[8] He offered her a job as his secretary. Kick was finally leaving home, and she would never go back. Her father sent her a congratulatory telegram:

WHEN I WAS IN PRIVATE BUSINESS I ALWAYS HAD A SIGN ON MY DESK WHICH READ AFTER YOU'VE DONE THE VERY BEST YOU CAN THE HELL WITH IT ANYWAY I AM PROUD OF YOU FOR TRYING ALL KINDS OF GOOD LUCK LOVE DAD[9]

30

Kick the Reporter

What's the stooory ...

Kick Kennedy[1]

'Can you lend me ten dollars?'

Kick Kennedy, the new secretary to Frank Waldrop of the *Washington Times-Herald*, burst out laughing at this impudent request made by the newspaper's star reporter, John White. She couldn't have known it then, but he was to be the man who got closest to driving Billy out of her mind. It certainly wasn't love at first sight. John was thirty-one years old, with thinning blond hair, and carelessly dressed. He had a tattoo of a serpent coiling up his bicep. Though he wasn't conventionally handsome, he was sexy, with a strong nose and sensuous lips. He had a piercing stare. He was brash, sardonic, argumentative and opinionated. He was nothing like the English noblemen Kick had dated and dreamed about marrying, or indeed the preppy boys that her brothers brought to Cape Cod from Harvard and Princeton. She didn't know what to make of him.

In some respects, he was similar to her brothers. He was Harvard educated, extremely intelligent and loved a good fight. He was a challenge, and sparks flew from the start. Unlike most of the men Kick had previously met, he didn't throw himself at her feet. For once in her life, she did not have the upper hand and this intrigued her.

Kick rented a modest apartment in north-west Washington DC, which she shared with a friend from Philadelphia called Betty Coxe. She was living for the very first time as a working girl. Kick did not want her colleagues to know about her wealthy, privileged background, so she kept quiet about being the Ambassador's daughter. She earned a meagre salary, and worked hard and efficiently to prove her worth. No one knew that she had been presented at court, dined with British royalty, dated the heir to Chatsworth, partied at Blenheim Palace.

Frank Waldrop, her boss, loved having pretty girls around him. Kick thought she had got her job because of her friendship with Page, but, as usual, her father was pulling the strings. Joe's friend Arthur Krock had called Waldrop up and suggested that he give Kick an opportunity, even though she couldn't type very well and knew very little about the newspaper business.[2]

The *Washington Times-Herald* was an isolationist newspaper, its founder an extraordinary woman called Eleanor 'Cissy' Patterson. She was no fan of Roosevelt, though she adored his wife Eleanor. Some people accused her of being a Nazi sympathizer. She bought and merged two newspapers, the *Washington Herald* and the *Washington Times*, making her title the most widely read in the capital. Cissy was one of the most powerful and most hated women in America.

Her quotes were legendary: 'I'd rather raise Hell than vegetables'; 'Women have always bossed men, although most of the time they don't know it'; 'the trouble with me is that I am a vindictive old shanty-Irish bitch'. Her father was a newspaperman, whose motto was 'when your grandmother gets raped, put it on the front page'.[3]

One of Cissy's writers was a beautiful blonde Danish woman called Inga Arvad. She was a daily columnist, penning a feature called 'Did You Happen to See ...', which profiled government officials. She was twenty-eight and on her second marriage, which was already in trouble. She exuded glamour and sensuality. She became Kick's close friend. In Denmark, Inga had been a beauty queen, but she was not just stunningly beautiful, she was intelligent and kind. She was cultivated and sophisticated, speaking several languages. She had attended the prestigious Columbia School of Journalism in New York before relocating to Washington.

Kick was intrigued by Inga. In the absence of her own beautiful but damaged elder sister Rosemary, Inga became a mentor and surrogate big sister. They became inseparable. Unlike so many other women, Kick was not intimidated by Inga's beauty. She was utterly secure in her own skin, thanks to her personality and effervescence.

Inga was wholly unlike her friends from Convent or England. There was nothing repressed about Inga. Kick was intrigued that she was apparently on her way to a second divorce, yet seemingly free of guilt. Everything that Kick had learnt from the nuns at school, and from her mother at home, was thrown into question by Inga, with her free spirit and her devil-may-care attitude to men and to life. Kick began, for the first time, to question some of the attitudes and tenets of her strict upbringing.

This was the beginning of a new and exciting epoch in her life. To Kick's delight, Jack had been assigned to the Office of Naval Intelligence in Washington, which meant that they could spend much of their social life together. Always close, their bond intensified as their lives entwined around work and play.

Waldrop recalled that, soon after Kick began working for him, he was called up by Joe Kennedy with an invitation to dinner. Waldrop remembered the dinner, to which Jack and Kick came along too. He noted the ebullience of the pair, the way that they described everything as 'terrific': 'a terrific day, a terrific movie, terrific this, terrific that, everything was terrific'.[4] Their enthusiasm could have been grating, but somehow he was charmed and he loved the way that Jack and Kick teased Joe. They mockingly referred to him as 'the Ambassador': 'Now that the Ambassador has stated his position we can go on,' Kick joked. Underneath it all, Waldrop was struck by the affection they had for him: 'I mean they loved the old son of a bitch for what he was because they knew he loved them.'[5] Waldrop also knew that Joe was sussing him out, ever careful of his adored daughter. Joe might have said, 'get out and get a job', but he wanted it to be the right sort of job and environment.

Kick, though, did not want it bandied around that she was Joe Kennedy's daughter. One day she was meeting her father for dinner. She dressed herself beautifully and put on her mink coat. Suddenly remembering that there was something she had forgotten to do in the office, she ran back, only to bump into some of her colleagues. They were astounded to see Kick dressed in such an expensive coat, and rumours soon abounded that she must have fallen into bad ways and have found herself a sugar daddy.[6]

When word finally got out that she was Joe Kennedy's daughter, some of Washington's elite frowned upon her. A wealthy girl was taking a job she didn't really need and thus depriving an ordinary girl of work. But it didn't take long for everyone to be won over by her charms. It was the same pattern that had been established in England when she had been teased by her aristocratic friends and then had won them over. She was so funny, so honest, with her radiant smile. She was irresistible.

She had been in her new job for just three weeks when she received the letter from Jack telling her that he was coming to live in Washington. Inga never forgot Kick's reaction to the news: Kick was 'curled up like a kitten her long tawny hair fell over her face, then she jumped up ... her Irish blue-eyes flashed with excitement as she leaped onto the floor and began a whirling dance like some delightful dervish. "He's coming to Washington, I'm going to give a party at the F Street Club. You will just love him!"'

Inga thought that Kick was talking about one of her many admirers, and then learnt that it was her brother Jack, who was in the navy: 'He came. She hadn't exaggerated. He had the charm that makes birds come out of their trees. He looked like her twin, the same thick mop of hair, the same blue eyes, natural, engaging, ambitious, warm and when he walked into a room you knew he was there, not pushing, not domineering but exuding animal magnetism.'[7] Inga and Jack embarked upon a passionate love affair. He was a handsome, charismatic male version of her beloved Kick, and she fell deeply in love.[8] Inga told John White that she was drawn to his ambition and single-mindedness. She also liked his honesty. Jack made it perfectly clear that the affair would not be long lasting. She thought that he had a lot to learn 'and I'll be happy to teach him'.[9]

Kick, who loved to tease Jack, wrote to him: 'Dear Twinkle-toes ... Inga returned with an infected throat. Torb and I want to know what you do to girls that causes T.B. or infected throats or causes them to marry someone else.'[10] Though she was putting on a brave face, that autumn she had heard the news that she had been dreading: Billy was engaged to another woman.

In October, she wrote to her father asking for his consent to travel to England: 'I have just had lunch with Dinah Brand (Lady Astor's niece) and I am nearly going mad. She said that everyone she say [saw] sent all sorts of messages to me and that there just never been such a missed girl as I am. I am so anxious to go back that I can hardly sit still.'[11]

Always closer to her father than her mother, and especially in romantic matters, she confided in him her fears about Billy Cavendish: 'I received a letter from Andrew and Debo pleading with me to come back and save Billy from Sally Norton who apparently has got him in the bag. No one wants him to marry her and all told [me] to come back and save him. Apparently they are going to announce it in Jan. I haven't heard from him for simply ages and that no doubt is the reason.'[12]

Her panic at not hearing from Billy was partly assuaged but partly increased by a letter from him announcing that he was engaged to Sally. He had told Kick that his parents were not happy about the match and did not think the Nortons 'respectable enough'. She told her father, 'The Duchess and Mrs. Norton had a tremendous fight but things have settled down and they are going to announce it in Dec.'[13]

Reading between the lines, Billy was still reaching out to Kick, and almost telling her that he thought he had made a mistake. She repeated back to Joe some of Billy's quotes, 'I have never been engaged before, thanks to you'; 'It was a very long time before I gave up all hope of marrying you'; 'what sense of humour I have I owe to you' and 'Please keep writing'.

She was clearly relieved that she still had a hold on him. 'Rather sad, don't you think?' But there was nothing she could do. Her father would not let her return to England. She also told him that she was going to the races and to a dance with Jack's Harvard friend George Mead. There was no mention of the man she was spending most of her time with, John White.

Anxious about the Billy and Sally situation, Kick wrote to her father that she had a plan. Her idea was to ask John G. Winant, the new American Ambassador in London, to get her a passport: 'The only thing that remains is your consent,' she wrote. 'I have a lot of great friends that I should really like to see.' She told her father that she wasn't worried about his unpopularity among the British: her real friends would not blame her and, as for the rest, 'the hell with them'. She added that her chances of being hit by a London bomb were the same as being hit by a car in Washington. Joe would not give his consent.

In the face of her father's intransigence, Kick finally accepted defeat. Billy was lost to her. He was tired of waiting for her and felt that the relationship was doomed. At least Kick now had Jack to distract her. With his bestselling book about England, he was a rising man in Washington. There were rumours that he might one day run for President. Kick's Washington set had a party game called 'Jack's future'. Inga remembered that they talked politics constantly. Kick helped Jack to send out signed copies of his book to important people. The directionless second son had found his way.[14]

31

Lobotomy

Rosemary's was the first of the tragedies that were to befall us.

Rose Kennedy

Kick was enjoying her time in Washington. Most evenings, she and Jack, together with his Harvard friends and Inga, would have dinner ('always the same menu: steak, peas, carrots and ice cream'). Inga was amused by the games of touch football played in the living room of Kick's apartment.

In the meantime, Kick was growing closer to John White. Their first encounters had been inauspicious. He teased her mercilessly and she retaliated, calling him 'a big bag of wind'. He was instantly intrigued by her feisty nature, her unwillingness to be intimidated by his age and experience, his self-confidence and swagger. It seemed that every time they were together in the office an argument would break out. Having discovered that she was a strict Catholic who had been convent educated, he simply couldn't resist teasing her about her beliefs. Kick was unused to defending her faith and her upbringing. Even when she was in England, away from her Catholic friends, it was unthinkable that she would have been teased or challenged about her religion. Her English friends respected her strong faith. Her tentative talks with Billy about their respective faiths had been careful and considerate. Often the subject was best avoided. With John, it was entirely different.

He loved to goad her. He knew that religion and sex were sensitive issues, so he delighted in pouring ridicule on Catholic teaching on contraception. One day at the office they had argued about the church. Later that evening, she couldn't resist carrying on the argument. She telephoned him, yelling, 'Birth control is murder.' Undaunted, he yelled back, 'It's the Catholic church's way of keeping membership.'[1]

John had a chip on his shoulder. Though Ivy League, he was the son of an Episcopalian minister, and had not had the advantages of many of the men Kick had met. He was the direct opposite of Billy. Billy was the perfect English gentleman, shy, self-effacing, polite and gentle. Courteous and kind, he would never force or expect even a kiss if he felt Kick wasn't ready. John White was rude, funny, irreverent, and despite his bravado and seeming detachment he truly loved her. Living in her own flat meant that Kick had freedom to develop her romance with John. She was too ambitious to take him seriously as a potential husband, but she liked him. He treated her like an equal. He understood her.

John scorned social skills and etiquette and fine dining and wealth. He was notorious for wearing shabby clothes. He once came into the office wearing a threadbare sweater that unravelled through the day.[2] Kick stood for everything he hated. She was rich, well travelled, socially adept, had led a life of privilege and luxury with holiday homes in Cape Cod and Palm Beach. But he couldn't get enough of her. Also, she had been raised arguing, and learning not to take it personally. Debating was meat and drink to her. John had never met a woman quite like her. Being so vivacious and clever, how could she be so thoroughly unspoilt? They began dating.

On their third date, he invited her back to his 'cave', a basement room in a Georgetown house which belonged to his married sister, Patsy. They spent most of the evening indulging in their usual banter and battle-of-wills. Suddenly, he pounced and tried to kiss her. Kick was horrified: 'I don't want any of this, John. You must understand. Please don't try. I don't want to do the thing the priest says not to do.'[3]

In an interview he recalled his surprise that this lively girl could somehow be sexually repressed. He told her that he wanted some physical affection, even if just hugs and kisses. At the same time, he was drawn to her innocence. He was shocked that she could not even say the word 'sex'.[4] But he could not give her up. Kick had confided in him that her father knew about her brother's sexual affair with the married Inga, and that Joe had encouraged the relationship. Her father thought it was good to have the sexual experience. There was nothing said about 'adultery' or 'fornication', as she had been taught by her faith. This sent such a confusing message. It was fine for her brother to be sexually active, fine for him to be having an affair with an older married woman, but not for her to have an affair.

One day that autumn, White remembered Kick showing an especial interest in a series of articles he was preparing about mental illness and 'retardation'. She probed him about the latest treatments and asked to accompany him on a research trip to a home for the 'retarded'. As White recalled:

> Kick would draw me out on the details – not just draw me out but absolutely drain me, although never saying why. This went on for a long time. One day we were walking in the park and she was, as usual, interviewing me to find out what new things I'd discovered … she finally admitted why she was so interested. It was because of Rosemary. She spoke slowly and sadly about it, as though she was confessing something quite embarrassing, almost shameful. I got the feeling that her family viewed Rosemary as a beloved failure, perhaps a disgrace.[5]

Rosemary was now twenty-three, and her problems had worsened. As she grew older, the gap between her and the rest of the family was widening, and she was becoming increasingly aggressive and frustrated. She had improved immeasurably at her school in England, where she had felt needed and useful, but since returning to America she had become isolated and her behaviour more erratic. In her memoirs, Rose talked of her eldest daughter's tantrums and rages, when she struck out at people and threw things, and there were convulsive episodes.

There was another troubling aspect to her conduct. As she reached sexual maturity, she couldn't understand why she didn't have boyfriends like her sisters. And there were embarrassing incidents when she had wandered out of the school at night and been found with strange men who did not realize her condition and tried to take advantage. She was still beautiful and voluptuous. She was at St Gertrude's Convent in the heart of Washington, not far from Kick and Jack. When she got out, the school would call to say that she was missing and the family would have to go out and find her before someone took advantage.

Fearful of the effect she would have on the lives and careers of the other siblings, the Ambassador decided to take matters in hand.

John White had investigated neurosurgical techniques such as the pre-frontal lobotomy. He was writing a six-piece series on St Elizabeth's, Washington's federal mental hospital. When John told Kick that the results of the pre-frontal lobotomy were 'just not good' and that afterwards the patient would be 'gone as a person, just gone', Kick was relieved and told her mother that this wouldn't do for Rosemary.[6] But Joe had other ideas.

John White had learnt about the work of Dr Walter Freeman, who worked at George Washington Hospital as well as St Elizabeth's. He also had his own private practice.[7] Joe went to consult him about his daughter. He was the leading doctor of psychosurgery and had performed eighty lobotomies with his partner James Watts. Freeman was a charismatic, articulate character who required little time to persuade Joe that the opera-tion would be a success. The hope was that the operation would calm her mood swings. What was highly unusual about Rosemary's case was that she was only mildly retarded. Most of the lobotomies Freeman had performed were on patients with severe developmental disabilities, who were brought to him as a very last resort.

On a cold day in November 1941, Rosemary was wheeled into the oper-ating theatre of George Washington Hospital. She was given a local anaes-thetic, because it was vital for her to be awake during the operation. Watts, who performed alongside Freeman, described what happened: 'We went through the top of the head, I think she was awake. She had a mild tran-quilizer. I made a surgical incision in the brain through the skull. It was near the front. It was on both sides. We just made a small incision, no more than an inch.' The instrument Watts used looked like a butter knife. He swung it up and down to cut brain tissue. As Watts cut, Freeman put ques-tions to Rosemary. For example, he asked her to recite the Lord's Prayer or sing God Bless America or count backwards.[8]

The operation involved severing neural connections between the frontal lobes of the brain and the thalamus. Rosemary was sent to Craig House to convalesce. No one knew whether she would regain mobility and speech. She did eventually recover her motor skills, but not her memory or her speech. She was left with the mind of a two-year-old child, unable to communicate or to walk, and almost certainly incontinent. Eunice, who was always closest to her, wasn't even told her whereabouts.

Rosemary and the botched lobotomy were seen as a failure that could barely be mentioned in a family where success was all. The Kennedys were masters at the power of denial. It was a survival strategy. Joe never referred to the operation or kept a written record, nor did Dr Freeman. In her 1942 round-robin letter to all the other children, Rose never mentioned Rosemary. In her memoirs, she wrote of the beloved daughter whom she had spent so many years nurturing, and how the neurosurgery had been such a failure: 'she lost everything that had been gained during the years by her own gallant efforts and our loving efforts for her'.[9] Rose never even told her friends; Joe lied and told his friends that Rosemary was teaching out in the Midwest.[10] Kick was quietly devastated, knowing her own small part in the sorry saga.

Rose was eventually sent to a convent in Wisconsin, St Coletta's. She was able to walk again, but her mental powers were gone. Joe built a private cottage for her in the grounds of St Coletta's. Rose later wrote, 'Rosemary's was the first of the tragedies that were to befall us.'[11]

In late November, shortly after Rosemary's operation, Rose shut up the family home in Brookline. The older children had gone for good, the younger ones were in boarding school. Family gatherings would now be confined to holidays in the Palm Beach house and at Hyannis Port.

Kick drew ever closer to John White in the wake of the Rosemary disaster. He would read to her from his favourite books and take her to the movies. On 30 November, he wrote in his diary, 'I held the hand of Kathleen Kennedy ... feel very friendly towards her and do now wonder what will become of us.'[12]

He had little idea that she was still thinking of Billy Cavendish and how to extricate him from Sally Norton while she was so far away from him – still plotting ways to return to England. Kick loved John, but in many respects, they had a fraternal relationship. He would tuck her up in bed at night, with Kick wearing a long nightgown. She didn't care that he saw her with her hair in pin curls, her face cleansed of make-up, slathered in cold cream. He would rub her back until she fell asleep, or he would read to her before returning home to his apartment.[13]

White said that after two or three dates Kick dropped hints about things she knew that she shouldn't know about him. For instance, once they were talking and she slipped in a reference to North Carolina, the place where he was from. He was simply astonished until she said that her father was doing a background check on him. She said, 'every time one of us goes out with somebody new, we have to call our father'.[14] She told him that her father had been investigating his past and concluded that he was 'aimless but harmless'.[15] She also told him that he did the same with the other children.

John chronicled their life in his diary. It reads a bit like a screwball comedy. She would call him a 'shrunken, bald-headed, irritable old man', and he would call her 'an ignorant, thickheaded Mick' or the 'Irish Catholic stupid fool'.[16] She would love this because it was so unlike the hero worship that she was used to. He would rise early to take her to work in his old car (nicknamed 'The Broken and Contrite Heart'), and they would quarrel incessantly. Once they even quarrelled about his height.[17] Despite his exasperation, he loved her ability to debate. He knew that her apparently wholesome and innocent exterior masked her keen intelligence and ability to manipulate and win an argument. He conceded that, despite his own prowess and skill in debate, she was 'a damn sight better than he was'.[18]

John White remembered that Kick loved coming to Patsy's house, mainly because of the family atmosphere, which she greatly missed. She liked his family because they were 'freethinkers'.[19] He remembered how 'she'd sit and talk about anything. She just loved to talk. She was like Jack in this regard – she had an insatiable curiosity about people'.[20] He continued to probe Kick's religious beliefs, her father's isolationist politics and her social views. 'It delighted her to see people somehow careless of appearances who were still not bad people … it was as though we were breaking the rules and not being thrown out.' He felt that he was the one who got her to challenge her faith, and claimed that Eunice later blamed him for it, accused him of 'talking my sister out of her religion'. This wasn't true, but he did sow the seeds of doubt.[21]

Her friends were surprised by the romance, amazed that she was so keen on this belligerent, scruffy man with a chip on his shoulder. They didn't understand that in his love of argument and debate he was like a Kennedy, and she felt extremely comfortable with him, despite the volatility of the relationship. There was also an undercurrent of sexual tension and excitement that was new to her. He also said 'she loved to cuddle. I don't think that there had been too much of that sort of thing when they were kids. But that had to take place apart from sex'.[22] Rubbing her back one night, he thought to himself that their relationship mostly resembled that of Clark Gable and Claudette Colbert in *It Happened One Night*. He was taking on the role of protector. As usual he would tuck her into bed before leaving. He was always amazed that whatever kind of day she had had, even if she were feeling sad or stressed, she would instantly fall fast asleep. But this one night was different. On the cusp of drifting off, she suddenly turned to John and said, in a tearful voice: 'Listen, the thing about me you ought to know is that I'm like Jack – incapable of deep affection.'[23]

On Sunday, 7 December, Kick had lunch with John White and his sister Patsy in a Hot Shoppes restaurant. An announcement was suddenly made that Japan had attacked Pearl Harbor. All eight US Navy battleships had been damaged, with four being sunk. Thousands had been killed or injured. There had been no warning, no declaration of war.

Thick smoke billowed from the Japanese Embassy in Washington as the diplomatic staff burnt their papers and documents. The next day, the President addressed Congress with the words that America was at war with Japan: 'a day that will live in infamy'. On 11 December, Hitler declared that Germany would unite with Japan in hostilities against the United States.

Overnight, support for non-intervention disappeared. Even an isolationist newspaper like the *Herald* changed its view. John White wrote in his diary that his household had 'jumped for joy' on hearing the news.[24] He immediately signed up for the navy. Billy Hartington wrote to Kick and asked if Jack still thought 'that the British were decadent'.

Joseph Kennedy, shocked and appalled, cabled the President: 'In this great crisis all Americans are with you. Name the battle post. I'm yours to command.'[25] It was too little too late. He never even received a reply. Joe had been wrong – catastrophically, irrevocably wrong. From this point on, he was little more than an outcast.

32

Scandal

No sooner in office than he became embroiled in the great case of the Ambassador's Son and the Beautiful Blonde Spy.

John White, January 1942[1]

In the busy newsroom of the *Times-Herald* a scandal was brewing, and it involved Kick Kennedy. One of the newsroom girls had been flicking through old news footage in the 'morgue', the basement where photographs were stored, when she saw what she thought was a photograph of Jack's girlfriend Inga taken with Adolf Hitler at the 1936 Olympics in Berlin. She told Page Huidekoper, who spread the gossip to Kick that Inga was a spy. Some whispered that Inga had attended the wedding of Luftwaffe chief Hermann Göring. Kick was outraged. Inga was Jack's lover and her closest friend and she refused to believe the malicious gossip. She told Inga, who immediately made her way to the boss's office: 'I can still see Cissy Paterson sitting in her office disgusted with the rumors, wishing very much to help me, and seeing a wonderful story in the whole thing.'[2]

Cissy thought it would be best for Inga to go directly to the FBI with chief editor Frank Waldrop. He summoned Page. 'OK. Get your coat.' They made their way to Lafayette Square. Both girls gave statements in which Kick was cited and a memo was sent to J. Edgar Hoover which said that Miss Huidekoper stated to 'Miss Kathleen Kennedy, a reporter on the *Times*

Herald and the daughter of former Ambassador Kennedy, that she would not be surprised if Inga Arvad was a spy for some foreign power. She remarked to Miss Kennedy that one of her friends had been going through some old Berlin newspapers and had noted a picture of Inga Arvad taken with Hitler at the Olympic games in Berlin … Miss Kennedy, a very close friend of Inga Arvad, told her of Miss Huidekoper's statement.'[3]

Though Inga protested that it was all a silly rumour, she had interviewed Hitler on two occasions. Struck by her good looks, the Führer described her as 'a perfect example of Nordic beauty'. She said of him: 'You immediately like him. He seems lonely. The eyes, showing a kind heart, stare right at you. They sparkle with force.' Inga later admitted that she had become good friends with Göring, and with the Deputy Führer Rudolf Hess, though she vehemently denied being pro-Nazi or a spy.

The damage was done. Jack and Kick were determined to stay loyal to Inga, but the FBI continued to monitor her closely. Jack was still in love with Inga and begged Kick and John White to double-date with him to play down the affair. Kick agreed, since she adored her brother and was extremely fond of Inga. Jack and Inga knew that they were being followed and wire-tapped. The FBI were convinced that she was using Jack to garner information, but as he was the former Ambassador's son they knew that the situation was delicate. It was time for Joe to step in. By the beginning of the new year Jack had been transferred to the Charleston Navy Yard in South Carolina.[4]

His health, as ever, was uncertain, but he was determined to get out of doing a desk job. He was still in love with Inga, but he knew that the relationship was doomed. The family gathered at Palm Beach that Christmas. Inga wrote to Jack, saying that she was glad he was basking in the warmth of Florida, and that he was 'one of the very rare people born to sunshine and happiness'.[5] Inga was shrewd enough to see that Jack was pulling back from her, and she knew that it was because of his parents and his loyalty to the family above all else: 'You belong so wholeheartedly to the Kennedy clan.'[6]

At the beginning of February 1942, Jack spent a torrid weekend with Inga at Charleston's Fort Sumter Hotel. They barely left their room for the whole weekend. Unlike the other women he had met and slept with, Inga was his match. She also understood that behind the jokes and wisecracks, he was deeply ambitious. 'You have just sufficient meanness in you to get along and enough brains and goodness to give to the world and not only take,' she wrote.[7] But they knew it was not to be. A few weeks later, Inga confided to Kick that her relationship with Jack was over, although they still saw one another sporadically. Kick was upset that Jack had been forced to leave Washington, and she spent hours with Inga talking about him. The one compensation was that she was able to move into his Washington apartment, much better located than hers. 'The apartment is swell, you are swell ... see you in my dreams,' she told him.[8]

She had been promoted from being a secretary to reviewing plays. She wrote to Jack to tell him of her numerous beaux: she was seeing a bit of Torby, and a Lieutenant Jones 'who claims ... he is a bosom friend of yours [and] is dropping in this evening for a drink of grape juice ... I still don't know what his first name is. Inga tells me he is a great admirer of feminine pulchritude. Are you sure I am his cup of tea?'[9] She also reported that Billy Hartington had been in touch.

Billy had written to her to explain that he had broken off his engagement to Sally. He simply couldn't stop loving Kick. His sister Anne later recalled Billy's misery about Kick and being engaged to the wrong woman. Billy had confided to his mother, to whom he was so close, about his passion for Kick. 'I long to come over,' Kick wrote to Nancy Astor, 'but it looks quite impossible.'[10]

Her father wrote to her in January 1942, urging her to make the most of her Washington experience by going to bed early and getting fresh air: 'You are only twenty-one and your type is very susceptible to fading fast.'[11] He sent shipments of oranges and grapefruits from Florida to freezing Washington. She enjoyed her work, writing to one of her priests: 'working round this office has certainly been an education. The people are from another world, but a world that has much more color than I ever dreamed possible.'[12] She told him that she was dreading the humid Washington summer, but that it was preferable to sitting 'on the Cape all summer and do[ing] nothing. So we shall just see how long Kick can hold out.'[13] Jack had continued to be plagued by back problems, and was now awaiting surgery in Charleston. Young Joe had just received his wings.

John White was still assiduously courting her. Without Jack to keep a beady eye on her, he began pressurizing her to become more intimate. He accused her of being cold and insisted that she should at least give him the occasional kiss. Inga often came along too and was witness to their arguments. Kick would telephone John to apologize, against Inga's advice, who warned her against 'crawling to the cross'.[14]

Even trying to make Kick jealous didn't seem to work. His frustration was evident from his diary: 'L'Affair Kathleen rocks along its windy way, very verbose indeed,' or 'Too many words and not enough action'. He also berated himself for his weak behaviour: 'For two weeks as of this day, I shall not see her alone … but do it I shall to see if I can't get some sort of control of myself.'[15]

Kick spent her twenty-second birthday in Florida with her friend Nancy Tenney. Having proved herself as a writer in the theatre column, Kick got a further promotion that spring, taking over Inga's column 'Did You Happen to See …'. Now she was interviewing notable Washington people as well as continuing to review plays and movies. She cut out all of her articles and pasted them into her scrapbook. She was proud of her journalism, which was improving all the time. She wrote in a crisp, eloquent style, with a light sprinkle of Kennedy wit. A feature on Maxine Davis began: 'Her father was a cynic, her mother an idealist. She struck a happy medium and has become one of America's leading magazine writers.'[16] She could almost have been writing about a possible future for herself. Her career was going from strength to strength and yet her heart remained in England. She applied to become the paper's correspondent in London, but was turned down.

In March 1942, Kick got a letter from Lady Astor begging her 'to stop all this foolishness and come right over and marry Billy'. She wrote to Jack for advice. He responded with characteristic forthrightness: 'I would strongly advise against any voyages to England to marry any Englishman.'

He wrote her a long, detailed letter explaining why he thought it was 'time to write the obituary of the British Empire. Like all good things it had to come to an end sometime, it was good while it lasted.' He outlined his theory, comparing Britain to the Roman Empire, and added, 'any time the Prime Minister of a country will admit to his own people that another country is going to save them – it's on the toboggan'. Jack's letter shows a new seriousness; there is none of their usual mocking banter. He explained to his sister his view that the war would mean the end not just of the British Empire but also of the old social order: 'the old school tie won't see much service in the future'.[17]

She wrote back, 'As for your words of advice Brother I'll take 'em. Boy the only persons you can be sure of are your own flesh and blood and then we are not always sure of them.'[18] Deep down, though, Kick just couldn't see it the same way. Days after she moved into Jack's old apartment she was paid a visit by Lem Billings. He noted with amusement the display of photographs of 'countless dukes and lords of the United Kingdom'. There was no photograph of her boyfriend John White.[19]

33

'Did You Happen to See …'

the drippings from my pen.

Kick Kennedy

On 2 March 1942, Kick received a letter from her father, kindly and lovingly berating her for listening too much to the opinions of other people: 'Without meaning any criticism of your very excellent character, I have noted that with you, popular opinions are frequently accepted as true opinions.' He advised her to trust her own judgement: 'So don't bum rides on other people's opinions. It's lazy at best – and in some cases much worse.'[1]

The trouble was that she disagreed with the father she had adored, who had been proven to be wrong and was now *persona non grata* in DC. Kick would never abandon her belief that the English would defeat the Nazis. She and her siblings were witnesses to their father's humiliation and ostracism, on both sides of the pond. She was still desperate to return to England, but she was concerned about how her English friends would react in the light of her father's unpopularity.

The President had offered him an ignominious job advising on bottlenecks in the shipping industry. He turned it down. Kick and her siblings tried hard to raise their father's depressed spirits as he sat aimlessly in the Florida sun. They wrote constantly and he visited them in Washington, but they could see he was a broken man. Kick wrote long, newsy letters. One of them was to tell him the latest joke that was circling Washington. It was about a man who was having terrible headaches and asked his doctor to remove his brain, dust it off and give it back to the patient. The patient didn't return for his brain, and when his doctor met him in the street he asked for the reason. 'Oh that's alright,' said the patient, 'I won't need a brain any more, I have just gotten a job in Washington.'[2] It was a good joke, partly at her own expense. However, given her sister's botched brain operation, it was insensitive, and perhaps an indication of some unresolved anger over the fate of the sister she had loved and tried so hard to protect.

Many of Kick's and Jack's friends were being posted overseas. There was Lem's farewell party in March. He was going to Africa as an ambulance driver. And in April there was a weekend party in South Carolina for George Mead. George had a huge crush on Kick and had often taken her out in Washington. The beloved eldest son in a family of five children, he had joined the Marines, and was headed overseas to fight the Japanese. That weekend, he was unusually quiet. Kick was puzzled and worried that he didn't seem happy to see her and her friends, who had all made such an effort to bid him farewell. George confessed to a friend that he was scared. His friend passed him Jack Kennedy's advice 'that if you didn't think you were going to be killed, you'd survive'.[3] The problem was that George thought that he would be killed, and he couldn't bear the thought of being a coward.

Jack, recovering from his back surgery, was his usual high-spirited self, not allowing anyone to see his agony. He was the life and soul of George's party, full of jokes about the navy versus the Marines. Despite his health problems, he signed up for combat action in high-speed PT (Patrol Torpedo) boats – sometimes known as 'bucking broncos'. He covered up his medical history in order to be accepted. He wanted action and nothing was going to stop him.

Kick sent John a telegram from South Carolina to say that she had been delayed from returning to Washington: 'Sickness prevents meeting.' He was furious and felt that she was excluding him.[4] When she came back, they quarrelled. To her surprise, he asked her what she thought about marrying him. 'Not the way you are now' was her response.[5] He felt that she was dropping him and it made him love her all the more.

One evening, as he said his farewell, he was struck by an overpowering feeling of love and affection. 'What a sweet, sincere, good-hearted little thing she is,' he thought. Then he truly let his guard down and whispered, 'I love you, Kathleen.' The next day at the office, he drew back and was cold with her. After accompanying her home, he walked down the hall and then heard her footsteps. She was crying. She asked him whether he meant what he had said. When he confirmed it, she told him that she loved him too. She said she was sorry for the mistakes she felt she had made in her relationship with him. He put in his diary, 'Think there are none.'[6]

The next day he sent her a dozen roses, took her out for dinner and enlisted in the Marines. By June, John, Jack and Joe had all gone. Jack made a special visit to Kick before he left for PT boat duty, in which he confided in her that he was thinking of renouncing the church. Kick was shocked. She found it unthinkable that he could hurt the family, knowing what this would do to her mother.[7] On the other hand, her relationship with John White had led her to question some of the strict tenets of her religion.

Inga had left Washington for New York, so Kick threw herself into her work on 'Did You Happen to See …'. One of her articles explored the idea of women running for office in times of war: 'What about it, girls? Are you ready to take on the responsibilities of the world? Well, and what does the stronger sex think about this proposal to displace them?'[8] As a Kennedy woman, she loved the idea of women in politics.

Kick was becoming a writer and had finally found her voice. She wrote to Jack with the 'drippings from my pen' and encouraged him to send his own literary endeavours for her to copy-edit.[9] Brother and sister exchanged letters, in which they discussed everything from politics to the ideals of England. Kick corrected Jack's spellings, and encouraged him to think carefully about his prose.

For the summer of 1942 Kick headed off for the Cape. For the first time other senior family members were missing. There was no Joe Jr, Jack or Rosemary. It simply wasn't the same without them, and the rest of the family felt subdued and dispirited. Kick left the family in August to meet up with White in the exclusive resort of Jones Beach. They spent a memorable day swimming, surfing and picnicking. White tried to kiss her underwater, and then they lay on the sand on top of his United States Marine Corps blanket. White kissed her passionately in front of the crowds. Somehow in this new and dangerous situation, she allowed him to take liberties.[10]

The weekend continued well. They took the train to Manhattan and met up with Inga, who had remarried quickly after her rejection by Jack. She told Kick she still loved him. Then Kick and John sipped brandy Alexanders at the Rockefeller Center and saw *Porgy and Bess* on Broadway.[11]

Kick invited John to Hyannis Port for Labor Day. He was anxious about meeting the family for the first time. Arriving late, he was given a stony reception by Joe and Rose, who made it perfectly clear that they disliked and disapproved of him. The rest of the family were pleasant, especially the funny and charming Teddy, who was now ten. But it wasn't a success. It was difficult for John to witness Kick back in the Kennedy fold; he saw that she was far more competitive than normal, and yet he also sensed that she was pulling back from the claustrophobia of the family, that she did not seek their approval in the same way as her siblings. He never saw the Kennedys again.

In August 1942, George Mead landed on Guadalcanal island in the Solomons and, after fierce fighting, was killed by a bullet in the face. His mother wrote to his friends, including the Kennedys: 'The love in our hearts for George certainly is there stronger, if possible than ever before, and always will be. What is death, then, but a physical change which does not interfere in any way with our power to love?'[12] Kick only learnt of his death at the beginning of September. She was devastated and wrote back to his mother:

> Your words to us meant more than all the things I have ever read, learned or been taught about death, war, courage, strength ... Future days may bring bad news to all of us, but remembering your words and the way you have acted, one cannot help but feel – Please God, let me act in a similar fashion.[13]

Kick also told Mrs Mead how much she had admired George for his strong sense of duty to his parents.

Back in Washington, without Jack or Inga, Kick continued to work hard at her job. She interviewed General Eisenhower's brother, finding him 'very interesting and very nice'. She had dinner with the 'future pres[ident] of the United States (aka Brother Joe)'. Her letters home to her parents were full of news about her life as a reporter: 'The column is going along very well.

Still have plenty of people that must be interviewed. Yesterday I had a woman in, who the paper has been trying to get for years. She never would consent to be interviewed before.'[14] Kick had the ability to get people to open up to her. They trusted her and responded to her warmth and good humour and intelligence.

She told her parents that she was still in touch with Billy, who was standing for Parliament: 'He still says that he is waiting for me to come to England.' She told them that he wanted her company 'more than ever because I would be such a help in advising him and helping him with his speeches'.[15] Her time in Washington and her long talks with Jack and Inga had politicized her further. She saw that she would make a good partner for Billy, and she thought again of how he had talked to her about Georgiana Duchess of Devonshire making Chatsworth into a centre of political power.

John White was to be transferred to Northern Ireland with the Marines, and as a parting gift he bought Kick a new nightgown. He teased her but loved her in her extra-long white nightgowns. They had made a pact that if she had not found herself another husband in five years' time they would marry. He wrote in his diary: 'KK WILL MARRY ME in 1947.'[16] He took with him a photograph of her on Jones Beach, the scene of that happy day.

In December she cut off her long, tawny hair, adopting the new short 'windswept' style. She went alone to a dinner at the Chevy Chase Club wearing a spectacular candy-striped dress which caused a stir. She was becoming confident in her ability to be herself without Jack and Inga at her side. In February 1943, she made a radio address, and though she felt nervous it only fuelled her ambition to do better next time. Kick was hatching a plan to be a reporter in London. She told her parents that she was arranging meetings with editors and publishers to pitch her storylines. The editor of *Women's Home Companion* had agreed to a meeting and she was determined to make him realize that it was 'essential for them to have a correspondent in London. Keep your fingers crossed and say a prayer.'[17] What she was also doing was letting her parents know that, whatever anyone said, she would return to England.

Now that John White had left, she was finally on her own, though it wasn't long before she found a new admirer. She was seeing much of Lord and Lady Halifax. He was now Ambassador in DC. They remembered her fondly from her London days. She dined at the Embassy and sat next to their eldest son, Lieutenant Charles Wood of the Royal Horse Guards, who was on leave after three years in the Middle East. Their second son, Peter, had recently been killed fighting in Egypt, and their youngest son, Richard, had almost lost his life in the same campaign – Kick told her parents that he had lost both his legs and was coming to America to recuperate. She was concerned about Lady Halifax, who 'looks awfully ill'.[18]

Lieutenant Richard Wood was born, like Kick, in 1920. He was to become very important to her. A tall, handsome Eton and Oxford man of great charm and courage, he served in the King's Royal Rifle Corps. His legs had to be amputated after a Stuka bomb fell on him. He often joked that he was very lucky that it had failed to detonate, and that he had had such a rough time at Eton that nothing else could be as bad. In fact, he was president of the elite society Pop at Eton and a good cricketer. He toured America to show war veterans how to cope with artificial limbs. He had his own artificial legs made slightly smaller than his real ones, to reduce his height from 6 foot 4 to 6 foot 1. He was not the sort to feel sorry for himself. Richard fell madly in love with Kick, and she never once considered his disability an impediment to his sexual appeal. She greatly admired his courage and humour. But he was also a reminder of Billy, and all that she felt she had lost when she left England.

John White, meanwhile, made an ignominious return to Washington, pending an investigation for espionage. He had been caught photographing British destroyers and suspicions were aroused that he might be a spy. He was imprisoned in the Washington Navy Yard, where Kick visited him. By now, the romance was truly over, John's disgrace the final nail in the coffin, but the friendship continued. He recalled that she talked increasingly about Billy. She was at last on her way back to England.

34

Red Cross Worker of World War II

Received from Military Liaison Officer, American Red Cross, New York Port of Embarkation, the following equipment:

1 Belt Pistol
I Helmet Steel M-1
1 Liner Helmet M-1, New Type
1 Can Meat M-1932
1 Canteen M-1910
1 Cover Canteen Dismounted M-1910
1 Cup M-1910
1 Fork
1 Haversack
1 Knife
1 Spoon
1 Headband Adj. New Type
1 Neckband, No. 4 Med.
1 Roll, Bedding
1 Pouch, First Aid Packet M-24
1 First Aid Packet M-24

Date: 6/21/43 Signature: Kathleen A. Kennedy[1]

At 7.15 p.m. on 23 June 1943, Kick Kennedy boarded the *Queen Mary*. She was equipped very differently from the time she had set off for England as the Ambassador's daughter decked out in fashionable hat and furs. Now she was a volunteer for the American Red Cross, dressed in a drab blue-grey uniform of skirt and jacket and hat. For once, she was like every other girl and not a celebrated Kennedy. She wrote to her family to tell them that, despite its being the hottest day of the year, she was dressed in winter uniform and a raincoat and wore a tin helmet. Like the other girls, she carried a gas mask and a first-aid kit strapped to her waist, and had packed her few belongings into a 35-pound musette bag.[2]

Kick's previous experiences of ocean liners was full of glamour and fun, dancing in the ballrooms, dining in the grand salon, swimming in the pool and promenading on the decks. She could hardly believe her eyes when she caught sight of the *Queen Mary*. The liner, originally intended for 2,000 wealthy passengers, now housed 18,000 American soldiers and 160 nurses as well as the Red Cross women. Kick told her family that the men were sleeping in the hallways and on the decks, wherever they could be squeezed in: 'It really is the most pathetic looking sight in the world to see the way they are living.'[3] She shared a cabin with eight other girls (one bath between them). At night, because of the blackout, they would cover the portholes. She was glad to find she could buy chocolate bars and cookies. During drill, which took place on the sun deck, she walked among the soldiers: 'it is amazing what the appearance of the fair sex gives them.'[4]

Kick had finally achieved what she had longed for: a return to her beloved London, and to Billy Hartington. How had she achieved the seemingly impossible? It seems that her parents had finally relented and let her become one of the 'Doughnut Dollies', as the press dubbed the women.

In early 1943, Kick left her newspaper job in Washington and began her Red Cross training. She was following in the footsteps of her Aunt Eunice in the First World War. Red Cross Clubs were being sent out to improve morale among American GIs. The girls would give out coffee and doughnuts and, more importantly, chat to the GIs about home. There were eight Red Cross Clubs in London, but many others around the British Isles. They worked from 'Clubmobiles', buses fitted with lounges, 'coffee and donut-making equipment, gum, cigarettes, magazines, newspapers, postcards, a phonograph and records.'[5]

The ARC (American Red Cross) training usually lasted for six weeks, and the girls were all expected to be college-educated and to possess extremely high social skills, which was no problem for Kick. They learnt management skills, programme planning and recreational games. They also learnt to drive a Clubmobile, to change a tyre and service their vehicles. But the main thing, as one volunteer said, was that 'you're female and speak English'.[6]

Kick was trained in Richmond, Virginia, befriending a woman called Tatty Spaatz, an ex-girlfriend of John White. The girls compared notes and discovered to their amusement that he had sent them identical letters declaring his undying love.[7]

Kick adored her time in Richmond, having what she called 'my real baptism as a Red Cross worker of World War II'.[8] She loved the 'beautiful & proud Southern town' of Virginia and the 'genuineness of Southern hospitality'. Wherever the Red Cross girls travelled on the trolley cars, they were given the best seats, men jumping to their feet. She noted in her diary that the people were 'first proud as Virginians, secondly as Americans'. She worked hard in the day, and then by night she danced with a range of partners from 'a plumber, a truck driver, bootlegger, heavy weight boxer, Cotton-Club dancer'. Everyone, she noted, 'had a story and it doesn't take much to get him started'.[9]

When she had finished her training at the end of May, she headed back to Washington, where she cleared her apartment. She accompanied a group to the FBI headquarters, where she met J. Edgar Hoover ('big personality and handshake'), who was 'worshipped like God'.[10] Later, she met up with Lord and Lady Halifax and their son Richard Wood. She enjoyed discussing Anglicanism and Catholicism with Lord Halifax. Halifax, she noted, was for unification of the churches but saw papal infallibility as the sticking point. They talked about the confessional and transubstantiation. It was a taste of things to come.

Kick had a gift for dealing with older people as well as young. She adored Lord Halifax who, she thought, 'bespeaks wisdom, spirituality', and she loved his sense of humour. She disliked the Director of the American Red Cross in Britain, Harvey Gibson: 'Rather Grumpy sort of person'. She dined with her father and Lord Beaverbrook, the Canadian newspaper tycoon and British politician, whom she found 'quick', with a 'nimble mind' and a desire always 'to get right to [the] core of the matter'.[11]

Kick had dinner with Richard Wood, who talked at length about his war wound. After the bomb had crushed his legs, he lay in his slit trench and told himself that he was going to live. When he awoke in hospital he heard two orderlies discussing whether he was going to make it through the night. His legs were amputated on a makeshift table in a tent in the middle of the desert. He asked if he would ever walk again and was told about Douglas Bader who had had both legs amputated after a flying accident. With the use of artificial legs, Bader learnt to walk and dance, and continued his career as a fighter pilot. Kick said Richard's worst fear was for people to pity him: 'I think he's the most courageous person I've ever known,' she wrote in her diary.

Ready to embark for England, Kick was issued with her regulation army equipment. In her diary, she observed that reality was hitting home.

Rose recalled many years later that once Joe and Jack had been sent to the 'theaters of war', Kick felt 'rather left out … she too wanted to be directly involved in the war and to make her own contribution that would be constructive'.[12]

Some of her friends had a more cynical view: that Kick's only motivation was her determination to win back Billy. As one of the conditions of her acceptance into the Red Cross, one of Kick's friends was required to sign a form verifying that Kick was not going overseas in order to be reunited with a boyfriend. Her friend Dinah Brand joked that having heard the news about Billy's engagement, Kick was getting on the first boat back to England.[13] Even Jack joked that his sister was likely to become a duchess soon.[14]

Rose admitted in her memoirs that she had little idea that Kick was in love with Billy. However, there was no guarantee that Kick would be assigned to London, where she so desperately wanted to be. Not unless her father could pull some strings.

Yet her father and Jack knew of her strong feelings for Billy. It seems likely that Joe did indeed pull some strings to ensure that Kick did not end up assigned to a Clubmobile in some remote city. One of his contacts at US Army headquarters in London ensured that she was posted there.[15] She was delighted when she heard the news.

The crossing was rough and precarious. Her sleep was interrupted by the ship's constant swerving to avoid German submarines. The cabin was cramped: 'and when I say on top of one another I do mean on top of one another'.[16] She thought the nurses were 'tough babies'. She liked the Red Cross girls but was rendered impatient by their giggling and gossiping until 1.30 a.m. She was always fond of an early night. To stop herself from feeling hungry she nibbled on chocolate and crackers. Then, always mindful of her weight, she would take exercise by pacing the deck (just 40 feet long), 'trying to eke a mile out of it'.[17]

She told Rose that she was attending mass and taking communion. She also spoke of her excitement at seeing England again, and was quite prepared for all the changes: 'This arrival certainly is going to be different from our last one. The life on an Army troop transport has been an eye-opener. It seems to me unreal and far removed from anything I've ever known that I can't believe I'm a part of it. Sometimes it almost feels like a dream.' But she added cheerily, 'Love to all and eat a lot of ice cream for me on Sunday.'[18]

Kick had not told many people that she was coming to England: 'What a shock they'll get when I get on the other end of the phone.' When she arrived, she scribbled a quick note home: 'Everything wonderful and it certainly doesn't feel like four years … to say that those I've seen were surprised is putting it mildly.' Her plan was to move into a flat with her old friend Jane Kenyon-Slaney: 'Certainly glad I brought an evening dress. As much gaiety here as in New York. Had steak for dinner last night, which is probably more than you all can say.'[19]

Most of her friends thought her unchanged, other than her new hairstyle with curls in front. On her first day in London she had tea with Janey, cocktails at the Savoy and then dinner at the Gargoyle with male friends, where she 'guzzled a steak'. Kick had been worried about the reception she would receive, and on her first night out two men abused her father for being anti-British. One was a journalist called Derek Tangye: 'an effeminate type and I think, completely inconsequential'.[20] Her father responded with a loving letter in which he advised her about the anti-Joe Kennedy feeling: 'After all, the only crime I can be accused of is that I was pro-American instead of pro-English … You have your own life to live and you needn't answer any of my problems, responsibilities or difficulties – so just smile and say "Fight with him; he can take care of himself."' He carried on reassuring her that 'no one has been more sympathetic to the British cause than you, so you shouldn't have to take any of the criticism, but I'm just saying this to you so that you'll be prepared for it. I don't mind; don't you.'[21]

There had been much interest in the English press about her return to England. One magazine article called 'Smart Set Society Hats Off' featured her: 'WE TAKE OUR HATS OFF TO Miss Kathleen Kennedy of the sparkling Irish eyes and unquenchable zest for life.' The report went on to detail her 'unhesitating response to her country's need in time of war and her gallant sacrifice in halting a brilliant newspaper career to serve overseas with the American Red Cross'. 'Her hair is a long, sweeping shoulder-length bob, and she has the radiant colouring of her Irish ancestors; a lovely colleen and a credit to her fighting lineage.'

Kick was relieved. In July, she wrote to her family to tell them about the warmth of her reception: 'I simply can't get over how nice everyone is. I must say that I expected old friends to be kind but they have exceeded all expectations.' Lord Beaverbrook had asked her to stay for the weekend, saying 'this admirer is the combined age of all your other admirers'. Kick was ecstatic: 'Anytime anyone says anything about the British in front of me they'll hear about it.'[22]

There was one man in particular who was overjoyed to hear that Kick was back. On the very night that she returned she received a telegram:

REACH LONDON 7.15 SATURDAY STAYING AT MAYFAIR. CAN YOU KEEP SUNDAY FREE. BILLY

35

Coffee and Doughnuts

I feel that my devotion to the British over a period of years has not been without foundation and I feel this is a second home more than ever.

Kick Kennedy to John F. Kennedy[1]

'First day back in London and I still can't believe I'm really here. It all seems like a dream from which I shall awaken quite soon.'[2]

She was assigned a position as programme assistant at an officers-only club in Hans Crescent in exclusive Knightsbridge, a stone's throw from Harrods. It's hard not to imagine Joe's handprint on this. Her days were long, and she was expected to stay on well into the evening, checking in female guests and then dancing with the soldiers. She wrote to her old boss, Frank Waldrop: 'As we get a day and a half off a week I am here recuperating from five and a half days of jitter-bugging, gin rummy, Ping-Pong, bridge and just being an American girl among 1500 doughboys a long way from home. (I'm not sure yet but I don't think this is what I was born for).'[3]

The 'doughboys' ate American food, had their clothes pressed and their shoes polished, went dancing and theatre-going in the West End, and had a warm bed for the night. Kick wrote of the GIs that they were 'very nice but most of them are so homesick and heartily dislike the British and everything about them'. She was constantly stopped on the street by the throngs of Americans who wanted to chat, but she was not terribly interested in the American boys: 'I hop on my bike and away I go.'[4]

She wrote to Lem: 'You wouldn't recognize old Kick who used to walk around with her nose quite far in the air if she had to go in the subway to get to the Automat with you'. She added, 'I'd give my two tiny hands, covered in warts for a meal in the Automat and I wouldn't care if I had to sit with two dirty truck drivers. As a matter of fact they are probably the only people I know how to charm now.'[5]

Jack wrote to Kick from the South Pacific to berate her for sending 'TERSE TELEGRAPHIC COMMUNIQUES' instead of proper letters. His entire letter was jokingly typed in capital letters to make his point.

He had assumed command of *PT 109* on Talugi in the Solomon Islands. He had written from his base to enquire whether Kick had left for Europe, telling his parents that he now had his own boat and went out on patrol every other night. He also told them that he had visited George Mead's grave: 'he is buried near the beach where he fell – it was extremely sad'.[6] This brought home the frightening reality of war, but his letters remained zestful.

Jack's sailing experience proved invaluable to him, and he joked to Kick that 'this job is somewhat like sailing in that we spend most of our time trying to get the boat running faster, although it isn't just to beat Daly for the Kennedy cup – it's the Kennedy tail this time'. He was his usual upbeat self with that vein of self-deprecating humour that Kick shared and loved: 'That bubble I had about lying on a cool Pacific island with a warm Pacific maiden hunting bananas for me is definitely a bubble that has burst.' He told her that he couldn't even swim because of a fungus in the water 'that grows out of your ears'.[7] He asked her to say hello to some of their English friends.

Kick wrote back to say that she was sunning herself in the garden of Sissy Gore: 'still recovering from a rather hectic trip over. That's about all I can say on that point!'[8] She told Jack that London seemed quite unchanged: 'food is very good – blitzed areas are not obvious'. Lady Astor had written her a note of welcome but was away at Plymouth. Many of her friends were in the country: 'Everyone is very surprised & I do mean very surprised to see me.' She confided in Jack that 'There's much more anti-Kennedy feeling than I imagined and I am determined to get my stories straight as I think I'll get it on all sides.'[9]

While she was waiting to see what she was going to be assigned to, she was having a 'terribly gay' time. 'Party about every week', she told Jack. What she didn't tell him was that one of the first people who had rushed to see her was Billy Hartington.

She had seen Tony Rosslyn (the former Lord Loughborough, who had now inherited his grandfather's earldom) who, as soon as he heard that she was back, had come to call at Hans Crescent, clutching a bottle of champagne. Tony played ping-pong with some of the GIs and chatted to them. 'I thought how amazed some of them would have been if they knew they were talking to a real live English Lord.'[10]

Tony then took her on to the 400 Club where she bumped into many old friends. She told her family that she had made a resolution not to discuss anyone 'because people do nothing but gossip these days. They are just so sick of the war that in order to get away from it they spend their time ruining people's reputations.'[11]

Tony Rosslyn wrote to Jack to reassure him that Kick was being well looked after: 'She is in great heart, looks divine & is surrounded by Beaux in her leisure time.' He bemoaned the fact that she didn't seem to be interested in any of her beaux, including himself: 'she is just the sort of girl I'd like to marry but I'm not the right type for her Jack & might make her unhappy'. He talked about the religious differences and the problem of raising children together: 'however ... I don't suppose she'd have me if I was the last thing on earth'.[12]

Tony also wrote to Joe, telling him how popular Kick was at Hans Crescent: 'I also saw her beat the pants off an American sergeant at "ping-pong".' He lent her a bicycle to get around town. He little knew that this would soon help to make her the poster girl of the American war effort: the American Red Cross Girl riding her bike. He took her to the cinema and when they left she jumped on her bicycle, wobbled and then fell off, smashing a bottle of pine essence he had given her as a present. The liquid spilt over her uniform and she and Tony descended into tears of laughter. He thought her unchanged except she was prettier than ever with the new hairstyle and a 'greater air of poise and self assurance'.[13] She teased him about having acquired a few grey hairs since she last saw him.

Kick couldn't understand the GIs who disliked the British and everything about them, 'the warm beer, the climate (I've slept with three blankets every night)'. She only ever experienced the British and England through rose-coloured glasses. Despite rationing, the cold weather and the privations of war, she saw only what she wanted to see, telling her family that she was dining on 'lobster, ice cream, chocolate cake, chicken salad' and sipping cocktails most nights.[14] After a party for the Free French, she wrote in her diary that 'It staggered me that a party here in London after four years of war could resemble the old days so much.' She was blind to the deprivations, the dreadful food and the blackout.[15] She noted that although a band called the Flying Yanks played the popular 'jitterbug', the 'Britishers danced sedately on'.

She wrote to her ex-boss Frank Waldrop to tell him how different her life was compared to the time when she was living in Prince's Gate as the Ambassador's daughter. Her work as a journalist had hardened her 'for come what may'. Her love for the British remained undiminished: 'You will be glad to hear that I am more pro-British than ever and spend my days telling the GIs about that great institution "the British Empire".' 'There'll always be an England' was her cheery farewell.[16]

Kick was excited about her reunion with Billy on 10 July 1943. How would he find her after four long years apart? He travelled down from Yorkshire and they met at the Mayfair Hotel, where they had dinner and celebrated their reunion with a bottle of champagne. They went on to the 400 Club until 3.30 and then walked home together in the rain.

36

Sister Kick

You'll never be happy in America now that England is in your blood.

Nancy Astor to Kick Kennedy

The day after her reunion with Billy, Kick set off for morning mass at Farm Street in Mayfair. She met Billy again later that day. They visited his cousin Arthur 'Boofy' Gore, son of the Earl of Arran. Along with his wife Fiona, they all talked about the havoc that war had 'wrecked with our lives'.

Back at the Red Cross, she learnt to dance the jitterbug ('it really is diffi-cult') and went to bed early 'to the sound of ping-pong balls flying across the net'.[1] The next day she wrote to the 'dearest little Kennedys'. Gossip was circulating around London that Billy and Kick were close to announcing their engagement, and some were even putting bets on when they were going to announce it publicly: 'It really is funny to see people put their heads together the minute we arrive at any place.' She told her siblings that 'Some people have gotten the idea that I'm going to give in. Little do they know. Some of those old Devonshire and Cecil ancestors would certainly jump out of their graves if anything happened to some of their ancient traditions.'[2]

She dined with A. J. 'Tony' Drexel Biddle Jr, Ambassador to the Polish and other Allied governments in exile, at his residence in Brook Street ('Only house in London where ice cream and chocolate cake are served'), where she noted drily that in the course of a spirited evening's conversation 'A few more characters and reputations hit the dust.' She thought Mrs Biddle 'very nice but rather hard' whereas Tony Biddle was charming: 'Adores Jack and Joe. Thinks we should rent them out.'[3] On the way home, she stopped off at the Dorchester 'for a dance or two'. The next morning she worked at the Club all day ('After the tea dance I thought I'd die if I ever saw another GI'), and then cycled around Hyde Park: 'the Serpentine looks as peaceful as ever'.[4]

The following weekend she lunched with her friend Jean Ogilvy, who was now Lady Lloyd, having married Lord Lloyd, a lieutenant in the Royal Armoured Corps, who inherited his title following the death of his father, a former Governor-General in Bombay. On a whim, they took the train to Cliveden to see Nancy, Lady Astor. Kick felt it was like 'old times' to be met by Arthur the butler, and take tea on the lovely, spacious terrace. She thought that there 'it would be easier to forget about the war than any other place I know'. She was amused that the much older Lady Astor (she was now sixty-four to Kick's twenty-three) played three extremely active sets of tennis during which she 'never stopped talking and rushing around the court', though Kick 'finally managed to beat her'. Lady Astor's first words to Kick were: 'the Pope is an out and out Fascist, you must marry over here. You'll never be happy in America now that England is in your blood.'

Cliveden was now a Canadian military hospital, and Lady Astor spent much of her time helping out. Kick recorded that her hostess had sent a bottle of champagne to 'some old soldier who literally couldn't keep a thing down'. Over dinner with three Canadian doctors, Nancy regaled them with anecdotes about her time in Russia where she had met Stalin. She had asked him why his enemies were shot without benefit of trial. The interpreter went white with shock, but Stalin, nonplussed, replied: 'this is war against the capitalist system and I am simply killing off my enemies'. She told the company that in the old days she preferred Hitler and Germany to the Bolshies and Stalin. Kick was, as ever, charmed by Lady Astor: 'her vitality, alertness is simply unbelievable'. She wrote later in her diary: 'This war has been a great shock to her nervous system as much as anything else. Four sons in it, and living through the horrible bombings of Plymouth are enough for any woman but she still keeps up her tremendous spirits.'[5]

The following morning, Kick was served breakfast in bed: 'How glorious it felt to lie lazily on these cool, white sheets and be waited upon.' After a quick game of tennis, she headed back to the Red Cross: 'the club is as depressing as ever'.

In London she improved her acquaintance with Fred Astaire's sister Adele, who had given up her own stage career when she married Billy's uncle. Kick found her 'full of charm', but noted that she was very critical of various other socialites. Then there was dinner with William Douglas-Home: 'He is quite fantastic in his beret and as a captain. Is he a phoney? I don't know.'[6]

One of Kick's qualities, shared with Jack, was being a good listener. She was struck by the war talk of a distinguished Eighth Air Force radio operator, Charles Patrick, who had just completed twenty operations and had received his 'Purple Heart' when he was wounded in a raid on St Nazaire. He told her that the Germans were 'great fighters', to be respected, and she loved to hear the air force slang: bombs were referred to as dropping 'eggs'. She noted, perhaps thinking anxiously of brother Joe, that the pilots 'definitely do not fly after 25 ops'. Patrick told Kick that the European 'theater of operations [was] much tougher than the Pacific'. She would think twice about these words when she heard the news about Jack's near miss in the Pacific.

On 29 July 1943, responding to Jack's reproach about telegrams, she wrote him a long, newsy letter describing how nice everyone had been to 'Sister Kick'. She told him how overwhelmed she felt by the welcome she had received. In Washington there had been a lot of criticism of their father by her fellow Americans. By contrast,

> Now here are the British who are directly concerned and not a peep out of them. Of course a lot of it I can put down to British reserve which feel that some things are better left unsaid but most I blame it on their ability to make friends which last all our lives. They are slow about it at first but once made then its lasting – wholly and completely.[7]

Kick had confided in Jack about the 'anti-Kennedy' feeling, but her return to war-torn London had done much to restore the family image. She was truly in her second home, among a people to whom she had grown devoted.

She confided in Jack that she had spent time with Billy at his Eastbourne home on the south coast, which had been heavily blitzed, but she loved it there. They had managed to get hold of some peaches, and walked on the beach: 'For 24 hours I forgot about the war.' She confided her feelings to Jack: Billy 'is just the same, a bit older, a bit more ducal but we get on as well as ever. It is queer as he is so unlike anyone I have ever known at home or anyplace really.'

Billy, as handsome as ever in his uniform, had grown in stature. The war had brought out the best in him. He was trying to put the Dunkirk experience behind him, and was showing a new sense of confidence. He was now a captain in the Guards, and was shortly expected to stand for Parliament, taking leave from the army to begin his campaign. Kick, with her interest in politics, was delighted.

But she also mentioned to Jack the insurmountable barrier to their relationship: 'I know he will never give in about the religion and he knows I never would. It's all rather difficult as he is very, very fond of me and as long as I am about he'll never marry.' Having for once revealed her deepest feelings and concerns, she reverted to her jokey tone: 'It's really too bad because I'm sure I would be a most efficient Duchess of Devonshire in the post-war world and as I'd have a castle in Ireland, one in Scotland, one in Yorkshire and one in Sussex, I could keep my old nautical brothers in their old age.'[8]

She was, however, keeping her options open and dating other men, such as William Douglas-Home: 'I can't really understand why I like Englishmen so much as they treat one in quite an off-hand manner and aren't really nice to their women ... That's your technique isn't it?' She closed off, 'Well, take care Johnny. By the time you get this so much will have happened. The end looks nearer now than ever.'[9]

Kick could never have known how prophetic her words would be. Four days later, on 2 August, the Japanese destroyer *Amagiri* ploughed through *PT 109*, slicing it in half. The hull was ripped in two, the fuel tanks burst into flames. Just before this happened, Jack had written to his parents: 'I myself am completely – and thoroughly convinced that nothing is going to happen to me.'[10] But at the moment of impact he thought: 'This is how it feels to be killed.'[11] Of the thirteen crew members, two were killed and three others badly injured.

The PT was reported as lost. A few days later Motor Torpedo Squadron 2 held a funeral mass for Jack and his crew. Joe Kennedy, in Hyannis Port, was informed, but he told nobody, not even Rose. He strongly believed that Jack was still alive and was waiting to hear some news. He carried on as usual, taking the younger boys riding, not letting anyone see his concern.

And Jack was not dead. He and his men endured a gruelling seven-day ordeal waiting to be rescued. After the PT had been hit, Jack rescued one of his injured men and swam him back to the wreckage of the boat with the other survivors. In the morning, the remaining bow section began to sink, forcing the men to swim 3 miles to a tiny island in the distance. As Jack swam, he pulled 'Pappy' McMahon, who was clinging on to a towrope with his mouth. Exhausted, the men reached the beach and collapsed. After sleeping for most of the day, Jack swam out at night to seek help. By dawn he was so tired that he gave himself up to the current, which washed him back to shore.

The men swam to another island, where they found limited supplies of food and drink and a canoe. After a few days, two islanders arrived, scouting for Allies. One of the men handed a coconut to Jack, suggesting that he carve a message into the green husk. They took it to the nearest naval station. After six days they were rescued. The men had been without food and drink for almost a week. Jack's back was badly hurt, and he was not in good shape.

The war needed a hero, and despite some criticism that Jack should have employed better seamanship (his was the only 'highly maneuverable' PT boat to be attacked by an enemy vessel), it was his conduct after the event that counted. He was front-page news and the family were ecstatic. 'Kennedy's Son is Hero in Pacific as Destroyer Splits his PT Boat', screamed the *New York Times*.[12] Telegrams and messages of congratulations poured in.

Jack scribbled a message to the family: 'Dear Folks, This is just a short note to tell you that I am alive – and *not* kicking – in spite of any reports that you may happen to hear … Fortunately, they misjudged the durability of a Kennedy'.[13] The family, without Kick and Jack, gathered at the Cape to celebrate the triumph in the Pacific and the Ambassador's birthday. Joe Jr was on leave and had to endure endless talk about his younger brother's heroism. Always fiercely competitive, he felt it keenly, and that night was heard weeping in his bedroom.[14]

Kick was especially proud of her brother. She wrote to tell the family that 'the news about Jack is the most exciting I've ever heard'.[15] She wrote to Jack himself: 'Goodness, I was pleased to get your letter. Ever since reading the news in all the newspapers over here I have been worried to death about you'. She told him how many of her friends had rung up with congratulations, and that Clare Boothe Luce (one of Joe's former mistresses) was crediting his survival to the Catholic medal she had given him when he went to war.[16]

Inga got an exclusive interview with Jack for the *Boston Globe*, in which he modestly rejected the title of hero (the headline read, 'KENNEDY LAUDS MEN, DISDAINS HERO STUFF'), and the wife of one of the saved men spoke to her about his courage: 'When my husband wrote home, he told me that Lt Kennedy was wonderful, that he saved the lives of all the men and everybody at the base admired him greatly.'[17] Kick, feeling out of the loop, wrote to Inga: 'Please, please send me the article you did on Jack. I was so pleased by your letter as it was the first one I had with a report on Jack's arrival home. Goodness I wish I had been there. I hope he doesn't go back for a very long time.'[18]

37

Girl on a Bicycle

The Soldiers have been flocking in during the last two weeks. I really can't see how this little Island is going to hold all the American troops that are arriving. Please send me any clippings from the American papers. One should be coming out soon of me on a bicycle.

Kick Kennedy[1]

Kick was bursting with pride about Jack's heroism, but life at the Red Cross was much more exhausting than she had expected. Long hours and enforced cheerfulness were not easy. She wrote a letter to Jack to congratulate him and to tell him about her own war efforts: 'It's a great joy, a great job but sometimes you don't know whether you are going to shoot yourself or that GI over there in the corner ... God bless you ...'[2] She told her family that the Club Director and the Programme Director drove her 'nuts'. The latter was a 'Jewess, ex-stage actress, hard worker but very jealous of me'. She would tough it out, however, happy to 'suffer them and stay in London'.[3]

Lady Astor had dropped in to see Kick at Hans Crescent, amusing her as ever, and remarking pithily, 'You don't work in a Red Cross Club, you work in a lunatic asylum.' To a 'big tough top sergeant', she said, 'You don't need to be entertained. I should give you a lecture on temperance.' She scoured the Club looking for boys from Virginia: 'Lord Astor just looked amazed, and I don't really blame him as the place looked like a mad house.'[4] Nancy, who still regarded Kick as a surrogate daughter, was kind underneath the sarcasm, telling her, 'I just wanted them to know that there are lots of people concerning themselves about you over here.' She kept up the invitations, insisting that Kick should appear at a ball 'in the cause of Anglo-American unity which at this point is anything but good'.[5] GIs were flooding into Britain at this time, in preparation for the opening of the Second Front. To many British people, ground down by years of air raids and rationing, the flashy Americans seemed 'overpaid, oversexed and over here'.

Brother Joe, newly stationed in England as a United States naval aviator, also arrived at Hans Crescent, bringing a food package from home of ham, beef, eggs, brownies, cookies, candy, oranges, lemons and apples. Then there was Rose Kennedy's London friend Marie Bruce. She would be a major player in the Billy and Kick drama that would soon unfold.

Joe Sr wrote to Tony Rosslyn about his fears that Kick was overdoing it. Lord Halifax had told him that Kick was 'the busiest person in England … available on the telephone at all hours of the night and day at Hans Crescent'. Joe, anxious parent as ever, told Rosslyn that he wished he would say to Kick, 'as I've said to Jack – that he doesn't have to win this war all by himself any more than she has to entertain the entire American Army or be the focal point for British-American relations, just do a little, that's enough'.[6] Joe couldn't or wouldn't see that she was overcompensating because of her father's damaged reputation in England. He told Tony that they missed her 'like the devil' but that she seemed to be happy: 'whatever she wants is all right with me'. Despite his own pessimism about the war and its outcome, he recognized that he hadn't influenced his daughter in this respect: 'She has been the steadiest battler that there is for England.'[7]

For all her difficulties with the management, she was popular with the GIs at Hans Crescent, playing golf with a mixed group to 'improve Anglo-American relations'. She bumped into one of Jack's ex-girlfriends, Stella 'Baby' Cárcano, daughter of the Argentine Ambassador: 'She's awfully sweet and very attractive but not the girl for Jack.' Baby hated the countryside, and as Kick remarked, 'It doesn't make for popularity over here not to like the country.'[8]

Kick missed all her 'wee brothers and sisters' and begged them to keep writing letters: 'I love their letters and read parts of them to the gang here. They all get a terrific kick out of them.' She was tickled to find that she was accused of having an English accent, 'but the boys keep me from going too "limey".[9]

She had a 'fantastic' time being an extra in a very popular film called *English without Tears*, which involved 'dancing about with various other representatives of the United Nations'. She loved the work, with directors, electricians and stars 'all screaming "darling" at each other'. She was taken to watch Laurence Olivier and David Niven, who were also making films for the war effort. When she finally saw the rushes, she found that she was covered by 'an enormous toy hanging from the Xmas tree right in my face … for all the rice in China, I wouldn't be a film star.'

Despite her popularity, Kick now excited jealousy among the other girls. The British girls, deprived of cosmetics and clothes, envied her the beautiful dresses and the make-up she had, most of which Joe had sent her on the black market. Some of the former debutantes who now found themselves working in factories, as army drivers or in other demanding uniformed roles felt resentment that she 'didn't have to do anything except for the odd stint at a canteen'.[10] The care packages sent over by Rose and Joe also aroused envy among her Red Cross colleagues. On one occasion, Rose dispatched a 'glorious chest full of little goodies' including golf balls, foodstuffs and a turquoise wool dress.[11] In the end, Kick asked her mother to stop sending her lovely clothes from America. She wanted to rely on clothing coupons like the other girls.

Kick was also admonished for taking too many personal telephone calls. She seemed to be permanently on the telephone, gossiping with friends. The real issue, though, was the sheer number of her male admirers. William Douglas-Home, Tony Rosslyn, Richard Wood over in America, and, above all, Billy Cavendish were in love with her. Some of the English girls were insanely jealous. As one of them said, 'She was after Billy. He had a nice big fat title and estate coming and all that. That was not a nice thing to say, but it was well known and so terribly obvious.'[12]

Little did they know the pressure that Kick was under because of her religious faith. She and Billy continued to discuss ways around their religious differences. That August, she met for the first time Father Martin D'Arcy, the Jesuit priest from Mayfair's Farm Street Church. He would become an important figure in the ensuing months. After a weekend spent at Cliveden, she wrote to her parents, 'Billy came down from Yorkshire and had to sleep on the floor. I wish his father could have seen him. It really is funny how much worried and how much talking is being done, by all those old Cecil and Devonshire spooks.'[13] Kick was anxious to go to mass on Sunday but was told that it was miles away. Undeterred, she 'hopped on a bike and was there in twenty-five minutes'.

Joe Jr was now down at the Coastal Command base in Cornwall in the far south-west of England, but they chatted on the telephone. During this time, Kick grew closer to Joe. She had always hero-worshipped him, but now she truly became more a friend and an equal. He had flown with the VB-110 squadron across the Atlantic, carrying a crate of eggs from Virginia as a present for his sister.

Taking on the fatherly role, he would phone Kick and lecture her. 'You talk to me like I was a member of the crew,' she would complain. During his leave he came to London, and visited the Hans Crescent Club. He listened to the jukebox and played card games with the other officers, and he was frustrated by Kick's bridge skills: 'Everyone makes mistakes, Kick, but you make too darn many ... Gee, Kick, aren't you ever going to learn?'[14]

They went off to the 400 Club together and then the next night to the Savoy as guests of William Randolph Hearst Jr, who was working as a war correspondent. One of the other guests was the beautiful, black-haired Pat Wilson, who was already on her second marriage, but whose husband was fighting in Libya. Pat was struck by the handsome young American GI with the dazzling smile. She and Joe Jr began an affair. Once again, Kick was living through a brother's adulterous relationship at close quarters. Once again, there was one rule for the Kennedy boys and another for the girls.

Private turmoil did nothing to dent her public image. In August 1943, a photograph appeared in the *Daily Mail* of Kick riding her bicycle dressed in her Red Cross uniform: 'MISS KATHLEEN KENNEDY, daughter of Mr Joseph Kennedy, former American Ambassador to Great Britain, has arrived in London to work for the American Red Cross. The picture shows Kathleen with her bicycle, which she uses to work in London.' She became known as 'the girl on the bicycle', a symbol of America helping the British to win the war.

38

Parties and Prayers

My British Buddy, we're as different as can be,
He thinks he's winning the war and I think it's me …
But we're in there pitching
Till we get to Germany.
When the job is done
And the war is won
We'll be clasping hands across the sea.

Irving Berlin

Irving Berlin was playing his latest song, 'My British Buddy', on the piano, guests 'swarmed in', all the girls were dressed in their finery. It was, according to Kick Kennedy, 'the first party London had had for the young for two years'. She was throwing it for her brother Joe and his friends in the home of her mother's London friend, Marie Bruce: 'Joe Jr. arrived with his entire squadron who were feeling no pain.'[1] It was just like old times.

Kick had been putting on her dress when Irving Berlin happened to telephone Marie Bruce. Kick insisted that he should come. She was expecting her guests to be rather overwhelmed by her coup of having Berlin performing at her party, but, as she discovered, 'People don't pay much attention to celebrities over here and when he walked in he might have been Joe Snooks for all the glances he got.'[2] She put him next to the Duchess of Devonshire, Billy's mother, 'hoping she'd strike up a lively conversation'. The guests gathered around the piano and sang along with Irving Berlin till past one in the morning. He closed with an old favourite, 'Over There'.

There was one dramatic incident when the new evening dress worn by one of Billy's sisters was set on fire by a young Guardsman who had had too much to drink. The seventeen-year-old Lady Elizabeth Cavendish told her mother: 'Before I was set on fire the boys didn't pay much attention to me, but afterwards I was very popular.' Kick told her parents that an American boy put out the fire, leading one of the guests, Angie Laycock, to ask her brave husband, General Laycock, 'Why didn't you do something about putting those flames out?' He replied, 'I thought it was a fireworks display.'[3] Kick found it difficult to enjoy the evening as she was so nervous about everything. Afterwards, she received many thank-you letters saying 'Why aren't more parties like that given?' Joe was proud of his sister. 'Kick handled herself to perfection as usual and made a terrific hit all around,' he wrote to his parents. 'The girls looked very pretty and made quite an impression on the love-wan sailors whom I brought.'[4]

Kick was seeing lots of Joe during his leave. They went shopping together and dined with friends. She was not being completely truthful when she told her parents that 'he has no special girl friend', since he was still seeing the married Pat Wilson.

At Thanksgiving, turkey was served to all the GIs. 'The Britisher hasn't seen turkey for four years,' Kick noted drily. She had a new duty at the Red Cross as official guide to the social scene: 'When a distinguished visitor arrives and wants to be shown about the London Clubs little Kick is going to do it.'[5] She was also giving lectures at the WVS (Women's Voluntary Service).

Kick and Joe made plans to meet up before Christmas. Joe had been ill early in December, but joked that his 'giant constitution, nurtured from babyhood by coca colas, nut sundaes and Hershey bars', had helped him on the road to recovery.[6] Joe Sr telegraphed Kick: 'we are all praying you will be with us next Xmas give Joe our love and wish him and all our friends a merry Xmas and a new year that will bring us all peace on earth.'[7] Jack managed to get home leave, and Rose wrote movingly about his return in her diary: 'He is really at home – the boy for whom you prayed so hard – at the mention of whose name your eyes would become dimmed ... what a joy to see him – to feel his coat & to press his arms ... to look at his bronze tired face which is thin & drawn.' She found it almost unbearable that he was so ill and weak that he couldn't eat the food produced by Margaret the cook. She would prepare all his favourite dishes and he would give them one look and say, 'just can't take it yet Margaret'.[8]

For all the maternal love revealed here, Rose was not the parent to whom Kick could turn as she faced the greatest challenge of her life. Billy had made up his mind that he was going to propose, and he was determined that this time Kick would not get away from him. They adored one another, but, as he acknowledged, it was a 'Romeo and Juliet' situation, families from opposite ends of the religious divide. Neither family would relent on the matter of religion.

The truth was that Billy Cavendish hailed from perhaps the most anti-Catholic family in England. Their wealth and position had been derived from their opposition to Catholicism, from the time when the 1st Duke fought James II in the seventeenth century. Kick was now fully aware of the extent of Billy's father's anti-Catholicism – even his own son Andrew called him 'a bigoted Protestant'.[9]

In January 1944, Billy plucked up his courage and asked for a meeting with his parents. On Sunday the 23rd he told the Duke and Duchess that there was only one thing he wanted to do in his life and that was to marry Kick.[10] He told them that he knew that it was impossible, but he knew it would make the whole difference to his life and that he was ready to do anything to bring it about.

The Duke replied that he could not give consent for his heir to marry a Roman Catholic. Seeing how upset Billy was, he went on to say that there was no one he would rather see Billy marry, and that he would do every-thing in his power to bring about a solution. He told Billy that he had discussed the situation with Joe Kennedy and would write him a letter if Kick wished. But there were huge barriers, practical ones as well as matters of principle. Billy's future son could not possibly be a Catholic and a duke of Devonshire. Quite apart from the family tradition, there was the fact that the Devonshires had within their gift at least forty livings (parish benefices) in the Church of England. How could a Roman Catholic be expected to perform the duty of appointing clergy in the Church of England?

The Duchess suggested to Billy that she should have a meeting with Kick. On the Tuesday, they had a long talk. Kick wrote that the Duchess was 'charming, felt rather embarrassed and said the one thing she didn't want me to think was that they were doing anything to make me give up something that was a part of me'. The Duchess asked Kick if she were prepared to meet with the Archbishop of Canterbury to discuss matters. In fact, the next day, Kick lunched with Father D'Arcy of Farm Street. Her friend Evelyn Waugh had suggested that she should take advice from the man who had converted him. 'Blue chin and fine, slippery mind' was how Waugh described him.[11]

D'Arcy was 'charming' and told her that he had known of the romance since before the war, but hadn't realized that it was still going on. He seemed to give a glimmer of hope when he told her that until twenty years ago mixed marriages had been permitted if the girls were raised as Catholics and the boys as Anglicans. Kick told him about her meeting with the Duchess and asked D'Arcy if he thought it a good idea to see the Archbishop of Canterbury. He replied that he felt 'quite safe' in sending her. She asked him if he thought that there were loopholes. There might be, but he doubted it. He told Kick that 'the Devonshires should be proud to get a girl of such strong faith and principles'. Before meeting the Archbishop, Kick decided that she should speak to a local bishop. Kick's parting words to Father D'Arcy were full of poignancy: 'I'm sure God would want two people to be happy.' D'Arcy 'smiled and said that's the language of wishing to make it so'. But he had to remind her that marrying Billy would mean 'living in sin' in the eyes of the Catholic Church.

These early months of 1944 were truly the most difficult that Kick, just turning twenty-four, had yet faced. To marry the man she loved and had loved for five years meant renouncing her faith. Few truly knew what renouncing her faith would mean to her. John White's probing had provoked some doubts about some of the dogma of Catholicism, but it had not shaken her faith. Rose believed that Kick had what she called 'the gift of faith'.[12] She also acknowledged in her memoirs, rather bravely, that her daughter had been 'thoroughly indoctrinated in her religious beliefs' from an early age. Writing with the gift of hindsight, in a world in which Catholic doctrine had been reformed by Vatican II, Rose admitted that Kick 'also knew how much the Church meant to me, to most of her close relatives, and, historically, to her ancestors'. It was Catholicism that had bound her Irish ancestors together: religion had been 'the main cohesive force, more important than language, custom, any circumstances that had enabled the Irish people to survive, and in some ways to prevail during the course of many centuries of domination by the English'.[13] Rose observed moreover that 'Billy's ancestors for generations had been occupants of highest offices in the English government of Ireland. As such they had done their best to suppress any sentiments for independence among or on behalf of the Irish … I think it would be fair to say that the Cavendishs and Cecils deeply mistrusted the Irish people.' She added, 'To put it mildly, there was little in the family backgrounds to encourage a romance between Billy and Kick'.[14] That was indeed an understatement. Rose also made the rather sly point that Billy's father was a Freemason, 'under condemnation by the Catholic Church for more than two centuries'.[15]

A friend remembered the sight of Kick on her knees 'for fifteen minutes, lost in prayers'.[16] Then, in the morning, she prayed again and then set off for mass. Her faith was perhaps deeper than Billy's. His was entwined with heritage, status, tradition, but he didn't feel it viscerally as she did. Rose was wrong about many things but she was right that Kick had the 'gift of faith'. It was much to give up.

Kick declared that 'she would marry Billy in a second' if there was a way out of the difficulty. She was dismayed that people around her were expressing disbelief that she would even think of rejecting Billy. 'Imagine an Irish Catholic saying no to becoming one of the richest and most important duchesses in England,' she wrote. 'Things like that make me want to show 'em.'

She was deeply upset at the pain Billy was enduring: 'Poor Billy is nearly going out of his mind.' Kick spoke to her brother Joe but felt that he didn't understand. She spoke endlessly to Marie Bruce and Nancy Astor, her surrogate mother figures: 'Everyone is trying to talk me into the marriage and I must say it's all rather difficult … I wish mother was here.'[17]

Marie Bruce wrote a long, loving letter to Rose to update her on the Billy and Kick situation. She told Rose that Kick had had many boyfriends, both English and American, and that she had advised Kick to court them in her Mayfair home rather than in nightclubs, where the newspapermen buzzed around her looking for stories. Then she got to the point, 'Well, dear Rose, suppose I better write to you about Billy.' She told Rose that she liked him very much indeed, that he was a very nice young man and would make Kick very happy.[18]

But it was not simply Billy's faith that was a problem. The rest of the Kennedy family had not warmed to him. He did not seem to be the right sort of personality for the gregarious, spirited Kick. Marie Bruce tried to assuage Rose's doubts, telling her that Rose had known Billy only when he was still a boy without responsibility. She explained that English men developed later than others, and that Billy's war experiences had made him into a man. She also told Rose that he loved 'little Kick' very much. Marie pleaded with her friend to accept the marriage. She told her that Kick was loved by Billy's family and liked English life. When she finally arrived at the sticking point, religion, she said that Kick feared greatly her mother's disapproval. 'If you could only see them together,' she urged her friend. She tried to convince Rose that a loophole could be found. Marie Bruce made her biggest mistake when she mentioned that she herself had been married by a Russian minister, so was in the eyes of the church 'happily living in sin'. This well-meant remark could only have reminded Rose that in the eyes of the Roman Catholic Church her daughter would, indeed, be living in sin. She was furious and felt that Kick was being badly advised.

In the meantime, Rose's secretary wrote to Kick, sending presents of clothes, including a beautiful silk dress and a pink bed jacket from her mother. Although there was not a single mention of Billy, Rose's secretary passed on a message that Kick should improve her grammar when writing home, telling her that her mother 'would also like you to watch the prepositions and pronouns ... whom is in the objective case and as such is principally used as the object of a preposition'.[19] Usually the Kennedy children made a joke of their mother's obsession with grammar, but this was not the time or the place.

Kick loved Billy. And she loved his deep, abiding love for her. She had fallen in love with England, and Billy was the embodiment of that love. The fact that British and American forces were massing in southern England in preparation for the opening of the Second Front, the Normandy landings, where casualties were expected to be high, meant that she was under extra pressure. She had to fulfil her destiny.

She now tried Bishop David Mathew, the Roman Catholic Auxiliary Bishop of Westminster, and a friend of Father D'Arcy. He was frank about her options: 'He had nothing to offer me as a possible solution and went so far as to say that in a case like this the Church would have to be very careful so as to avoid all criticism.'[20] At an inopportune moment, she discovered a newspaper article by the Archbishop of York which said that 'any Anglican who gave in to the Roman Catholic Church at marriage was guilty of great weakness'. She assumed that 'He must have got wind of something.' There was no doubt that the possibility of an impending union between Billy and Kick was big news in the Church of England.

That January, Billy's father, mother and sisters helped him with his campaign to persuade Kick to accept his proposal. His sisters recalled gifts of jewels and other lavish presents. The Duke gave her pearl and diamond earrings to match a diamond cross given by the Duchess. She was invited to parties to meet fascinating family members, such as Lord David Cecil, one of Jack's heroes.[21] So much would be hers, if she would only renounce her faith. But Kick was still thinking through her decision.

39

Rosemary Tonks

She was a more effective envoy to the people of Britain from the
people of America than her father, our pre-war Ambassador.
Unidentified newspaper clipping in Rose Kennedy Papers

There was a brief hiatus from the marriage dilemma, as Billy had taken
leave from the army to stand for Parliament in the West Derbyshire
by-election. He was to fight for a seat that had been in his family for over
two centuries. He was obliged to request leave from the regiment. This
troubled him, at such a key time in the war. According to some, he didn't
want to stand for Parliament at all. There were whispers that it was at his
father's insistence. A family friend remembered: 'He never should have
come back. He should have stayed with his Regiment. He was just too nice.'[1]
Likewise, Andrew, Billy's brother, thought the by-election 'a grave error of
judgment on my father's part'. Billy may also have been persuaded to run
because he knew that Kick would be impressed to see a different side to
him.

By 6 February, she had made up her mind. She wrote to Inga Arvad to
tell her that she had decided to 'marry an Englishman and if it wasn't for
this religious difficulty I'd be married to him now'. She told Inga, 'Yes, it's
the same one as before. He's standing for Parliament at the moment so
there's lots of excitement about whether he'll get in.'[2]

Kick took part in the last few days of the campaign, using up her precious leave to be at Billy's side. She wrote an excited round-robin letter to her family with details of the election. On 12 February, she left London for York, and was met at the station by Richard Wood, who was still in love with her. She told her family that he had new wooden legs and was able to drive, though he still found it difficult to walk. 'But he'll do it sooner or later,' she wrote loyally.[3] Kick probed Richard about his own family's relationship to the tenants on their estates. She was curious about everything and Richard felt that she was weighing up her future as the Duchess of Devonshire: 'All this interested Kick very much indeed in that she was going to be in a position one day of great authority and responsibility for masses of people who lived at Chatsworth.'[4]

She stayed with Richard's sister, Anne, for a few days in the Yorkshire Dales, and was spoilt by her, having breakfast in bed every morning, though Kick suffered from the inclement weather: 'I have never felt such cold.'[5] From there she went to Derbyshire to meet with Billy on the campaign trail. They agreed that it would look bad for Billy if appeaser Joe Kennedy's daughter were to be publicly connected to him ('news of me wouldn't add any votes', she told her father), so they gave her a pseudonym, 'Rosemary Tonks', the village girl. She told her family that she 'wasn't allowed to open my mouth, although I did go canvassing for votes with Billy's sister'.

It was very much a family affair, with Billy's mother the Duchess speaking on five different hustings. Kick thought she was absolutely wonderful up there on the platform. She was imagining herself in the role. Billy was worked off his feet, and in one evening he had to speak in six towns. Kick sat in the back of the car to hear the comments from the crowd. Billy, she reported, 'was asked every sort of question from the Beveridge [social welfare] plan right on down to "Why isn't the park at Chatsworth ploughed up," "Why didn't your father pay more death duties? What do you know about being poor?"'[6] He was also attacked for his relationship with the Mosleys, who had recently been released from prison (they had been interned as Fascists) but remained under house arrest. Billy calmly replied that he and his brother and his brother's wife were all 'violently anti-Fascist'.

The Duchess later told Jack Kennedy that the 1944 by-election was 'the worst & dirtiest fight I ever came across in all the 9 or 10 elections I have fought'. She was proud of Billy, who endured the heckling and remained perfectly calm. His mother felt that towards the end his performance improved considerably.[7] Having Kick beside him gave him great confidence. She helped him by handing out leaflets saying 'A Vote for Hartington is a Vote for Churchill'.[8]

Kick thought his speeches 'absolutely terrific', though she was angry if a member of the public asked him a question he couldn't fully answer. She explained to her family: 'Billy has been in the Army for the last four years and hasn't had much chance to keep up on every political bill that has passed the House of Commons.' Loyally, she went on, 'He did awfully well. He had everything against him, every vote he got, he got despite who he was, not because.'[9]

Churchill wrote a public letter of support, which backfired because it only drew attention to Billy's aristocratic pedigree and connections. According to Kick, the Duke 'pulled a few fast ones which made every one rather mad' (quite what he did is not clear). Kick concluded that Billy's 'own personal charm was the only thing he had in his favour'.[10] Billy was so handsome, so elegant with the press. His 'bobby-dazzler' of a smile helped: the press joked he and Kick could make his fortune in Hollywood if his career in politics failed.[11]

Kick loathed his opponent, the socialist Charlie White: 'He hates the Cavendishes like poison … looks absolutely repulsive.'[12] She resented the way he was turning the campaign into a class war. He was the 'cobbler's son', the voice of the working man. White got his boys to boo and hiss and stamp on the floor when Billy made his speeches. Billy just spoke louder.

In Kick's view, the people running White's campaign 'know just what the working people want to hear and they give it to them'. Billy never really stood a chance. He represented a hierarchical class of wealth and privilege that no longer had the upper hand and that the war had shown to be redundant. Kick noted: 'There is no doubt about it, there is a terrific swing to the Left.'

On polling day she rode around with Billy to the various polling booths, and then on to Matlock Town Hall for the counting of the ballot. The Duchess was relieved that the campaign was over, and was amused when Billy said, 'It's a pity we are not just starting, isn't it?'[13] When the votes were finally counted, White had won, with over 16,000 votes to Billy's 11,775. The socialist victory in this by-election was an augury of what was to come in the 1945 general election at the end of the war.[14] Kick was upset that 'poor Billy had to walk around looking cheerful and not too disappointed'.

Although Billy had lost the election, Kick loved her involvement in the world of politics. She was Joe's daughter and the Mayor of Boston's grand-daughter: politics made her feel alive and invigorated. Her time in Washington with Jack had sharpened her mind and her intellectual appetite. The long talks through the campaign evenings had now stimulated her even more: 'We all used to sit up far into the night discussing trends, elections and the world in general. I just sat and listened and thought how lucky I was to be there.' She told her family that she'd never spent such an interesting week in her whole life. It was her political epiphany, as her mother had had her religious epiphany all those years ago: 'That's really the way I like to spend my time.'

And she saw Billy in a new light. White had repeatedly tried to humiliate him and present him as a spoiled, out-of-touch aristocrat. 'Can you milk a cow?' one of his supporters shouted. Billy calmly responded, 'Yes I can milk a cow, and I can also spread muck. Some of my opponents seem rather good at that too.'[15] Kick loved his witty response, which made him seem a little like Jack. Billy challenged White to a competition on a local farm to see who could rake the most muck. White, at age sixty-three to Billy's twenty-six, refused the challenge.

Kick saw how fired up Billy had been by the campaign. She was proud of him, saying 'Better luck next time.' She saw herself as the new Georgiana, canvassing by Billy's side. She loved it when his mother made a reference to Georgiana and her campaigning on behalf of Charles James Fox in the key Westminster constituency in the famous 1784 general election: 'Duchesses' kisses are not what they used to be.'[16]

Kick told her family that Billy didn't really mind losing, though he was surprised by White's victory. She knew that what he most wanted was to go back to the army. But what really stung Billy to the core were assaults on his courage. One woman had yelled at him: 'Young man, you ought to be in the front line, not standing here talking politics.' He tried not to show how much this got to him: 'I've been in the army five years and have seen action overseas. I hope to take my place in the front line shortly.'[17]

The Duke was mortified by the result. According to Kick, 'he kept saying "I don't know what the people want"'. Billy replied, 'I do, they just don't want the Cavendishes.' His father was shocked to hear Billy speaking in this way. When Billy gave his speech at the declaration of the result, he told of his intentions to go back to his men: 'It has been a fierce fight. Now I am going to fight for you at the front, perhaps die, for my country.'

One woman remarked to Debo Cavendish, 'It's a shame to let him go, a great tall man like he is, he's such a target.'[18] Kick wrote to her family of her fears about the war as it began to reach its final stages: 'We've been so lucky so far that it scares me.'[19]

40

Agnes and Hartie

This situation, Daddy, is a stickler.

Kick Kennedy

Billy returned to his regiment and was stationed at Alton in southern England, so Kick and her friends gathered together for weekends at Pat Wilson's cottage in the grounds of nearby Cradstock Farm, which they christened 'Crash Bang'. Kick would dash into the cottage and run upstairs to shower and wash her hair free of the doughnut grease of the canteen. Everyone would bring a treat, such as eggs or chocolate. There would be chat, fun and games.

Joe's affair with Pat had intensified, though she was still married. It was Inga and Jack all over again, but worse because Pat had three small children. This was the time when Kick and Joe grew even closer together, and she was able to confide in him about her feelings for Billy, and her concerns about Rose. 'Never did anyone have such a pillar of strength,' she later wrote.[1]

Joe was feeling the strain of living in the shadow of Jack's success. Jack was not only a bestselling author, but he had brought glory on the Kennedy name by becoming a war hero. Joe Jr and Jack, so close in age, had always experienced sibling rivalry, but he had been the first-born, his father's favourite. Now, in Kick's hour of need, he took on the role of father figure.

The ex-Ambassador wrote to his eldest son: 'I do hope you'll give her the benefit of your counsel and sympathy because after all she has done a swell job and she's entitled to the best ... as far as I am personally concerned, Kick can do no wrong and whatever she did would be great with me.'[2]

To her, Joe Sr wrote, 'As far as I am concerned I'll gamble with your judgment. The best is none too good for you, baby, but if you decided it's a Chinaman, it's okay with me. That's how much I think of you.'[3] Rose said nothing.

Kick was impressed that when fastidious Billy visited her at Hans Crescent, he would happily sleep on the floor just to be close to her. When Kick stayed with Fiona and Arthur (Boofy) Gore in their tiny, cramped house, she would sleep in the bathtub ('more like a bed') and Billy would turn up, sleeping bag in hand. Those family members and friends who knew Billy and his particular ways and his taste for elegance and luxury saw that he was demonstrating his love for Kick. Jean Lloyd, who now had a baby daughter, remembered Kick and Billy sitting up all night, 'to talk and talk and talk'.[4]

After the by-election Kick tried to find a way to marry Billy without losing her immortal soul. They went back and forth over the arguments and possibilities, trying to find a solution. Who would make the ultimate sacrifice? That February, Kick wrote to her family to tell them that the Duke had given her a 'lovely old leather book' for her twenty-fourth birthday. The Duchess insisted that she had had nothing to do with it, and when Kick opened it, she saw that it was the Book of Common Prayer. She laughed and thanked him for it. But she knew what the symbolic present meant. The Duchess and Kick had a long talk about the 'situation' and Billy's mother said, 'It's a shame because you are both so good and it would please everyone so much.' Kick begged her parents, 'Please try and discover loopholes, although I keep feeling that the particular parties involved would make any compromise impossible. The Catholics would say it would give scandal. This situation, Daddy, is a stickler.'[5]

Kick always thought that her father could find a way. The plan now was to get a special dispensation. Bishop Mathew had told Kick that the process would put the Anglican Church in a very difficult position and that it would be better to wait until after they were married.

The Catholic Church's 1917 Code of Canon Law prohibited marriage between a Catholic and non-Catholic unless there was a dispensation,

Coming out: Kick, Rose Fitzgerald Kennedy and sister Rosemary
on the day of the girls' presentation as debutantes at court.

Girl about town: Kick in London and, right, at Goodwood races.

The charismatic smile: Kick at an evening party, with an admirer.

Transatlantic girls: Kick (*right*) and Eunice, smartly dressed in furs at La Guardia airport, New York.

Girl on a bicycle: the iconic press photograph of Kick, the Red Cross worker of World War II.

Father and daughter: Kick in Red Cross uniform, with Joseph P. Kennedy.

Kick, flanked by Joe Jr (*left*) and Jack, walking down Whitehall to Parliament on the day that war was declared.

Billy and Kick.

Engaged.

Married: at Chelsea Register
Office, with Billy's mother,
the Duchess of Devonshire,
and Kick's brother, Joe Jr.

Chatsworth.

Marquis Weds With The Doors Locked

MISS KENNEDY
A MARCHIONESS

THURSDAY—ENGAGED: TO-DAY—MARRIED

"*Evening News*" Reporter

THE MARQUIS OF HARTING-
TON and Miss Kathleen
Kennedy, daughter of the former
U.S. Ambassador, whose engage-
ment was announced only on
Thursday, were married to-day
before the Chelsea registrar.

Duke At Heir's 'Secret' Wedding

The Marquis of Hartington
was married "secretly" in
London yesterday to Miss
Kathleen Kennedy, daughter
of the ex-U.S. Ambassador.
In the picture below are the
newly married pair, the
Duke and Duchess of Devonshire, parents of the bride-
groom, and Lieut. Kennedy,
brother of the bride.

Press reports of the wedding.

Lismore.

Peter Fitzwilliam dancing with a girlfriend.

Political Kick: the house in
Smith Square, Westminster.

The crash.

The grave at Edensor, on the Chatsworth estate, with flowers laid by President John F. Kennedy on the occasion of his private visit in 1963, shortly before his assassination.

which would require the Catholic to assure the priest that there was no danger of apostasy, and that any children would be brought up in the Catholic faith. The non-Catholic would have to be catechized on the nature of marriage in Catholic theology. Would Billy and his family consent to this? The arguments went back and forth, back and forth to no avail.

The Kennedy family had a codename for the 'situation' – Agnes and Hartie (Agnes being Kick's middle name, and Hartie for Hartington). Rose wrote to her daughter in late February 1944: 'There is no news about Agnes and Hartie ... frankly I do not seem to think that Dad can do anything. He feels terribly sympathetic and so do I and I only wish we could offer some suggestions: When both people have been handed something all their lives, how ironic it is that they can not have what they most want.'[6] There were numerous transatlantic telephone calls, letters and cables. 'Enough material', Rose later observed, 'for a novel'. As she said, it would have been a 'marriage made in Heaven' except for the special and ironic circumstance of religious loyalties.[7]

Throughout the crisis Kick went frequently to church, taking Holy Communion whenever she could, as if she were making the most of it while she was still allowed. Rose wrote to say, 'do not be exhausting yourself and running your little legs off going to Church as your first duty is to your job ... We had a letter from someone in Boston whose third cousin watches you go to Communion frequently, so the news has been carried across the waters.' Joe continued to tell his daughter that anything she did was all right by him, that it was hers and Billy's decision, and all the rest could 'go jump in the lake'.[8] Rose was the one to apply moral pressure: 'I understand perfectly the terrific responsibilities and the disappointment of it all.'[9]

It seemed that everyone was involved in the Agnes and Hartie situation. Rose appealed to Archbishop Spellman of New York, Enrico Galeazzi and Pope Pius. Everyone was trying to find a way through.

In her friend Evelyn Waugh's Catholic novel *Brideshead Revisited*, the beautiful aristocratic Catholic heroine Julia Flyte is faced with Kick's dilemma when she falls in love with an Anglican. Waugh was writing the novel during this time, and there is a scene in the novel where the heroine visits a priest from Farm Street to talk about her problem: 'not in the confessional, but in a dark little parlour kept for such interviews'. The priest, like D'Arcy, is a 'gentle old Jesuit ... unyielding as rock'. Waugh was clearly drawing on Kick's experience: 'She barely listened to him; he was refusing her what she wanted, that was all she needed to know.'[10]

This was Kick's dilemma as she went back and forth on visits to D'Arcy's parlour to discuss the situation. D'Arcy was unrelenting as he painted a bleak picture of a Godless life. Marriage to Billy meant 'living in sin' in the eyes of the Catholic Church. She would be unable to take Holy Communion, unable to make an Act of Confession. She would not go to Heaven and nor would her children.

In March, Billy's mother had arranged for Kick to meet with Father Ted Talbot, a prominent High Anglican clergyman and former chaplain to the King. His role was to explain to Kick why Billy was so adamant that his children should not be brought up as Catholics, what the Cavendishes stood for in the English Church. 'He also took a great deal of trouble to explain to me the fundamental differences between the Anglican and Roman Churches.' The clear intention of the meeting was to persuade Kick to convert to Anglicanism, so that they could at least be married in a church. As Billy was the eldest son and heir to one of the greatest dukedoms in the land, it was expected that, despite wartime restrictions, the wedding would be an important social occasion. Kick was undaunted, defending her faith to the hilt: 'I explained that something one had been brought up to believe in and which was largely responsible for the character and person-ality of an individual is a very difficult thing for which to find a substitute.'[11] She was not slavishly following her faith simply because she was born that way, but proclaiming that Catholicism had shaped her character and personality, had made her who she was. She went on to say that 'I had been blessed with so many of this world's goods that it [would have] seemed rather cheap and weak to give in at the first real crisis in my life.'[12]

In an addition to her round-robin letter to 'dearest Family', headed 'THIS IS FOR MOTHER AND DADDY ONLY', she wrote, 'The Duchess is so wonder-ful and so kind.' And then, 'I want to do the right thing so badly and yet I hope I'm not giving up the most important thing in my life … Poor Billy is very, very sad but he sees his duty must come first. He is a fanatic on this subject.'[13] Kick made it clear to her parents that Billy's parents were being remarkably supportive. He would not be 'cut off' if he married her – they 'would make the best of it'. Kick was 'discouraged and sad'. She said that the Duchess and Father Talbot understood perfectly about the importance of her faith, but 'they just hoped that I might find the same thing in the

Anglican version of Catholicism'. The Duchess wrote Kick the kindest of letters, and she took the trouble to quote a lengthy passage of it in her letter to her own parents:

> You are always in my thoughts and how I feel for you alone here with-out your mother and father when you are going through so much and have had such overwhelmingly difficult things to decide about. It is desperately hard, that you should have all this great unhappiness with the second front always at the back of one's mind. I know how lonely you must feel and almost forsaken but we must trust in God that things will come out for the best in the end. I do hope you know how much we love you and if there is even the smallest thing we can do to help you have only to say.[14]

Sensing his daughter's deep unhappiness and loneliness, Joe was quick to send a telegram: 'CONTINUE WRITING LETTERS AS ALWAYS THEY ARE WONDERFUL ... I FEEL TERRIBLE UNHAPPY YOU HAVE TO FACE YOUR BIGGEST CRISIS WITHOUT MOTHER AND ME YOUR CONFIDENTIAL MEMORANDUM WORTHY OF CHESTERTON MAGNIFICENT'. He told her: 'with your faith in God you cannot make a mistake and remember you are still and always will be tops with me'.[15]

By April, Kick felt that she was going mad, and that matters had to be resolved one way or the other. Worn down with all the talks, she succumbed to an attack of laryngitis. Her two surrogate mothers stepped in. First Mrs Bruce nursed her in London and then she went to Cliveden in the country to recuperate with Lady Astor. She was well looked after, and Joe Jr came down on the Sunday night to see her, and they walked together. She thought he was 'slightly dejected'. That night the young people just wanted to sit and talk but Nancy insisted on games, one called 'Subjects'. Joe had to talk for two minutes on the subject of 'Jam'. He didn't do a very good job. Kick called her hostess the 'soul of generosity', adding, 'of course she still hopes I'll marry Billy and keeps telling me I'll only be happy in England'.[16] Nancy Astor wrote to a friend, 'I have had Kick Kennedy here for three days. She is a very nice girl and I believe that if she says she will not bring up her children RCs that she will honourably keep her promise. I had a most inter-esting talk with her on the subject and warned her against the traps that would be set'.[17]

41

Telegrams and Anger

'They [Catholics] seem just like other people.'
'My dear Charles, that's exactly what they're not … they've got an
entirely different outlook on life; everything they think important is
different from other people.'
  Charles Ryder and Sebastian Flyte in Evelyn Waugh's *Brideshead Revisited*
(1945)

On 4 April 1944 Kick told her parents that she and Billy and young Joe had
seen Bishop Mathew, who had said that there would be no immediate
'dispensations' nor 'concessions' from the Catholic Church. The only possibility was to 'be married in a registry office' and then 'perhaps at a later date'
their marriage 'could be made valid' by some sort of special dispensation.[1]

  She reiterated that fifteen years earlier her marriage could have been
'solemnized in the Church – the boys being brought up in the father's religion – the girls in the mother's'.[2] Kick also told them that the Duke was 'very
worried about having A Roman Catholic in the family. In their eyes the
most awful thing that could happen to our son would be for it to become a
Roman. With me in the family that danger becomes immediate even though
I would promise that the child could be brought up as an Anglican.'[3]

  What Kick was really preparing her parents for was the idea that she
would more than likely be married in a registry office. For a Roman

Catholic this would have been the greatest disappointment. Kick refused to have an Anglican ceremony, so this was the compromise position. Not a Roman Catholic church but also not the beautiful English church in which Billy's ancestors had been married.

It was sad, and disappointing and grim, but wartime made this compromise seem not so terrible. She told her parents: 'The Church would not marry us and the result would be that I would be married in a registry office. I could continue to go to Church but not Communion.' Her anguish was clear. Then Kick got down to the real issue of the letter: 'If I do marry Billy within the next few months, please be quite sure that I am doing it with the full knowledge of what I am doing and that I'm quite happy about it and feel quite sure that I am doing the right thing.' No doubt for her mother's sake, she added, 'As my Bishop said, "No one can say that you are committing a sin because a sin is done from a selfish motive. What you are doing is done entirely from a non-selfish motive."'[4] Her P.S. was typically upbeat: 'Feeling happy & well – Don't worry! Sorry you'll have to face the McDonnells.' She well knew how humiliating it was for Rose to face her friends, knowing that her daughter was renouncing her church.

On 20 April Kick went to Yorkshire to stay with Jean Lloyd, who had broken her foot. Kick was glad to help. The door suddenly opened and there was Billy carrying a sack of oranges: a great rarity in wartime. He had also managed to procure champagne and lobster, and they had a sumptuous supper. Jean remembered Billy's joy that evening, as he had heard the news he had long desired: that the Allied invasion of France was afoot. Billy's smile was radiant and he rubbed his hands together with the words 'We're off.'[5] He had never truly recovered from the ignominious defeat at Dunkirk and had longed for honour to be restored. Kick, terrified by the prospect of Billy fighting in what she knew would be a fierce and bloody invasion, finally agreed to marry him. On his terms. It was one of the happiest days of Billy Hartington's twenty-six-year life. He had Kick and he was off to fight for his honour and that of his country. Jean took a photograph, capturing his look of complete joy.

On 24 April, Kick typed a long round-robin letter to her 'Dearest family' to prepare them for the inevitable. It was the most difficult letter she had ever had to write. She began talking about how the war had changed her friends. Jean Ogilvy, daughter of the Earl of Airlie, was living in a tiny house in

Yorkshire, with no phone and no domestic help, and was not at all regretful about the loss of her luxurious, pre-war life. Like many of his fellow aristocrats, Billy knew in his heart that the old world would never come back. He had no expectations of being able to afford to maintain Chatsworth in a new age of post-war austerity and swingeing death duties. 'But', wrote Kick, 'he won't give up all hope'. She then dropped her bombshell: 'I have definitely decided to marry him.' With the thought of the war coming to an end, and gaining the woman he loved, Billy was in 'tremendous spirits … he has been sending for rings from all the jewelry stores in London'. And then the painful news: 'You understand that the ceremony would have to be performed in a registry office which is rather sordid but the only thing to do as I wouldn't have an Anglican service.'[6]

Rose and Joe were genuinely shocked. Joe wrote back, saying that even Jack, 'much to my amazement because I am not particularly impressed with the depth of his Catholic faith', felt that 'some sort of concession should be made on the part of Billy … In the meantime, I want you to know that I feel for you very deeply.' But she had to live her own life.[7]

Kick had promised her parents that she would 'let them know in advance' the date of the wedding. On 29 April she sent a cable to her parents to say that she was definitely going to be married in a registry office.

Rose was distraught. In normal circumstances, she was scrupulous about punctuation and grammar, always writing in lucid, perfectly formed sentences. But on this occasion her anguish is clear. She wrote down her feelings in a haphazard, broken, stream-of-consciousness fragment that she entitled 'Notes on My Reactions at Kick's Marriage':

Personal Reminiscences Private
K – sent cable Sat April 29th that she would marry in a registry office – Joe phoned me said he hadn't slept – Naturally I was disturbed horrified – heartbroken – Talked for a minute on our responsibility in allowing her to drift into this dilemma then decided we should think of practical way to extricate her. I said I would think it out & then call him later.[8]

Rose was convinced that there was still hope. She had been furious that Joe had not flown out to exert his powers of persuasion, and now they were paying the price. Her panic is evident. As she continued, her normally impeccable prose fell to pieces: 'Later we decided we would send a cable about like this Heartbroken – think-feel you have been wrongly influenced – Sending Archie Spell's friend to talk to you. Anything done for our Lord will be rewarded hundredfold.' Rose was reasoning with herself about why she was so distraught: 'I thought it would have such mighty repercussions in that every little young girl would say if K— Kennedy can – why can't I? – why all the fuss, then everyone pointed to our family with pride as well behaved – level headed & deeply religious. What a blow to the family prestige.'[9]

Rose was on the edge of a nervous breakdown. Cables flew back and forth as she tried to prevent the inevitable. What should have been a joyous time for Kick, the happiest time of her life, was marred by her mother's misery. Rose had never really thought that Kick would capitulate. She believed that her daughter's faith and her respect for Rose would win out over her love for Billy. She simply could not and would not believe that her compliant, sweet-natured daughter would rebel in this, the most disastrous of ways.

On 30 April, Billy wrote a beautiful letter to Rose, apologizing for not having written before: 'I have loved Kick for a long time, but I did try so hard to face the fact that the religious difficulties seemed insurmountable, and I tried to make up my mind that I should have to make do with second best. I felt too that if she could find someone else she could really be happy with, it would be much better & more satisfactory for her.'[10] Billy then explained that after Christmas he had made up his mind to propose: 'I couldn't bear to let her go without ever asking her if we couldn't find a way out.' He added that he knew he was going back out to fight and time was getting short.

He told Rose, 'I could not believe, either, that God could really intend two loving people, both of whom wanted to do the right thing, and both of whom were Christians, to miss the opportunity of being happy, and perhaps even useful, together because of the religious squabbles of His human servants several hundred years ago.' Rose would not have warmed to this. For her, Roman Catholicism was the only true religion, and for her, religion was never about men but about God.

Billy also explained his strong feelings about the religious upbringing of his own children. He told Rose that the reason he wanted his children to be raised as Anglicans was bound up with the national Church of England. As

England was not a Roman Catholic country, and as he benefited from many of the advantages of his position, he felt that he should be setting a very bad example if he gave in and allowed his children to be raised as Catholics: 'I do feel terribly keenly the sacrifices I'm asking Kick to make, but I can't see that she will be doing anything that is wrong in the eyes of God … I do think in my heart that she is so holy and good that God will continue to help her and that she can be happy, and I know that selfish though it sounds, I should never be happy or be much good without her.'

He thanked Rose for her consent, which she hadn't given, and told her that he felt 'punch drunk after the emotional battering of the last few months'. He wrote of his 'amazing good fortune in being allowed to have Kick as my wife; it still seems incredibly wonderful'. He apologized for his 'dopey & after reading over, pompous letter', and for 'what must seem to you a tyrannical attitude' and closed by saying: 'I promise that both Kick & I have only done what we really believed in our hearts to be right.'[11]

By this time, Billy's parents were reconciled to the marriage. On 27 April 1944, the Duke of Devonshire wrote to his 'darling mother' on the headed notepaper of the Zoological Society (London Zoo), of which he was President:

> I am afraid that you will not like what I have to tell you, which is that I do not feel justified in opposing Bill's engagement any longer. He & Kick are so desperately in love and so unhappy, and have both been so good and so dutiful, and, alas, Bill's tenure of life is so uncertain that I should feel almost like a murderer if I refused him the chance of being happy while he can.
>
> Kick is seeing [Archbishop] William Temple on Monday with a view to her conversion, which is, of course, the best that can happen.
>
> I do not think she will come over now, but it may bear fruit in the future.
>
> You will be unhappy, as I am. The religious question apart, I would not choose as a wife for Bill a Boston Irish girl, but she is a good and a nice girl … Both Bill and Kick are for some reason against an announcement, but I want one very much and I think it will appear early next week.[12]

The Duke and Duchess were readying themselves to attend the wedding. The British establishment was, for the most part, duly reconciled. Nine days later, the Duke received a letter from King George VI:

> I am very glad that you have gone into the matter of her religion so carefully, and that she has promised that the children shall be brought up as Protestants and that she herself may come over to the church later ... I am sure the girl takes after her mother and not her father, as his behaviour here as ambassador in the early days of the war was anything but helpful.[13]

* * *

The week before her marriage was torture for Kick. She wrote to her mother that it had been a 'most difficult' week: 'The clergy of both churches were after me.'[14] She had a meeting with the Archbishop of Canterbury, 'charming and so desirous to be helpful', and Archbishop Spellman, her parents' cardinal friend in America, sent a papal delegate, 'absolutely charming and made me feel very sad about Mother'.[15]

'Brother Joe' was indeed Kick's rock. Every time she received a letter or cable from the family she would telephone him for advice. 'Once she had made up her mind, I did the best I could to help her through,' he explained to their parents.[16] He also told them of the terrific strain she was under. He took on the paternal role, in his father's absence, and went to London to meet with the Cavendish lawyers. The terms of the marriage settlement were set out: in the event of Billy's death (the stark reality was that he would soon be embarking for the Second Front), Kick was to be given an annual allowance of £3,000, but if she remarried it would be cut down to £1,000. The children were to receive a lump sum of £25,000 pounds and an income of £1,000 per year for education and maintenance, but 'All this is conditional on them not becoming Catholics, which would automatically cut them out of the gift and income.'[17]

The Duke wanted the Archbishop of Canterbury to give a blessing. The Archbishop wrote to the Catholic Bishop to ask if they might both say a few words of blessing. The Catholic Bishop declined. Joe Jr wrote, 'the Duke's idea on this is that it would lift the marriage from a purely civil ceremony to something which would have the blessing of God'.[18]

Young Joe persuaded the lawyers not to force Kick to sign papers agreeing that the children should be brought up as Anglicans, though the Duke had wanted her to do so. Joe met up with the Duke at the Colonial Office, where he was Under-Secretary of State (i.e. a junior minister). Joe described him as 'a shy old bird' who was 'as jittery as an old duck'. The conversation was strained, but the Duke wanted the Kennedy family to know that they had not put pressure on Kick to become an Anglican. The Duke told Joe that he had asked Kick to convert to the Church of England as it would make more sense for the family, but Kick had refused to do so. He also explained that he wanted the Archbishop to give a blessing as it would make his wife feel so much better. Joe thought this a bad idea, and they agreed to let Kick make the final decision.

Kick wrote that her brother exemplified great 'moral courage' and 'once he felt that a step was right for me, he never faltered'. She knew that Rose was capable of blaming Joe for supporting her decision and she was always deeply grateful for his strength in standing up to the formidable matriarch: 'in every way he was the perfect brother doing, according to his own light, the best for his sister with the hope that in the end it would be the best for his family'.[19]

Meanwhile, Tony Rosslyn made a last-minute intervention. He was in close contact with Joe Kennedy and had been keeping him informed. Tony took Kick out for dinner. They had always had a pact that if either of them were to marry, they would tell the other. It was a tense and unpleasant meeting. She told him she was engaged and was getting married. Tony was shocked and distraught and spoke frankly to Kick about the mistake she was making. 'I'm afraid she got rather angry with me,' he told Joe. Tony asked Kick to clarify her feelings towards Richard Wood, and then asked her about her religion and where she stood in relation to Billy's Anglicanism. Kick told him that the decision she had reached was her own secret. Tony begged her, with the imminence of the Second Front, to wait for a while, and then she would be sure of her feelings for Billy. Kick said that if she had even one week with Billy then she would be happy. She told Tony that she was fated to be Billy's wife, that she had felt this way for six years, that she loved him and that if you wanted something badly enough, you were sure to get it.[20]

Tony was not the only one to think that Kick was acting hastily because of the war. Evelyn Waugh thought it was 'second front nerves' that were driving her to commit this 'mortal sin'. He made no bones about her 'apostasy'.[21]

On 3 May, Kick sent a rather terse letter to her parents. She seemed firm and resolved and not quite so compliant. Rose had been lashing out at everyone she thought was unduly influencing Kick, and Marie Bruce was the chief target. Kick was distressed by the telegrams that were being fired across the Atlantic: 'Marie Bruce is most upset about your cable. She has been more than kind. Please do not be angry with her.' Her letter was short and her sentences pithy and stiff by her usual loving standards: 'You have both been so wonderful to me all my life – given me every advantage and whatever I have or am stems from you both. Many thanks … Please try and understand and pray that everything will be all right in time. I'm sure it will be … Billy is so pleased and so kind. It would delight your heart to see how solicitous he is … Joe comes tomorrow. He is a great strength.'[22]

Frantically, the Kennedys asked Archbishop Spellman to make one last intervention on 4 May, the day the engagement was announced. Spellman contacted Archbishop William Godfrey, who saw Kick and begged her to postpone the wedding on behalf of her greatly distressed mother. 'Effort in vain,' he cabled Spellman. Kick cabled back to her father the night before her wedding day: 'Religion everything to us both will always live according to Catholic teaching. Praying that time will heal all wounds … please beseech mother not to worry am very happy and quite convinced have taken right step.'[23]

Rose, defeated and broken, checked herself into New England Baptist Hospital in Boston for a 'routine physical checkup'. She refused to give an interview, saying only to reporters: 'I'm sorry but I don't feel physically well enough to grant an interview now. I'm sorry it has to be this way.'[24]

42

'I Love You More Than Anything in the World'

The greatest gesture for Anglo-American relations since the Atlantic Charter.

Life magazine[1]

6 May 1944.

Kick Kennedy, pale and thin, dressed herself with care at the home of Marie Bruce. It should have been the most spectacular wedding of the year: the heir to Chatsworth marrying the daughter of the former American Ambassador. For a well-heeled Catholic girl, the day of her wedding should have been the most important of her life. There should have been a dress made from yards and yards of white satin, a train and a long, long veil. There should have been hundreds of guests, including prominent members of the Roman Catholic world; Kick's parents were on close terms with archbishops, and the Pope had received them in a private audience on the occasion of his coronation, which they had attended as official representatives of all the Catholics in America. There should have been a full nuptial mass, hymns and a choir and glorious flower arrangements, wedding photos galore, all her sisters (except Rosemary) as bridesmaids, her little brothers as pageboys, her father proudly walking her down the aisle and Rose Kennedy as mother of the bride. As it was, Rose was in hospital and Joe, for the first time in his life, had gone completely quiet.

If Kick had converted to Anglicanism, she could have been married in even more lavish style by the Archbishop of Canterbury. Even in wartime, the marriage of the future Duke of Devonshire, the heir to Chatsworth, would have been the society wedding of the year.

Instead, it was a short ceremony at the redbrick Chelsea Register Office.

Marie Bruce was more than a mother to Kick. It was she who organized the wedding dress. Clubbing together the clothes coupons of everyone who was willing (even the milkman contributed), they had bought pale pink crepe fabric, and the best fitter in London had copied one of Kick's plain black American dresses. In February, Billy had given Kick a beautiful square-cut sapphire ring set with diamonds either side for her birthday, and in the haste they decided to use it as a wedding ring.

Kick fastened aquamarine clips to her simple dress: 'Couldn't have been prettier'.[2] She wore a half-hat made of two very pale pink and one pale blue ostrich feathers, with a pale pink veil. She carried Marie Bruce's gold mesh bag with sapphires and diamonds (her 'something old and something new'). The Duke had sent Kick a basket of pink camellias from Chatsworth that morning, and she carried a small posy.

The press had picked up on the story but Kick refused to give interviews and kept the door to Mrs Bruce's house firmly closed. On the morning of the wedding, Joe Jr picked up Lady Astor, Marie Bruce and Kick. They got lost on the way and, when they arrived, were met by a crowd of press photographers and spectators. The Duke and Duchess and Billy were already present, and Kick's small party waded through a throng of reporters to get to the room where the ceremony was performed.

Although the wedding invitations had been sent out only the day before, people came to support Billy and Kick; some were illustrious, such as society hostesses Lady Cunard and Laura Corrigan, but Kick had also invited porters from the Club ('needless to say they all showed up'). She invited thirty of the Red Cross girls, and was amused when one of the guests said that she had heard the Kennedy girl had a lot of sisters, but not that many. Billy's sister Anne was just fourteen, and she adored Kick, describing her on the day as a 'shining light of gaiety and pleasure and enthusiasm. She was absolutely nonpareil.'[3]

Charles Manners, Duke of Rutland, was Billy's best man. Joe and the Duke were the two witnesses. Joe reported that the whole thing took ten minutes: 'Kick looked very pretty, and she repeated her statement without a falter. I think I was more nervous than she.'[4] Billy, dressed in his army uniform, looked radiantly happy.

The reception was held at Lord Hambledon's house in Eaton Square. Marie Bruce bribed the head waiter at Claridge's to make an 'enormous chocolate cake' (the ration was one egg per person per week). Kick reported that 'the Dukie-Wookie supplied the champagne.'[5] She loved 'every minute' of her reception party, and especially the strange mix of people. She observed a few GIs, tipsy on champagne, chatting with Lady Cunard, 'who looked more terrifying than ever'.[6] An American sergeant came up to Billy and said, 'Listen, you dog [sic] damn limey, you've got the best god damn girl that America could produce.'[7]

Young Joe reported back to the family that the couple received some beautiful presents, and that 'everyone seemed delighted'. Marie Bruce had given Kick exquisite Porthault lingerie from Paris, the Duke and Duchess a diamond bracelet. Mrs Biddle gave her a Cartier ruby and sapphire clip. Her close friends Boofy and Fiona gave her a gold, diamond and pearl brooch. And Billy himself gave her an 'enormous old diamond clip' which Kick said she wouldn't wear until after the war – 'but it really is absolutely lovely', she told Rose, knowing how much her mother loved jewels.[8]

Kick's going-away outfit was a red coat over a pink and white print dress; her hat was made of white gardenias. She and Billy set off for a honeymoon at Compton Place by the sea on the south coast. On the wedding ring that Billy placed on her finger were inscribed the words, 'I love you more than anything in the world'.

The minute the wedding ceremonies were over, young Joe sent a cable to the family: 'EVERYTHING WONDERFUL DON'T WORRY SHE IS VERY HAPPY WISH YOU COULD HAVE BEEN HERE.'[9] He promised to follow up with a long, descriptive letter. Marie Bruce and Nancy Astor, deeply worried about Rose's reaction, also sent a joint missive: 'DEAREST ROSE YOU WOULD REJOICE IN THEIR YOUNG HAPPINESS ONLY GRIEF YOUR SORROW KATHLEEN LOOKED LOVELY PALE PINK.'[10]

There was no response. The next day, young Joe had had enough and cabled a terse message to his parents: 'THE POWER OF SILENCE IS GREAT.' The ex-Ambassador finally took the hint and cabled Kick. She had heard that Rose was ill in hospital: 'MOST DISTRESSED ABOUT MOTHER PLEASE TELL HER NOT TO WORRY YOUR CABLE MADE MY HAPPIEST DAY.'[11] In the meantime, young Joe sent his letter to the family describing the wedding day.

Photographs had been taken by the press, including one of Joe: 'I saw no point in looking extremely grim throughout so I looked as if I enjoyed it.' Joe warmed especially to the Duchess: 'I like her very much. She is the one who is so much in favour of it.' He reassured the family as best he could: 'Billy is crazy about Kick, and I know they are very much in love … I think he is ideal for Kick.' He told them of his pride in her conduct: 'Kick handled herself like a champion.'

Joe was worried about the press coverage in America: 'I suppose Boston went wild.' He tried his utmost to reassure his mother that he hadn't unduly influenced Kick, and that her soul was safe: 'As far as Kick's soul is concerned, I wish I had half her chance of seeing the pearly gates.' Joe knew that the gossip in Catholic circles that Kick had married out of the faith was hard for Rose to bear: 'As far as what people will say, the hell with them. I think we can all take it. It will be hardest on Mother, and I do know how you feel Mother, but I do think it will be alright.'[12]

Joe had hit on the nub of the matter when he talked about Kick's soul. As a devout Roman Catholic, Rose truly believed that Kick was damned and would go to Hell. It was a view shared by the devout Catholic Evelyn Waugh, who had also told Kick that her soul was in mortal danger and that her 'apostasy' was a 'grave sin'. In the weeks following the marriage, Kick would be sent furious letters by irate Catholics telling her that she had sold her soul for a title. 'They don't bother me a bit,' she said. Billy answered every one of them, calmly and courteously.

Just a couple of days into her honeymoon, Kick took the trouble to write a letter to her 'Dearest Mother', telling her that she was sick with worry as the newspapers had reported that Rose was 'very ill'. 'They made out that it was because of my marriage. Goodness mother – I owe so much to you and Daddy that nothing in the world could have made me go against your will.'[13] She was keen to emphasize her understanding of her mother's position: 'Please don't take any responsibility for an action which you think bad (and I do not). You did everything in your power to stop it. You did your duty as a Roman Catholic mother. You have not failed. There was nothing lacking in my religious education.' She also stressed yet again that she had not given up her faith: 'it is most precious to me. Billy wants it to remain as such.' She told Rose that until the time when her marriage could be made valid by way of a special dispensation, she would continue 'praying and living like a Roman Catholic and hoping. Please please do the same.'[14]

Kick begged Rose not to blame Mrs Bruce: 'Marie Bruce saved my life. She took full charge of buying me what little trousseau I had … I can't tell you how generous and kind most people were.' She admonished Rose, 'Marie feels very badly about being in your bad graces, as she loves you more than anyone else in the world. Please do write to her and make it all right as she was only doing what she thought right.'[15]

Billy's sister felt that Kick was perfectly at peace with her decision. Kick deeply valued all the support she was getting in England: 'I never realized how many friends I had in this country (some of them are just impressed but most of them are genuinely pleased).'[16]

Jack, still recuperating from his adventure in the South Pacific, was unimpressed by his mother's coldness. He thought it was a coup for his little sister to marry into such a family, and bag England's most eligible bachelor. He wrote to ever-devoted Lem: 'Your plaintive howl at not being let in on Kathleen's nuptials reached me this morning … You might as well take it in your stride and as sister Eunice from the depth of her Catholic wrath so truly said, "It's a horrible thing – but it will be nice visiting her after the war, so we might as well face it."'[17] Jack added, with his usual wit: 'At family dinners at the Cape, when you don't pass Hartington the muffins, we'll know how you feel.'[18]

Joe Kennedy wrote to Lord Beaverbrook on 24 May: 'She was the apple of my eye and I feel the loss because I won't have her near me all the time, but I'm sure she's going to be wonderfully happy and I can assure you that England is getting a great girl.'[19]

43

The Marchioness of Hartington

This Book is the PRIVATE PROPERTY of Billy & Kick ... Much has been written. Much has been said. I'm going to write down all the things that we shall ever know.

Kick Kennedy[1]

The weather in Eastbourne was wonderful. After the turmoil of the previous six months, Billy and Kick were badly in need of a rest. Kick sunbathed and turned as 'brown as a berry'.[2] It was a time of perfect happiness, marred only by Rose's silence. Kick had not felt so well since returning from America to England.

Once the honeymoon was over, Billy was to go back to the army, and Kick to the Hans Crescent Club. She told her mother that she intended to live with Marie Bruce while Billy was away. The night of her wedding, Kick started a new diary, calling it the joint diary of Billy and Kick, and getting her new husband to contribute. She wrote down her impressions of the wedding day, and reflected on the curiously successful mixture of Billy's 'ultra-conservative relations' and her American friends from the Red Cross.

Billy wrote down their plans to go to Eton for 4 June (the school's special annual celebration). He teased Kick by mirror-writing jokes and limericks. 'He thinks he's made a joke! He just doesn't begin to know how lucky he is,' she wrote.[3]

From Compton Place, they went to Hatfield to see Billy's grandmother, and Kick enjoyed chatting to his uncle, Lord Robert Cecil, finding him 'wonderful to listen to'. She told her parents that 'all the old relatives and servants continue to give me the eye, but now I feel I can stand anything'.[4] The press were more indulgent. *Vogue* did a feature on Kick, and the editor of *Life* wanted to write a piece about the marriage between Billy and Kick as 'The greatest gesture for Anglo-American relations since the Atlantic Charter': that idea greatly appealed to her.[5]

Kick and Billy took rooms in the Swan Hotel near to where Billy was stationed. She painted a wonderful word picture of her life as a new war bride, joking that it wasn't to be compared with her father's set-up at the Waldorf, 'but as I have often said it takes all sorts of experience to make life worthwhile'. Billy had a motorbike to ride back and forth from the hotel to his camp, and Kick had her bicycle.

Billy wrote a tender love letter from his barracks, 'to my own darling', telling Kick that the last week had been the 'most perfect week of my life, and has no blemish of any kind'. He was only sorry that it had gone so quickly. He told her that he missed her terribly, and was feeling sorry for himself in this dump, but, now that he had her, nothing else mattered to him. He told her that he 'loved her so much, more and more every day, and it is Hell being separated from you'.[6]

Kick was beginning to realize what it was to be the wife of a marquess, and was rather amused by the deference shown by the hotel's bellboy (also an Irish Kennedy called Tom) who 'rushed headlong into our room' saying 'Good Morning Marquis, good morning Marchioness'. It was a 'preview of things to come'. He dashed around opening doors, pulling out chairs, 'in fact never let us alone'. The hotel was run by an Irish couple, and she noted that what they lacked in efficiency, they more than made up with in kindness: 'The whole place obviously loves a Lord'.[7]

They had been given an 'enormous room' with a gas fire and running water, where supper was laid out on the table. Kick loved meeting the other guests, English eccentrics, including an old army major who gave them a print of one of Billy's ancestors for a wedding present. Tom told Kick that people were ringing up the hotel wanting to have a look at the married couple: 'of course we're pleased to death'.

One day they ordered a delicious picnic from the chef and headed off on bikes into the countryside. Billy picked out the 'longest hill in England to climb but we just managed it'. Billy had borrowed Tom's bicycle: 'the seat was so low that I felt I was riding uphill a spike'. 'Another wonderful day,' he wrote in their joint diary.

Not quite everyone was a fan of the titled guests. Billy was met in the hall of the inn by an ugly woman who said, 'You're Lord Hartington, you don't [know] me, do you?' Billy looked at her blankly, until she explained that she was the sub-agent of Charlie White, the man who had defeated Billy in the by-election. 'What a small world,' he scribbled in the diary.

They were amused that the chef, whom they thought excellent, had created a new savoury dish called 'Croûte Cavendish'. When they asked to speak to him, he told Kick that he had almost gone to work for the Kennedys when they lived in the Embassy, but his letter of application had gone astray. Kick thought that the savoury was 'filthy' but Billy insisted on eating it. Back in their bedroom they laughed until they were 'nearly sick'. Then Tom called on them to tell them that he was becoming a Jesuit priest. 'Never a dull moment': another lighthearted memory for the diary.

Their happiness was marred by Rose's distress and the hate mail that they continued to receive about the marriage. What Rose didn't reveal was that she too was receiving letters criticizing her for Kick's behaviour in marrying a Protestant. One priest wrote to her, 'May the Blessed Mother give her the necessary grace to see the error of her ways, before many weeks have passed.'[8] There was also negative press in Catholic Boston. Kick sent letters to try to cheer her mother up: 'Please do not be sad about anything. I'm very, very happy and quite certain about what I have done. My only regret is that none of you were here for the 1st Kennedy marriage. What an event!!! I missed you all so much. You have no idea!' She also said, 'I think you knew I'd marry B— some day.'[9] She asked her parents to send her a bathing suit, shorts, cotton dresses and a summer dinner dress, a pink dressing gown and a pair of gold and silver evening sandals. It was still so difficult to find lovely clothes with rationing.

Friends who came to stay were impressed by how she handled her new status as a member of the aristocracy. Never one for giving herself airs, she was dignified and kind and took all the extra attention in her stride.[10] The Duke, who 'owns half of Eastbourne', had 'given orders for a Kennedy Street'. She made light of the honour: 'I have chosen to have flowering cherry trees up and down.'[11] Though distressed that she was unable to receive communion, she carried on attending mass.

Kick spent much of her time writing to friends and relations. John White congratulated her on her nuptials, and she wrote back: 'At the moment I am living in a pub, but don't worry, things will get better and I've been in worse places (mainly with you!).'[12] In his journal, White, no doubt jealous, was less kind, saying that Billy 'looked something of a fool'. The staff at the *Times-Herald* sent their congratulations and she wrote back, 'When the revolution comes I shall come begging for another go at "Did You Happen to See".'[13]

Billy and Kick were dreaming about their life after the war. They planned an American trip to see her family, though Billy was extremely nervous about meeting all the boisterous Kennedys en masse. Kick planned to continue working at the Red Cross until the end of the war and then take up her social duties in Derbyshire. But, for now, she was enjoying herself: 'Have put on some weight and am getting plenty of sleep. MARRIED LIFE AGREES WITH ME!'[14]

44

Operation Aphrodite

We are all looking forward now at having Joe home and we only
wish you and Billy were going to be along too.

Rose Kennedy to Kick

6 June 1944, D-Day.

'When we awoke this morning,' Kick wrote in the joint diary, 'Billy said
he was sure the 2nd Front had started. Planes had gone over unceasingly
for two hours. He was quite right. London quiet.'[1]

Their precious days of uninterrupted joy were coming to an end. The
Duchess joined them for the evening and they talked about what lay ahead.
The rain poured down. 'Planes not so plentiful,' Kick wrote in the diary, but
'tanks, with waterproof equipment and heavy trucks rumbled by all day.'
The atmosphere was heavy with expectation: 'The men look ready for what
awaits.'[2]

Fiona and Boofy came for the weekend: 'B got rather tiddly. He'll hate
that fact remaining for posterity,' Kick teased. Billy left to get his T.A.B.
(typhoid) injection. Kick noted that he was 'looking very worried'. For
once her teasing failed to amuse him: 'I was in my most maddening
mood.'[3]

The next morning, 13 June, Billy wrote down his feelings in their diary,
quoting the schoolboy end-of-term refrain: 'This time tomorrow where

shall I be / Not in this academy'. Now, of course, it was the end of honeymoon and potentially the end of everything:

> Although I have been expecting it daily, it is quite a shock too that it has come. I shall always remember these last months as the most perfect of my life. How beastly it is always to be ending things. This war seems to cause nothing but goodbyes. I think that is the worst part of it, worse even than fighting.[4]

Billy was ready for the fight, but hated saying goodbye to Kick. They had had just five weeks together since their wedding day. She wrote down her own feelings of joy and sorrow: 'This is the saddest evening. Ever since May 6th I have had a wonderful sense of contentment. B is the most perfect husband.'[5]

By 15 June, Kick was 'ensconced in Marie Bruce's apartment'. She felt truly alone: 'I miss B so much. Things seem quite empty without him.'[6]

Besides the pain of having to say goodbye to Billy and the anxiety about what he would face in France, Kick had to face the terror of the Luftwaffe's latest weapon, the V1 flying bombs, known as 'doodlebugs', that might drop with hardly any warning at any time of the day or night. The worst thing about them was the moment when the engine (said by the novelist Elizabeth Bowen to sound like a hundred diabolical sewing machines) cut out and there was a twelve-second wait before the explosion.

On 14 June a doodlebug dropped dangerously near to Kick: 'It shook us up quite a bit … Nervous night.' Her diary is full of references to the bombs: 'Nervous day with doodlebugs expected at any moment … they haven't stopped all day … people are absolutely terrified and one senses that the people are always listening first for them to arrive and next for the sound that the dreaded engine has stopped.'[7] More than 200 bodies were dug out of the Guards' Chapel – a place dear to Billy's heart – after a doodlebug hit during a service. Kick pasted newspaper articles about this tragedy in her diary and noted again that Londoners were far more frightened of the doodlebugs than of any other bombs: 'the eeriness and the inability to hit back at a human element make them more disliked'. One of the clippings cited remarks from an eighty-year-old woman: 'Seems 'orrible queer to me. I believe I'd rather have bombs.' Another article talked of Anglo-American unity in the face of the latest Nazi weapon: 'They really feel now that when Germany bombs London she is also bombing America … The flying bomb has done more than anything could have done to destroy any complacency in America that the war in Europe is won.'[8]

Perhaps the danger of the doodlebugs, together with Billy's departure for the Second Front, was the catalyst for Rose. She finally broke her silence at the end of June, sending Kick a cheerful and supportive letter. The Duchess of Devonshire had written a warm note to Rose, telling her how much Kick was loved. 'It made us very happy to know they all love you so dearly,' Rose told her daughter. She said that she felt bad that she had written an angry letter to Billy (now lost) in the aftermath of the wedding, and she had the grace to apologize. She assured Kick that Billy would be given an 'equally warm welcome into the family'. Her behaviour, she emphasized, was the result of shock, 'but that is all over now, dear Kathleen, and as long as you love Billy so dearly, you may be sure that we will all receive him with open arms'. The rest of the letter was news about friends and family, and discussion about clothes. 'Have you ever thought of wearing woolen gabardine slacks in the country?' Rose also told Kick that Jack was recovering from yet another operation on his back. She asked Kick to send love to Marie Bruce, and added that she had written to her: 'I told her that we hope to see her as soon as the war is over, which we think may be soon.'[9] Relationships were healing.

On 7 July, Joe Sr wrote to a friend: 'We hear from Kathleen and she is very, very happy but a little worried about her husband as she hasn't heard from him for quite a while. You know they stick those Grenadier and Coldstream guards with the Irish guards right out in front.'[10] Kick had indeed been worrying about Billy and was relieved when 'a glorious letter' from her 'darling hub' arrived saying that his regiment was 'resting'. She told him that she had been staying with his family, and that they had been picking raspberries and his father chopping logs, his favourite pastime. She sent so much love: 'I doubt it will fit into this tiny envelope.'[11] With the war drawing towards its close, her letter was full of references to their future together. The press was beginning to talk about how one day Kick would rank 'next to the Queen as the most powerful woman in England'.[12]

*   *   *

The Kennedys, now based on Cape Cod, were looking forward to the return of young Joe. 'We are all looking forward now at having Joe home and we only wish you and Billy were going to be along too,' Rose had written in the letter in which she had softened her position on the marriage.[13]

Joe had completed all his missions successfully, so was due for home leave. But he had other plans. To their surprise, Joe and Rose received a letter from him which stated that he was not coming home: 'I am going to be doing something different for the next three weeks. It is secret, and I am not allowed to say what it is, but it isn't dangerous so don't worry.'[14]

He and his crew had volunteered for what was in fact an extremely dangerous mission. He told his parents, 'I persuaded my crew to do it, which pleased me very much,' but he didn't reveal anything about the mission.[15] The truth was that young Joe had signed his own death warrant.

Meanwhile, his married lover Pat Wilson and Kick planned a short holiday in Eastbourne. Hurrying to catch the train at Waterloo they noticed that a doodlebug had exploded close to the station. The minute they arrived at Eastbourne station, they saw in the sky a group of fighters going after other doodlebugs: then there was a tremendous crash when a V1 landed five minutes away.

Young Joe told the family that Kick, normally so intrepid, was 'terrified of the Doodles, as is everyone else'.[16] The only brightness for Kick was being reunited with him, her great supporter throughout the build-up to her marriage. It was his birthday on 25 July, so Kick and Pat Wilson threw him a party: 'there was champagne, and a delicious dinner, so I really enjoyed it'. Joe seemed very happy. He was deeply in love with Pat, though he couldn't see a future with a married woman.

Joe and Kick took a short holiday in the seaside resort of Torquay, and went swimming, despite the terrible British weather. He reported that Kick looked marvellous and joked that he was going grey: 'I'm getting on, and I had better get a gal while there is some life in the old boy.' He and Kick teased one another over a typewriter that Joe had and Kick wanted. 'The Kennedy clan on this side of the Atlantic is doing OK,' he wrote.[17]

Joe had kept up Kick's spirits by reassuring her that fighter planes were chasing the doodlebugs. What few people knew was that, as a response to the flying bombs, a new secret plan called 'Operation Aphrodite' had been developed.[18] An empty bomber, stripped and filled with 10 tons of TNT, would fly by remote control across the Channel, precision-guided to explode on the launching site of the doodlebugs in Normandy. There was one hitch: these drones could not take off without a pilot. So a crew of two was required to take off and fly to 2,000 feet before activating the remote-control system, arming the detonators and parachuting from the aircraft. Joe Kennedy volunteered his services.

On 10 August, Joe wrote to Jack telling him of his secret mission and praised a recent *New Yorker* article about his brother: 'The whole squadron got to read it and were much impressed by your intestinal fortitude.' He was proud of Jack, but was also writing as a competitive elder brother, a professional and a father figure: 'What I really want to know, is where the hell were you when the destroyer hove into sight, and exactly what were your moves, and where the hell was your radar?'[19] It was typical of Joe to question his brother. Jack loved his brother's honesty while everyone else was calling him a hero.

Joe joked about his female conquests, and told Jack not to worry: he was not risking 'my fine neck (covered in the back with a few fine silky black hairs) in any crazy venture'.[20] Joe was very well aware of the risks of his mission, but he wanted to return a hero, to outdo his brother.

On the night that he flew, he was given two warnings that the electric circuitry of his plane was faulty. He left Kick a message asking her to explain to Pat that he was going to be a day late. He added, 'I'm about to go into my act. If I don't come back, tell my dad – despite our differences that I love him very much.'[21]

One of Kick's presents to Joe had been a velvet-lined casket in which he stored his fresh eggs. The night before the mission he and a friend had a fry-up, using up most of his precious eggs. He leant out of the window of his plane, and joked with his men who had gathered around to wish him luck that, if he didn't come back, they could eat the eggs that remained.[22]

Twenty minutes after take-off from Fersfield Aerodrome in Norfolk, his plane exploded in mid-air.

Sunday, 13 August 1944.

It was a beautiful sunny afternoon on the Cape, and the Kennedys had just finished a picnic lunch on the big porch of the family home in Hyannis Port. The children sat in the living room chatting quietly and listening to the Victrola playing Bing Crosby's 'I'll be Seeing You', while Rose read the Sunday newspaper. Upstairs, Joe had retired to his bedroom for a nap.

Suddenly a car pulled up. Two priests got out and came to the house. There was nothing unusual about this; priests often called at the house, so Rose did not feel particularly alarmed. They asked to speak to Mr Kennedy. Rose invited them in and asked them to wait until Joe had finished his nap, but they told her that it was urgent. Their eldest son was missing in action and presumed lost. Young Ted recalled that all the children heard were the words 'missing' and 'lost': 'All of us froze.'[23]

Rose ran upstairs and shook Joe awake. Her mind was 'half-paralyzed', but she managed to blurt out that two priests were here with a message. Joe Sr 'leaped from the bed and hurried downstairs … we realized that there could be no hope, and that our son was dead'.[24] Ted recalled that when his parents emerged from their conversation with the priests: 'Dad's face was twisted. He got out the words that confirmed what we already suspected. Joe Jr was dead … Suddenly the sunroom was awash in tears. Mother, my sisters, our guests, myself – everybody was crying; some wailed. Dad turned himself around and stumbled back up the stairs; he did not want us to witness his own dissolution into sobs.'[25] Jean, only sixteen, got on her bike and rode to church. Jack turned to Teddy and said, 'Joe wouldn't want us sitting here crying. He would want us to go sailing. Let's go sailing.'[26] And that's what they did. They went sailing.

Rose recalled it slightly differently. In her memory, it was Joe Sr who urged the children to go on with their plans, to be brave, as that's what Joe would have wanted them to do. She remembered Jack walking on the beach for a long time.

Back in England, Kick was having her first serious taste of her life as a Cavendish. On 8 August, four days before Joe's fateful mission, she performed her first official public engagement in Derbyshire. Lady Hartington, dressed in her Red Cross uniform, gave a spirited speech at the Derby Red Cross and St John Carnival in the market town of Bakewell. The Duke of Devonshire's political agent observed her carefully and then wrote to tell his master what a great asset she would be to the family once the war was over and Billy could resume a life in politics.[27]

Kick had been spending much of her time with the Duke and Duchess as they waited for news of Billy. In her diary, she pondered on Anglo-American relations, and the differences within the English class system. At Compton Place an American colonel came to tea: 'I'm always interested in seeing the effect an American has upon an English family such as my own,' she wrote. She was amused that when she used the word 'faze' nobody understood what she meant. Other Americans were invited to tea at Compton Place. One of them was terrified at the thought of an English duchess and had a mental picture of a character from *Alice in Wonderland*.

Kick spoke at length to Edward the butler about the position of servants in America as compared with England. They discussed why Americans always used people's first names, 'which I always do'. He asked her, 'Would you go to a movie with me?' She replied that she would 'do what Lord Hartington wanted and I don't think he'd approve'. She was puzzled by why the English thought it 'queer' that Americans 'speak to everyone in a normal, friendly fashion'.[28]

It was to the great relief of Billy's parents that Kick was with them in Derbyshire when she heard the news of Joe's death. The Duke later wrote how proud he was of the courageous way that she handled the news. The next day, one of Joe's friends, Mark Soden, telephoned to say that before he flew Joe had made a will in which he left Kick the typewriter that they had fought over, his beloved Victrola and a radio and a camera. She wrote to Mark: 'I'm so sorry I broke down tonight. It never makes things easier … I don't know whether I'll even want to use the much discussed typewriter but it will make me always think of the hard-talker Joe. I still can't believe it. It's hard to write. I don't feel sorry for Joe – just for you … and everyone that knew him 'cause no matter how he yelled, argued etc. he was the best guy in the world.'[29]

Joe was awarded the Navy Cross (the highest honour) and also the Air Medal. In death, he was the hero he had longed to be.

Kick wanted to be home in Hyannis Port with her family. On 16 August she was granted leave and priority air travel, flying to New York in an army transport plane. From there she took a flight to Boston. Jack, whom she had not seen for two years, met her at the airport. According to the *Boston Globe*, she was wearing an American Red Cross summer dress in robin's-egg blue, and she smiled wearily before she 'ran into John's arms and wept'. 'After a moment, she squared her jaw, faced the crowd and walked resolutely up the ramp, arm in arm with her brother.'[30]

Part of the reason for her tears was her shock at seeing her beloved brother so emaciated from his war ordeal. Jack was painfully thin and his skin a yellowish colour from a bout of malaria. That evening the family attended mass together.

Kick had been the last Kennedy to see Joe alive and she brought great comfort to her family. Furthermore, despite her great sadness over Joe, her own happiness at being married to Billy shone through.

Some of Kick and Jack's friends who gathered at the Cape that summer were rather shocked to see the family coping so well in the aftermath of Joe's death. There were the usual highly competitive games of tennis and touch football and sailing. That was the Kennedy way. Kick put on the same brave front as the others, writing to Frank Waldrop: 'It's a great treat to be back in the land of "the free and the brave" – No place like it.'[31] Jack and his friends teased her about her title: 'Excuse, the Marchioness of Hartington is trying to get through,' one of them joked. The only person unable to cope was Joe Sr. When the young people made too much noise, he reprimanded them, accusing them of lack of respect for their dead brother. But of course they did have respect. Jack began plans for a book in his memory, and Kick wrote that without him 'there would always be a gap in the Kennedy family circle, but we are far, far luckier than most because there are so many of us … I know the one thing Joe would never want is that we should feel sad and gloomy about life without him. Instead he would laugh with that wonderful twinkle shining out of his Irish eyes and say, "Gee, can't you learn to all get along without me?"'[32]

At the end of the summer Kick sent a telegram to Marie Bruce announcing her plans. She asked her friend to find out whether Billy was coming on leave. If he was, she would return at once, but if not, she would stay with her mother till the end of September – the younger children were returning to school and Jack was going back into hospital. Her parents were insisting that Billy should be her priority. She said of her current circumstances that 'it was still quite sad, but nothing would stop me coming home if Billy has the chance to get back'.[33]

45

Billy the Hero

I have a permanent lump in my throat and I long for you to be here as it is an experience which few can have and which I would love to share with you.

Billy to Kick

He was riding atop an army tank, festooned with garlands of flowers and brightly coloured streamers, as they crept at a snail's pace into Brussels among the cheering crowd on an early-September evening. Lord Hartington, a major in the Coldstream Guards, just twenty-six years old, a stoical, cool-headed Englishman, was close to tears as he witnessed the ecstatic reception from the thousands of Belgian citizens lining the streets crying and waving. His battalion, the 5th, serving in the Guards Armoured Division, was one of the first units to liberate the city, having travelled 430 miles in six days, with the German army in full retreat.

They had pressed on through France, liberating town after town, village after village, encountering cheering all the way. Many of the villages had been occupied by the Germans fewer than ten hours before, and the excitement was intense. Some people came out in their nightshirts to wave at the Allies. A soldier, Frank Clarke, writing to his sister, recalled: 'The French people were glad to see us but the Belgians went mad. Their villages and towns were gaily festooned with flags, Belgian and Allied, and the streets were a mass of colour. Before we had gone many miles, our vehicles were covered with flowers and every time we halted we had fruit and wine showered on us. We looked like flying greengrocer's shops.'[1]

Banners proclaimed 'Welcome to our Allies' and 'Bienvenue aux Libérateurs', and bands played music in the path of the advancing army. Clarke wrote: 'From early morning till we arrived [in the capital] I ate, ate, ate cakes and biscuits, fruit and wine. My god how hysterically crazy and excited were these people to see us ... On and on we drove towards Brussels, the excitement getting more intense every hour. The people were getting frantic! The route was a blaze of colour and my arm fair ached with waving to the excited crowds.' The tanks and jeeps crawled through the seething masses, and people climbed on to the trucks, kissing the soldiers and crying. As they finally entered the capital, it took the troops three hours to get from the suburbs to the centre, thanks to the crowds. 'Bands, screams, singing, crying, all these sounds rent the air.'[2] Once the tanks had drawn to a halt, the soldiers were hugged and kissed and applauded as their photographs were taken again and again. Soldiers were given babies to kiss, and mothers were weeping tears of joy.

It was dark by the time they reached the city centre, but lights blazed in cafés and there was a red glow in the sky. The Germans had left their own welcome: they had set fire to the Palace of Justice. But when the Allied tanks arrived there, they discovered that the Germans had stored thousands of bottles of wine and champagne, which had been rescued and brought up into the streets. The party in the main square went on all night.

The next day, Monday, 4 September 1944, Lord Hartington wrote a beautiful letter to his wife, telling her that the past week had been 'truly incredible and unforgettable'. Billy, usually so languid and composed, told Kick of his deep emotion: 'we have advanced and advanced and advanced and the reception we have had makes one want to cry'. He told Kick what a terrible time the people had had and of their loathing for the Huns.

Billy had been in the vanguard, leading No. 3 Company into the central square of the city. He and his devoted batman Ingles were 'mobbed' by the crowd: 'Ingles was literally carried out of the vehicle and covered with kisses and hugs for nearly half an hour.' Billy managed to keep control, but soon gave in to the 'crying and the kissing'. He told Kick with great emotion:

There is nothing, absolutely nothing in the world that they would not do for us. I would not have believed that the human race could be capable of such emotion and such gratitude and one feels so unworthy of it all, living as I have in reasonable safety and comfort during these years whilst they have been suffering such terrible hardships under the Germans. I have a permanent lump in my throat and I long for you to be here as it is an experience which few can have and which I would love to share with you.[3]

This was recompense for the ignominy of Dunkirk. Those long years of war, deprivation, fierce combat, separation from his beloved Kick, were all worth it for this moment. But he wanted to share it with Kick, knowing that she would understand what it meant to him.

He told her of his fatigue after travelling non-stop for days. He described the 'exhausted and demoralized' Germans they met: 'I cannot believe that they can go on much longer. They come in weary, unshaven and ragged, without weapons and with their boots worn out.' Most Germans were incredibly young: 'I've seen a lot that can't be more than 15 years old.' And yet, he said, 'one can't feel sorry for them. They have been guilty of such appalling wickedness.' The local mob were ready to lynch them. He also told Kick that the French Resistance had been 'tremendously well-organized' and helpful with information: 'they are worth several Divisions to us.'[4] He reported that French women who had slept with German soldiers had had their heads shaved in public and been paraded through the streets.

In the weeks before reaching Brussels, Billy had been involved in heavy fighting in France.[5] A week after he left Kick, his battalion landed on Pereira beach in Normandy, but he was held back in England with a reinforcement unit. Then on 8 July, he joined the battalion in France, promoted to the role of commander of No. 4 Company, in place of the Major who had been killed in action. He was now Major Hartington. The Coldstream Guards suffered many casualties as they advanced. On 1 August the Battalion Diary recorded a busy day:

0900 hours

The Brigade Commander came to Battalion H.Q. and ordered an attack on the enemy holding up No. 3 Company in the ORCHARD at 675585.

The attack is to be made by No. 1 Company passing through No. 3 Company and supported by a Squadron of tanks.

Artillery support is not possible as the distance to the objective is only about 400 yards.

1000 hours

The attack was put in but after the first 200 yards came under very heavy fire from enemy tanks and was unable to get on.

Seven of our own tanks were knocked out and both Nos. 1 and 3 Companies had a number of casualties, including the Commanding Officer and Major THORNTON Commanding No. 1 Company, who were both wounded.

After several unsuccessful attempts to stalk the [enemy] tanks with PIATs [hand-held anti-tank weapons] the Company withdrew back to the Start Line.

1100 hours

Major The Marquess of HARTINGTON took over command of the Battalion.[6]

For the next few days, until a colonel arrived to take over, Billy was left in command of the entire battalion. As casualties rose and tanks were knocked out, different companies were amalgamated. By 18 August Billy was in command of the merged 2 and 3 Companies. Kick later received a letter from his fellow officer, James Willoughby (Nancy Astor's son-in-law), describing his courage:

Billy was magnificent, he never lost his head or his good spirits in spite of the hard time his Battalion was having, no sleep, no food and continual casualties and kept up the spirits of his men the whole time. On the last day we were counterattacked continuously from 6 o'clock in the morning until 10 o'clock at night and Billy's Battalion had to stand the brunt of the attack. Again he organized the defence in the most cool headed manner, and the position was held in spite of the most determined efforts by the Germans to capture it.[7]

Billy was highly regarded by his men. Another fellow officer recalled: 'I can still see his dismay when told that his company had done enough and must hand over the lead to another.'[8]

One of the ways that Billy kept up morale was to observe social niceties. When his men fortified themselves with rum, he would insist that they should drink out of glasses. He always ensured that he looked smart. He carried a small steel mirror in his left breast pocket so he could shave every morning. He insisted on his company carrying a fold-up table and chair. When they set up camp, he would scan the field and announce, 'Now … where is the Company office going to be? Ah, we'll have it here,' he would say pointing at a bit of grubby land. His men were devoted to him, and none more so than his batman Ingles. The men loved to hear Billy shout: 'Ingles! Some watah for my feet!'[9]

One of the privileges of his position as a major was that he could wear non-regulation clothing. He chose pale-coloured corduroy trousers and a bright, white Macintosh. He refused to wear a helmet. It was a courageous (or foolhardy) symbolic gesture to show that he wasn't frightened of being taken down by a sniper. Everyone knew that the Germans targeted officers, easily identified by their clothing.

One of his platoon commanders recalled that Billy rarely mentioned Kick, keeping his feelings private, except for one rare instance when he disclosed what he felt about the bad press Kick had received about supposedly abandoning her faith and marrying in a registry office.[10] But he was thinking about her all the time and writing when he could. On an unusually calm morning in August he wrote a letter that she would always treasure:

> I have been spending a lovely hour on the ground and thinking in a nice vague sleepy way about you & what a lot I've got to look forward to if I come through this all right. I feel I may talk about it for the moment as I'm not in danger so I'll just say that if anything should happen to me I shall be wanting you to try and isolate our life together, to face its finish, and to start a new one as soon as you feel you can. I hope that you will marry again, quite soon – someone good & nice.[11]

During other moments of respite, there was a Battalion Sports Meeting on 22 August and a concert the following night in honour of the Liberation of Paris, with the local French as guests. They crossed the Seine at the end of August, then made rapid progress towards Brussels. Back home, the Duchess of Devonshire wrote to Kick in America with the news that their beloved Billy would be 'out of the line in about a week which is a great comfort'.[12]

Billy's unit moved onward, east from Brussels. After the jubilation of those early days, the mood changed at the end of the week, as the Germans fought back. On 8 September, Billy lost a quarter of his men in attempting to capture the village of Beverlo. During the fierce battle, he showed enormous courage and fortitude, walking across to one of his sections 'as calmly as if he had been in the garden at Compton Place'.[13] He stood on the back of a tank, all 6 foot 4 of him, directing the fire on to the German tanks, 'All the time, under fire'. A fellow soldier observed: 'Many of our guardsmen asked me who was the officer from the 5th Battalion, for it was impossible not to be inspired by his presence.'[14]

The next day, Billy's unit set out to capture the German-occupied town of Heppen near Limburg. There was fierce fighting and the British losses were great; six tanks were left behind on the battlefield. No. 3 Company, led by Billy, attacked across an open field, raked by concentrated fire from about fifteen machine guns. Major Hartington stopped his tank near a farmhouse and walked out, leading the infantry forward. He was 'completely calm and casual, carrying his cap'. Rather languidly he said, 'Come on you fellows, buck up!'[15] He was wearing his white coat and corduroy trousers. He was carrying only a hand grenade and a pair of pliers for cutting barbed-wire defences.

The events of the day were recorded in the Battalion Diary, with the military precision of timings and map co-ordinates:

1944 September 9
    At 0845 hours the attack was continued and the Battalion attacked HEPPEN 2481.
    Right No. 3 Company with objectives the ROAD & TRACK JUNCTION 249821 and Left No. 2 Company objective ROAD & TRACK JUNCTION 241816.

During this attack the enemy put in an attack along the line of the Canal bank towards the bridge site, and our F.2 Echelon became involved, but managed to drive them off without difficulty.

No. 2 Company reached their objective at 0915 hours and reported little opposition.

No. 3 Company met much greater opposition and were held up for some time, so that No. 2 Company was ordered to clear the village Eastwards, and try and link up with No. 3 Company when they had got their objective.

The Company Commander Major The Marquess of HARTINGTON was killed during this attack.[16]

A more detailed account was provided by an eyewitness. Young Frans Mangelschots was the son of a local farmer. He heard the sound of heavy shooting, and realized that the battle for Heppen had begun. From his hiding place, he witnessed what happened next: 'Major Cavendish attacked our farmhouse from the rear, and threw a hand grenade through the window, knowing the Germans were inside. (We could see from the ruins afterwards what had happened.) Major Cavendish was hit simultaneously by a bullet.'[17] He had made it across the field but had been shot at close range at the very moment when he took out the Germans in the farmhouse with his grenade.

Some hours later, at three o'clock in the afternoon, the fighting armies having moved on, Frans returned with his father. The place was deserted, with the exception of a couple of neighbours living on the outskirts, who had been permitted to stay, with a sick aunt. They were 'still hiding, scared to death'. The only living person in the village was the priest, hiding in his church. At the farmhouse, they saw a scene of carnage. In all, they found eleven English and thirty German corpses. The battle had been ferocious. Frans saw two bodies lying next to one another, men who had strangled each other to death. 'Some had bayonets in their bodies, some even had spades. It had been a hand-to-hand battle, eye to eye.'[18]

It was Frans and his father who found Billy's body. They could see it was an officer 'as his uniform was quite different from that of the soldiers'. Frans recalled the bright trousers, the white Macintosh, no beret or helmet. He was lying on his back with his feet against the outside of the kitchen door of the farmhouse: 'He had a small wound beneath his left arm' but 'No blood, nor scar was seen on his face.'[19] Lord Hartington had been shot through the heart.

46

'Life is So Cruel'

I feel like a small cork that is tossing around.

Kick Kennedy

After Labor Day, Kick, Eunice and their parents headed for New York to their respective hotels, Joe to his suite at the Waldorf Towers and Rose to the Plaza with Kick and Eunice, the younger girls being back at school. On 19 September 1944, Kick went shopping alone at Bonwit Teller's department store on Fifth Avenue. Having being deprived of beautiful clothes in war-torn England, she was looking forward to the day. She was a good shopper.

Kick was meeting Eunice for lunch, so she was faintly surprised to see her sister on the second floor seeking her out. 'Before we go, I think we ought to go back and speak to Daddy.'

'Something's happened?' said Kick.

'Why don't you go talk to Daddy?'

They walked back to the Waldorf in silence. Eunice had been told by her father that Billy was dead. When they arrived at the hotel, Kick was taken into her father's suite, where he broke the news. She returned to the Plaza and stayed in her room by herself until evening, when she arrived downstairs for dinner, red-eyed. That evening at supper, nobody talked about Billy's death. They acted as though nothing had happened. After some time, Joe asked Kick if she would like to have a friend with her. 'Patsy White,' she replied. Joe didn't like Patsy, or her brother John, Kick's former Washington boyfriend, but he put in the call at midnight and said: 'I hate your guts, as you well know. But I have a favor of you. Will you come and stay with Kathleen.'[1]

Patsy came the next day, but was first taken to see Joe at the Waldorf to be briefed. When she finally got to Kick at the Plaza, she found 'a great cloud of misery was hanging over everything'.[2] She was desperate to be alone with Kick, and when she finally got the time she asked her friend what she had been doing since she heard the news: 'Mostly going to Mass. Mother keeps saying: "God doesn't give us a cross heavier than we can bear."' They talked for hours. Kick told Patsy that her only regret was not being pregnant with Billy's child. She wanted something of him. Kick told her: 'The amazing thing was that Billy loved me so much, Patsy. I felt needed. I felt I could make him happy.'[3] Patsy, looking at Kick's deathly pale face and ringed eyes, asked her if they'd given her anything to sleep. She took out some sleeping pills and gave them to her friend. Patsy told her that Kennedys don't cry. She was shocked that everyone was carrying on as normal. Kick spent most of her time staring at a photograph of Billy.[4]

Letters and telegrams poured in. The President sent a telegram: 'Please tell Kathleen I am thinking of her in her crushing sorrow. Mrs. Roosevelt joins me in heartfelt sympathy.'[5] The most poignant letter was from the Duchess, written just four days after Billy's death:

> I want you never, never to forget what complete happiness you gave him. All your life you must think that you brought complete happiness to one person. He wrote that to me when he went to the front. I want you to know this for I know what great conscientious struggles you went through before you married Billy, but I know that it will be a source of infinite consolation to you now that you decided as you did. All your life I shall love you – not only for yourself but that you gave such perfect happiness to my son whom I loved above anything in the world.[6]

The Duchess, thinking only of Kick in her sorrow and not of herself, concluded: 'May you be given the strength to carry you through these truly terrible months. My heart breaks when I think of how much you have gone through in your young life.'

That night Jack stayed awake with Kick while she talked about Billy. He later said that it was the worst night of his life.[7] It was so tragic that she had lost Billy so close to the end of the war, when she had allowed herself to believe that he would come through. Her only comfort was that she had defied her family and sacrificed her religion to make him happy, and it had been worth it. Her family had been wrong, and she had been vindicated.

Kick called Richard Wood's father, Lord Halifax, at the British Embassy. He told her that the War Office in London had confirmed the bad news: 'She seemed very good and brave on the telephone ... She is going up to Quebec tomorrow to fly home ... It is a melancholy business.'[8] He had arranged to get her without delay on to a top-secret flight back to England.

From Quebec she wrote to her parents: 'We depart tonight some time – I am so glad to be going.' She told her parents that losing Billy felt very different from losing Joe: 'When a brother dies, a sister is very sad but she doesn't get the gnawing pain which one gets when one loses a part of oneself – that was Joe to you both – And Billy to me.' Heartbreakingly, she told her mother: 'Remember I told you that he got much holier after we were married. Now he is the one to bring me closer to God – what a funny world.' She wanted the family to know how much she had loved Billy, and how happy she had been: 'I don't mind feeling sad cause why should I mind. If Eunice, Pat & Jean marry nice guys for fifty years they'll be lucky if they have five weeks like I did.'[9]

Before heading for the airport she had got out the diary inscribed 'This Book is the PRIVATE PROPERTY of Billy & Kick' and written:

> September 20th 1944
> So ends the story of Billy and Kick. Yesterday the final word came. I can't believe that the one thing that I felt might happen should have happened. Billy is dead – killed in action in France Sept 10th. Life is so cruel. I am on my way to England. Writing is impossible.[10]

Since Billy's battalion had moved on after the battle of Heppen, his body had been recovered by a following unit. This led to the assumption, in the casualty report to the War Office, reiterated in the telegram to next of kin and the official records, that he had died on 10 September. But the battalion diary and the recollection of Frans Mangelschots reveal that he was actually killed the day before.[11]

On the special flight from Quebec, Kick found herself in the illustrious company of Britain's top brass, the Chief of the Air Staff, Sir Charles Portal, and Field Marshal Sir Alan Brooke, the Chief of the Imperial General Staff, returning from an Allied conference. Each was accompanied by two aides-de-camp. She observed that 'They all kept opening up important looking boxes and rushing around always clutching a very, very secret looking brief case'.[12] She was treated royally, and given champagne and a meal of soup, meat and vegetables and ice cream. Her sense of humour never left her. Three days later, back in England, she wrote, 'I must say the last thing I thought I'd be doing last week at this time was watching the Chief of the Air Staff and the Chief of the Imperial Staff drinking champagne in the mid-Atlantic'.[13]

Throughout the flight she put on a brave face. She was shown round the cockpit, 'watching the landings and takings-off, which was terribly exciting and Portal took great pleasure in showing me everything about an airplane'. For official purposes, they pretended that she was a nurse. Charles Portal chatted to her for much of the flight and told her that if at any time she wanted air passage he would arrange it on her behalf. On landing in Plymouth, the group were taken from the plane and whisked into a private train with luncheon served on board.

The Duke of Devonshire met her at the station in London and took her down to Compton Place on the south coast. Elizabeth and Anne Cavendish and Debo were there: 'they are all wonderfully brave. What you and mother went through has only now just been brought home to me as I feel such a funny pain and that must just be what you had'.[14]

Being back in England was a double-edged sword for Kick. She desperately wanted to mourn Billy among people who knew and loved him, and yet the memories of him were ever present and she suffered deeply: 'The realization of Billy's death has come to me very acutely here and I should probably have spared myself a great deal of agony if I had remained in America,' she told her family. She recognized, however, that she needed to be with her in-laws: 'I am so terribly pleased that I came and the Duke and Duchess were so glad and I couldn't have borne not being able to talk to them all about Billy'.[15] The Duke, shattered by Billy's death, was impressed by Kick's fortitude and selflessness. He finally saw what Billy had seen all along.

Tributes poured in and the Cavendish family devoured them all, trying to piece together the very last moments of Billy's life, taking comfort from the wonderful words that were written about him. 'The letters about him', declared Kick, 'have been perfectly wonderful … saying how well he had done during the whole course of the summer.'[16] They learnt that he would certainly have won the DSO (Distinguished Service Order) had he not been killed. Letters were read and re-read and passed around, as if they could somehow bring Billy back from the dead. The Duke received a letter saying how furious Billy's men had been when they heard the news about their commanding officer. 'We took no prisoners that day,' one of his friends later wrote to the Duke.[17] A twenty-five-year-old corporal from Essex was so incensed by Billy's death that he killed forty-five men in one hour: 'so the death of Lord Hartington was avenged'.[18] Another comrade wrote to Kick to tell her that Billy was 'brave and fearless … just and fair' and 'admired and respected by all whom he commanded'. He told Kick that he could still hear Billy shouting 'Sergeant Major'. He was full of energy, 'a real live wire'. He and Billy had spent hours talking in the slit trenches and Billy had spoken endlessly about wanting a career in politics and his desire to be an MP. He told Kick that he had helped to bury Billy.[19]

Another soldier, James Willoughby, wrote to the Duchess to say that he had visited Billy's grave by a little chapel in Heppen: 'He lies with five other guardsmen and the local people have made it all very beautiful with flowers and a private hedge.' He added, 'I am thankful, too, that he lived to see the welcome we received all the way across France and Belgium for the look of happiness in the people's faces made us all realize that almost any sacrifice is worth while.'[20]

Kick was keen that her family should recognize Billy's courage. She faithfully copied out paragraphs commending his courage from friends who had written letters to her and to the Duke and Duchess. She asked her parents to show the passages to 'all the brothers and sisters. Since they didn't know Billy very well they might like to know how well he did.'[21] Praise for Billy even came from the unlikely source of one of Britain's leading left-wing academics: 'Prof Harold Laski has written the most wonderful impression of Joe as he taught Joe for a year at the London University. In the letter he sent me he said "I met your husband often and on each occasion I thought he combined charm with integrity in an exceptional degree." That's praise indeed coming from one of England's most rabid Socialists, don't you think?'[22]

But Jack was the one who truly understood. He sent the Duchess a beautiful condolence letter, comparing Billy with his own hero, Raymond Asquith, who had faced death so bravely in the trenches of the Somme. Billy's death, he wrote:

> was about the saddest I have ever had. I have always been so fond of Kick that I couldn't help but feel some of her great sorrow. Her great happiness when she came home which even shone through her sadness over Joe's death was so manifest and so infectious that it did much to ease the grief of our mother and father. It was so obvious what he meant to Kick and what a really wonderful fellow he must have been that we all became devoted to him, and now know what a really great loss his is. When I read Captain Waterhouse's letter about the cool and gallant way Billy died [the tribute in *The Times* describing Major Hartington's bravery at Beverlo and Heppen], I couldn't help but think of what John Buchan had written about Raymond Asquith 'Our roll of honour is long, but it holds no nobler figure. He will stand to those of us who are left as an incarnation of the spirit of the land he loved … He loved his youth, and his youth has become eternal. Debonair and brilliant and brave, he is now part of that immortal England which knows not weariness or defeat.' I think those words could be so well applied to Billy. I feel extremely proud that he was my sister's husband.[23]

*　*　*

A service was going to be held for Billy at Chatsworth, which Kick worried would make her feel so 'very sad'. She told her parents that everything in England reminded her of her husband: 'I just feel terribly, terribly sad.' She acknowledged her father's belief that she and Billy might have had future difficulties as a result of the religious difference: 'That's all quite true, but it doesn't fill the gap that I now feel in my life. Before it had its purpose, I knew what it would be. Now I feel like a small cork that is tossing around.'[24]

Kick had also received a letter from Bishop Mathew telling her that she was able to receive Holy Communion. Since Billy was dead, she was no

longer living in a state of sin. She was gratified that he now spoke sympa-
thetically of her decision to marry Billy: 'I have always been convinced that
the reason why you took the line you did about the marriage was because
you wanted your husband to be happy in what might prove the last portion
of a small life.' 'Isn't that nice,' Kick wrote to her family. She was also having
a mass said for Billy and Joe 'at which I shall receive Communion. I hope
that makes Mother as happy as it makes me.'[25] Rose was indeed delighted
that she had her daughter back in the fold, though she told Kick that she
had been so exhausted that she had spent a night with the nuns at Noroton.
She also told her that she had been to mass frequently, to say prayers for
Billy's soul: 'After I heard you talk about him and I began to hear about his
likes and dislikes, his ideas and ideals, I realized what a wonderful man he
was and what happiness would have been yours had God willed that you
spent your life with him.' In Rose's mind, it was not God's will that Billy
should survive and stay married to her daughter. 'A first love – a young love
– is so wonderful, my dear Kathleen, but, my dearest daughter, I feel we
must dry our tears as best we can and bow our head to God's wisdom and
goodness. We must place our hand in his and trust Him.'[26]

Joe wrote to Billy's parents, sympathizing with them as one who had lost
a beloved eldest son himself. Whenever he talked about the war and his
losses, he always included mention of his son-in-law, whom he never really
knew. He was upset when he visited the President in October and the
President got Billy's name wrong.[27] He wrote to Lord Beaverbrook, 'I have
had rather a bad dose – Joe dead, Billy Hartington dead, my son in the
Naval Hospital.'[28]

He knew that Kick was suffering badly: 'She is frightfully courageous but
I think deep in her heart, completely inconsolable.' But Joe could not and
would not change his views about the war. He refused to believe that 'the
death of the two boys' had any positive effect. His friend Arthur Houghton
lost his son in May 1945 and Kennedy wrote: 'I don't think you ever get over
the shock … I won't offer you that hocus-pocus that some people offer –
that he died for a great cause – I don't believe he did. I believe he died like
young Joe as a result of the stupidity of our generation.'[29]

This was a view that Kick did not and would not understand. She had to
believe that Billy had died for a cause that he believed in. Jack knew this.
She told him that it would be 'a long time before I get reconciled inside …
little things happen every day that make me think "what would Billy have

thought of that"'. The 'pattern of life for me has been destroyed. At the moment I don't fit into any design.'[30]

But now she had to make decisions about her future without Billy. She had not given Chatsworth an heir, and Debo was now the Marchioness of Hartington. Kick was given a small inheritance and was able to retain the title of 'Lady Hartington'. Debo came to stay to help her through her grief. She was saddened to see her bubbly sister-in-law so changed. Kick refused to sleep alone, so a family member slept in the same room. Younger sister-in-law Elizabeth Cavendish felt 'she had never met anyone so desperately unhappy'.[31]

Kick spent Christmas 1944 quietly with the Duke and Duchess. Then in January she went to a Sacred Heart convent near Kendal in the Lake District for a retreat. She had been staying with Sissy Gore, who now had two small children. Kick said other people's children made her feel sad, as she would have loved to have some of her own. It was freezing at the Convent, but the nuns were charming, kind and solicitous. Kick was still traumatized, and she was glad that she had made the retreat: 'it still somehow doesn't seem right. Rather like an awful dream.' Here at the Convent, she didn't have to worry about being courageous or thinking of others. She could give in to her grief for all that she had lost. There had been moments of anger towards God – 'I guess God has taken care of the matter in his own way, hasn't he,' she had written to a friend[32] – but now a process of spiritual healing began. One of the nuns wrote to Rose after Kick's visit, describing her as 'the sweetest, most simple, unspoilt child you could wish to find … she is looking very well … quite lovely – her great innocent eyes, and very sweet face makes one long to have her portrait painted. The grace of God is shining from her face.' The nun was convinced that sorrow over Billy's death had not turned her away from God. Kick, she said, was a 'really holy girl, a deep thinker'. She was coming to the realization that her life was 'not over, or spoilt, or wrecked, but beginning anew'.[33]

The retreat was an important turning point. Kick was in two minds about her future. Her friends and the Duke and Duchess were begging her to stay in England. When she returned from Kendal, she concurred that for now England was her home. She moved into a flat in a building called Westminster Gardens in Marsham Street with Billy's aunt Anne Hunloke. She loved the flat, which was 'furnished quite simply, but very cosy'. The sitting room had an open fire and there was a small dining room. Her linen and silver were from Chatsworth. She liked her cook: 'I have completely destroyed all her illusions about Marchionesses, slouching around in overalls or stark naked.'[34]

She returned to the Red Cross. True to Kennedy form, she wanted to keep herself busy. Her job was to arrange hospitality in English homes for GIs and she also worked with wounded soldiers. She still cycled to work every day, as in the old days before she married Billy.

Kick was being mothered by the Duchess and by Marie Bruce. She also had a new maternal figure, Lady Anderson, whose younger brother had been in Billy's battalion. Ava Anderson was married to Sir John Anderson (after whom the Anderson shelter was named), Home Secretary and Minister of Home Security, then Lord President of the Council, in the war cabinet. Billy had been extremely kind to Ava's brother after he was wounded and Lady Anderson was repaying him by taking an interest in his beautiful young widow. 'Please don't worry about me,' Kick told her family, 'because I am well taken care of and Billy always seems quite near.' She told them that 'with the passage of time I miss Billy more but feel the sense of loss less. Rather difficult to explain.'[35]

Letters from the family kept her going during the harsh winter of 1945, as snow fell deep on the ground and food rationing was making her miserable. Bobby Kennedy, Kick's favourite little sibling, wrote to her constantly. She liked his style. She was also deriving great comfort from reading poetry. The poet Maurice Baring had sent her some autographed verses, which she loved: 'Because of you we will be glad and gay / Remembering you, we will be brave and strong / And hail the advent of each dangerous day / And meet the last adventure with a song.'[36]

The family also sent presents from America: pineapple juice, ham, chocolate, stockings, records and clothes. Her friends were rallying around her and most evenings her little dining room was filled with people. She had a small but intimate party for her twenty-fifth birthday in February 1945. The Duke and Duchess gave her a Crown Derby tea service. The Duke brought claret and port, and her friend Fiona Gore made her a cake, using up all her sugar ration for the month. Her birthday present from the Kennedy family was a diamond and sapphire watch: 'There is no doubt I LOVE large expensive gifts.'[37]

She wrote to Lem to tell him that she was looking to the future: 'One thing you can be sure of life holds no fears for someone who has faced love, marriage and death before the age of 25. It's hard to face the future, without someone who you thought would always be there to help and guide and for whom you'd sacrificed a lot. Luckily I am a Kennedy. I have a very strong feeling that makes a big difference about how to take things ... I know we've all got the ability to be not got down.'[38]

Kick took great comfort in the fact that Billy had been so brave and a wonderful leader: 'I have so much to be proud of.' And she never relented from her belief that, for all the anguish it had caused the families, she had been right to marry him: 'I thank God every night I married him and I think it must have been God's way of making Billy's life, though short, completely happy.'[39]

47

The Widow Hartington

During the war everybody lived in a state of flux but now we must
all settle down & make definite plans.

Kick Kennedy Hartington[1]

It was Tuesday, 8 May 1945 and Kick was playing bridge in her flat with her
friends Major-General Bob Laycock and his wife Angie, and an American
who had been out in the Pacific. Kick had been staying in Yorkshire but
returned hurriedly to London to hear the announcement about VE Day.
She turned on the wireless to hear that the Prime Minister was going to
speak. Kick thought it funny that Bob remarked to her, an American, how
quietly the British were celebrating the end of the war. But 'At that moment
bedlam broke loose and never stopped for two days.'[2]

That evening, Kick, accompanied by the Gores and Hugh Fraser, joined
the crowds outside Buckingham Palace: 'I must say it was a most moving
sight.' Everyone shouted, 'We Want the King!' and finally the royal family
appeared on the flood-lit balcony, the Queen wearing her tiara. The people
screamed and cheered as the King and Queen waved. Behind her in the
crowd, Noël Coward was signing autographs. Many were dressed in red,
white and blue.

Later, Kick and her friends gathered around a huge bonfire in Green
Park, where effigies of Hitler were burnt. Then they headed off to Piccadilly,

'which was absolute bedlam. Fire-works, dancing in the streets.'[3] The day after VE Day, Kick lunched at the House of Commons and then climbed to the top of Big Ben to survey the crowd.

Kick wrote to her parents to say that during the week of celebrations she felt that she had 'lived five years rather than five days'. Joe wrote back, 'Mother and I were talking it over last night and decided that nobody in the world twenty-five years of age has had the kind of life you've had or as interesting.'[4]

The spring and summer of 1945 was a bittersweet time for Kick. The returning soldiers only brought back memories of Billy. The Duchess noticed how her face would suddenly look ineffably sad, which caught at her heart.[5] Kick still felt rudderless without Billy. She also felt isolated by the fact that so many of her friends were married to husbands who had survived the war while she had lost so much. She decided that she wouldn't wear black widow's weeds, though Evelyn Waugh began calling her the widow Hartington.

The Duke had been in Burma in his capacity of Under-Secretary at the Colonial Office and then had accompanied his son Andrew back from Italy, where he had been fighting. He brought Kick a beautiful white and gold sari. Seeing Andrew, and thinking that he, not Billy, would one day be Duke of Devonshire, was difficult for Kick: 'It nearly kills me to see him, not that he is really at all like Billy but the whole idea of seeing Andy makes Billy's absence much more noticeable.'[6] She was upset when she saw Billy's poodle, Lupin, bounding about looking for his master. Kick sorted through Billy's things and sent his diamond and sapphire cufflinks to his godson, Andrew Parker Bowles, with a kind note.[7]

Kick's new cook was working out well: 'looks like the sort that would stick around and not disappear into a factory seeking a higher wage.'[8] Post-war Britain was changing at a rapid rate. After the freedoms of the war, domestic servants did not want to go back to a life of servitude. That March Kick had been asked to give a speech at the Women's Institute on the subject of the American housewife in wartime. She was initially nervous but once on her feet she was fine and by the end the housewives were 'screaming Give the English country housewife the recognition she deserves – more freedom for women'.[9]

In March the family had heard the news that Billy had been mentioned in dispatches. She immediately cabled the family and then wrote to express her delight and pride: 'Isn't that wonderful? We are all so pleased.'[10] There had even been talk about Billy getting a posthumous VC and Kick told her parents that the King and Queen had sent a condolence message on Billy's death. Billy's servant Ingles had been to see Kick and told her that after the war she would be able to get a photograph of Billy entering Brussels with Billy on top of the tank. Ingles said that Billy had 'volunteered for everything ... was always in a good humour and he was the best-liked company commander'.[11]

She had planned a political life at Billy's side, which had now been snatched away from her, but Kick had not lost her interest in politics. She had been reporting back to Jack the news about the upcoming general election and urging him to come to London for a ringside seat. She joked to her parents: 'Tell Jack not to get married for a long time. I'll keep house for him.'[12] She warned her brother of the 'terrific swing to the left' in Britain. Kick also promised that she had a few girls lined up for him for when he came to London to cover the election for the Hearst newspapers.[13] He arrived on 31 May and was met by an excited Kick. Jack's friend Pat Lannan joined them. He thought Kick was an Anglicized version of Jack, completely at home in England:

She was a very industrious, animated young woman, and by that time very English, or British orientated. I felt that she had really melded herself into the city of London and England, as though it were her adopted home – that was my very distinct impression ... Whereas I felt that Jack was an outsider, he was an American visiting there, as I was an American visiting there – but I never felt that way about Kick.[14]

Kick, keen to be involved and to spend as much time as possible with Jack, offered to drive the young reporters around in her car, a little Austin Seven:

When the two of us got in it we were filled. I remember it ran like hell – the windshield wipers didn't work and a lot of things like that, but we were grateful to have it because in following Churchill around, he was delivering speeches at racecourses, dog tracks and what have you and they were very difficult places to get to.[15]

Kick's little flat became the centre of activity and political gossip.

Jack, who had so impressed the Duchess with his condolence letter, was invited to Compton Place. On 29 June he dined with the Duke and Duchess and was a great success. He saw that Kick had been, in the words of her youngest sister-in-law Anne, 'completely amalgamated into our family – it had become her family'.[16] The Duke and Duchess, he noted, treated her like a daughter, and therefore Jack was to be treated as a family member.[17]

Kick also took Jack to Chatsworth. She made speeches to the Red Cross in Derbyshire. He told the family, 'Kathleen is fine – does very well with her speeches by looking extremely girlish and sweet and looks like a possible candidate to me.'[18] When he went into hospital for yet another operation on his back, a diplomatic correspondent visited and saw the 'beautiful young widow of the Marquess of Hartington, was sitting on foot of Jack's bed'.[19]

In July, Kick spent a weekend at Hatley Park, the new home of Jakie Astor. Kick took William Douglas-Home out to ride on a donkey to cheer him up, after his release from incarceration following a court martial for disobeying orders. William was still besotted with Kick. He began writing a play about post-war socialist England, in which a beautiful, spirited American heiress called June is engaged to the hero, an English peer, who wants to be a politician. June was based on Kick Kennedy.

In July, Kick stayed for the first time at the Devonshires' Irish home, Lismore Castle in south-east Ireland. She described it as 'the most lovely old castle ever'.[20] The chatelaine was Adele Cavendish, Fred Astaire's sister. This mesmerizing, vibrant woman had nursed Billy's uncle Charlie through alcoholism, which in 1944 had claimed his life at the age of thirty-eight. Adele, like Kick, was perceived as part of the Cavendish family and they gave her Lismore Castle as her home. She saw Kick as a kindred spirit. Kick adored the Castle. She swam in the pool, sunbathed and had a good rest. The place prompted her to think of her Irish ancestors, and she made plans to return. She told her parents how Billy had loved to come to Lismore to fish. Adele wrote to Joe to say how much she had loved Kick's company, 'overflowing with big political talks'.[21]

She stayed for the whole summer. Towards the end of her stay, she attended the opening meet of the autumn hunting season at Shillelagh, a little further north in County Wicklow: 'I must say to see them all in red coats moving off with the hounds into the Irish countryside is one of the most lovely sights imaginable.'[22] She was beginning to fall in love with Ireland. The hunt was led by the local aristocrat, Peter Wentworth-Fitzwilliam, who two years before had inherited the title of 8th Earl Fitzwilliam.

Jack had fallen ill again and in August, on the day that the first atom bomb was dropped, he flew back to recuperate at Hyannis Port. After the second atomic bomb was dropped on Nagasaki, and the surrender of the Japanese, Kick celebrated with Evelyn Waugh and Hugh Fraser in London. Hugh had been a tremendous support to Kick in the months after Billy's death. Hugh had won a seat in the Commons in the 1945 general election, and Kick often went along to listen to him speak in the House.

This was the famous election that Churchill lost to Clement Attlee. He moved out of 10 Downing Street and into a flat above Kick's. People came every night to sing under his window. She was unimpressed by Attlee: 'the Prime Minister's [i.e. Churchill's] definition "a sheep in sheep's clothing" fits perfectly'.[23] She talked at length with Harold Macmillan (Billy's uncle) about Eisenhower in North Africa and Italy. When he told her that Churchill had no eggs or milk she left some outside his door.[24] She dined at the House of Commons with Evelyn Waugh, Christopher Hollis and Hugh Fraser, and was pleased to insult the left-wing journalist and MP Tom Driberg who had written a 'terrible' article about Billy when he lost the by-election.[25]

Billy's sister Elizabeth recalled the change in atmosphere following the end of the war and the defeat of Churchill. Britain had changed irrevocably. From living in the moment, people were beginning to think of the future. Kick told her parents that during the war everyone had existed in a state of flux, but now it was time to 'settle down & make plans'.[26] That summer of 1945, she pondered her future: America or England. Her friend Janey Lindsay (née Kenyon-Slaney) recalled her once saying, 'It's such a wonderful day. You don't think Billy would mind if I wore a really flowery dress, do you?'[27] She was moving on.

Jack's departure left a hole in Kick's life and she began to think about returning home to America. After VJ Day, she resigned her post at the Red Cross.[28] The first anniversary of Billy's death in September was difficult. All of his family wrote her 'the nicest letters': 'I must say that it is difficult to realize it has been a year but then sometimes it seems like a hundred years … even though one is surrounded by friends etc there are always moments when one feels very lonely.'[29]

She was back in Hyannis Port with the family for Thanksgiving and then headed off to Washington, where she met up with old friends, including John White, who had recently broken up with his fiancée. But Cape Cod no longer felt like the place where she belonged. She began to think about returning to England and making it her permanent home. She wanted to be among friends who had loved Billy, and who wanted to talk to her about him and keep his memory alive. She wrote to her mother-in-law, 'Darling Dutch', and told her that staying in England was what Billy would have wanted.[30]

In the meantime, she stayed at the Chatham Hotel in New York. Winston Frost, a lawyer from an old Virginian family, dated her and she began to fall in love. Frost – tall, blond and handsome – was a ladies' man and he did not meet with Joe's approval. Having made his usual investigations, Joe told his daughter that Frost was seeing another woman, and that she should break off the romance. Joe got his way. Kick thanked her father: 'You told me what you thought. I listened. The rest was up to me and in the cold light of morning after having the life I have had one doesn't waste it going from El Morocco to the Stork Club.'[31] But she had had enough of her father's interference and her mother's controlling ways.

When she returned to her London flat, the sitting room was 'swamped with flowers' welcoming her home.[32] Back in England, Kick found herself attracting more suitors than ever before. At twenty-six, she was at the height of her loveliness. Her sadness seemed only to enhance her attraction. She had lost weight, which suited her. She was no longer the all-American girl with the gorgeous smile, or the quintessential Red Cross girl on the bicycle. She was the impeccably dressed Lady Hartington, with beautiful jewels, the most elegant wardrobe, her own car: an independent woman of means. She now seemed more English than American. She had finally thrown off the shackles of family, confiding to a friend, 'it's rather nice not having to be a Kennedy. Lord knows there are enough of them as it is.'[33]

Men, young and old, fell in love with her. The forty-nine-year-old Anthony Eden, who had been Churchill's Foreign Secretary, was smitten and asked her to continue writing her wonderful letters: 'For then I can imagine that you are here. How I wish that you were, and I do believe that you would enjoy it too.'[34] Her friends admired not only her courage and her dignity, but her enduring vivacity. One of them, Angela Lambert, put it especially well perhaps: 'Gaiety, like honesty, is a kind of social courage. It is not easy to be unfailingly charming, lively and original. It requires energy and generosity always to make the effort to be on one's form.'[35] Kick wrote to the Dowager Duchess, Billy's grandmother, telling her that it was her duty to be strong and brave, and that if men like Billy found 'the courage to die so one must have the courage to live'.[36]

Kick had resumed a romantic affair with Richard Wood. She admired him greatly for not allowing his disability to affect his life, and he was determined on a political career. He had been fitted with new artificial legs, and walked with just a cane. They came close to becoming engaged, but, once again, she would have the obstacle of a mixed marriage. Richard, more flexible than Billy, and without the encumbrances that came with his status, agreed that their children could be raised as Catholics, and he even agreed to convert if it made her happy. In the end, she decided not to marry Richard. He was overwhelmed with sorrow. When he was a very old man, he met a female relation of Kick's and asked if they were related. He then told her that he had thought about Kick Kennedy every single day of his life.

The problem for Kick was that nobody, it seemed, could come close to Billy. She stayed with Lord Dudley at Himley Hall in Staffordshire, but was unimpressed by the stuffiness and formality of the place: 'I keep thinking how Billy would laugh at it all – there's even a coronet on the butter. That was a great thing about him. He hated show or ostentation of any kind.'[37] The Duchess was the one person who really understood. Kick wrote to her from Compton Place, where she had spent her honeymoon with Billy two years before: 'the hot weather always makes me think of Billy ... sometimes it seems like six years at other times six minutes'.[38]

48

Politics or Passion?

> Mother, if possible, will you please bring me some evening shoes
> (gold and silver), an evening bra (strapless, size 34), a black evening
> sweater or one in fuchsia colour, any pretty wool dress.
>
> Kick Kennedy, letter of 3 August 1947[1]

Kick kept a close eye on Jack's political career as he campaigned to get to Washington to represent the Eleventh Congressional District in Boston. Kick was delighted when he won the Democratic primary in June 1946. She wrote to congratulate him from Garrowby in Yorkshire, where she was staying with Richard Wood and Lord and Lady Halifax: 'Everyone says you were so good in the Election and that the outcome must have been a great source of satisfaction. It's nice to know you are as appreciated in the 11th district as you are among your brothers & sisters. Gee, aren't you lucky?' She added that everyone on her side of the Atlantic 'thinks you are madly pro-British so don't go destroying that illusion until I get my house fixed. The painters might just not like your attitude.'[2]

The house she was referring to was her new home in Westminster. Her beloved brother she believed was on the way to the White House, but she had her own plans too. She had been looking out for a house near Westminster where she could preside over a political salon. Her suitor Richard Wood thought that she perceived a role for herself as a political hostess: 'I think she was ambitious to play a part as great ladies have played a part in the past.'[3] In part this was a tribute to Billy, who had seen her as a second Georgiana. She would never now be the Duchess of Devonshire but she could carve out a place for herself as Lady Hartington.

Number 4 Smith Square was a lovely three-storey Georgian townhouse in the heart of historic old Westminster, close to the Houses of Parliament. From the three sash windows of her first-floor drawing room, you could see the beautiful Baroque Church of St John's. The dining room opened on to a small courtyard garden, perfect for entertaining. Jean Lloyd remembered the tiny drawing room 'crammed with armchairs – and nothing else!'[4]

Kick hired a cook and a housekeeper called Mabel, bought herself a fridge and filled the house with antiques, mostly given to her by the Duke and Duchess. Her two most prized possessions were a large photograph of the eleven Kennedys, taken just before the war, and a large oil painting of Billy in his uniform by the society portraitist Oswald Birley. She kept herself busy, fixing the garden, painting window boxes and choosing fabrics. Nancy Astor gave her china. She was starting her new life and there was a renewed sense of purpose.

Being so close to Westminster meant she could dine at the House of Commons and listen to the speeches. She went to the state opening of Parliament. Evelyn Waugh, Anthony Eden and George Bernard Shaw dined at her house. That summer, she threw herself into charity work, becoming involved in a fundraising event for the widows and dependants of the Commandos. She was given the position of chair of the Commandos Benevolent Fund Ball at the Dorchester. She was delighted that they sold 500 tickets. She bought herself a beautiful new dress for the ball, and had never looked lovelier.

The Dorchester Hotel, 12 June 1946.

It was a ball reminiscent of the glorious days before the outbreak of war. The women were once again dressed in their finery, the men no longer in their uniforms, but in white tie. Kick, chair of the committee, was dressed in a floor-length dress of blush-pink satin with aquamarine diamond clips. She was back to her best Kennedy self, lighting up the room with her personality and her dazzling smile. One eighteen-year-old debutante was heard to whisper, furiously, 'It's absolutely maddening, Kick's taking all my dance partners.'⁵ It was inevitable, with all eyes on her, that she would catch the eye of Peter, 8th Earl Fitzwilliam. His reputation as one of the most dashing and fearless of the Commandos was assured.

It was Kick's friend Bob Laycock who during the war had been commissioned to raise an independent company of army Commandos. They were recruited from the 'smarter regiments' such as the Household Cavalry, the Grenadiers and the Coldstream Guards. They were the most raffish of soldiers. Evelyn Waugh, one of them himself, described them as 'Mr. Churchill's private army or Buck's toughs'.⁶ Peter, handsome and dashing, with swept-back black hair, was one of the most notorious of them. Evelyn Waugh called him 'king dandy and scum', but even he fell for his charms. Chips Channon dubbed him the 'Fabulous Lord Fitzwilliam'.⁷

Kick knew that he was a decorated war hero who had been awarded the DSO for a highly dangerous mission, reminiscent of her brother Jack's. Peter had manned high-speed motor boats known as 'grey ladies' in extremely dangerous conditions in the North Sea, right under the noses of the German navy. 'The boats didn't cut through water, they bounced,' one crew member recalled.⁸ At first the men were suspicious of Peter because he was an earl, but they quickly warmed to him: 'He seemed to take it all in his stride. He came down to our level, he didn't expect us to go up to his.' Peter, acting under the codename 'Peter Lawrence' (his aristocratic pedigree would have made him especially vulnerable in the event of his being captured), completed twelve missions, earning the respect and admiration of all his men.

Peter came from an extremely privileged background. His seat, Wentworth Woodhouse in Yorkshire, was said to be the largest house in England. It had 365 rooms, was twice the size of Buckingham Palace and was set in 22,000 acres. The family also had an ancestral stately home near Peterborough on the edge of the East Anglian fens, and a beautiful Irish estate, Coolattin in County Wicklow (from where he had ridden to hounds the previous year).

Peter was a womanizer and a gambler. He married a glamorous and spirited woman called Olive (known as Obby), but disappeared for a tryst halfway through the honeymoon, a habit that he never fully broke. He couldn't be tamed. He loved racehorses, fast cars and beautiful women. When he saw Kick dancing at the Dorchester, he was smitten. Despite the fact that he was married with a young daughter he was determined to win her. To the disapproving looks of the bystanders and the humiliation of his wife, the Earl Fitzwilliam took Lady Hartington in his arms and danced with her. Her friend Charlotte McDonnell, now married to a man called Harris, said, 'it was overnight and it was the real thing – illicit, passionate, encompassing'. Charlotte continued, 'One got the impression that she'd discovered something she didn't really plan to experience in life.'[9]

Kick's friends were horrified when they heard about the romance. Nobody could understand the relationship, as she and Peter appeared on the surface to be so different. Kick's friends were literary, cultivated, intelligent, politically minded. She was a devout Catholic who rarely missed mass and always went to confession. She had a brother on the way to Washington. She was not part of Peter's playboy, hard-drinking, gambling, fast-living set. Janey Lindsay was especially upset:

> Peter and Kick were absolutely different personality types with absolutely different friends. She was totally different to him. She had intellectual friends. His world wasn't a bit like that. He belonged to a set where you gambled terrifically and drank a lot. He was terribly naughty – frightfully – with loads of girlfriends. And that was just not Kick. Not a bit Kick. As time went by, I got the impression that he must have been a very good lover. It was the only way to explain it. It's awful, but it can have such a major impact.[10]

Janey thought that Kick would not have been happy with him for any length of time. The best that could be said of him, and it wasn't very much, was that, since there was no substitute for Billy, Kick had found a replica of her father: 'older, sophisticated, quite the rogue male. Perhaps in the last analysis those were the qualities required to make her fall deeply in love.'[11]

Whatever the reason, Kick was smitten hard. She told Janey that no one she had ever met before had made her so completely forget herself.[12] But she said nothing to her family, reporting only that the ball had been a major success. Princess Elizabeth attended and 'stayed until the bitter end'.

Lismore Castle, County Waterford, Ireland.

'The first sight of Lismore Castle as you come over the Knockmealdown Mountains in County Waterford makes your jaw drop. A place of mystery and romance, the huge grey castle – half giant, half fairy – rises from the rocks above the banks of the River Blackwater.'[13] This was Debo's description of the magnificent Cavendish property in Ireland. Sir Walter Raleigh had once lived there, in what many described as a fairytale castle. It had a Rapunzel tower, and a forest encircled it. Silver fish flickered in the waters, and in the early summer the grounds were covered in rhododendron blossom. The writer Patrick Leigh Fermor found it so magical that 'one would hardly have been surprised to see a pterodactyl or an archaeopteryx sail through the twilight'.[14]

Lismore had been given to Charles Cavendish, Billy's uncle, as a wedding present when he married Adele Astaire. In the Pugin banqueting hall, with its star-covered ceiling and chandeliers, photographs of Adele's brother Fred nestled by those of King Edward VII. Adele remained at Lismore until she remarried in 1947, when the castle passed into the hands of Billy's younger brother Andrew.

Kick loved Lismore, describing it to Lem as 'the most perfect place' in the world.[15] She took her sister Eunice there in November 1946. They drove around Ireland sightseeing. Kick took the opportunity to drop in at Lord and Lady Fitzwilliam's house in County Wicklow. Eunice had no idea that Kick had become Peter's mistress.

Eunice had arrived in London in September for an extended stay with her sister. Kick wrote home with newsy letters, telling of a visit to the Duke and Duchess of Devonshire at Compton Place, where the Princesses Elizabeth and Margaret stayed overnight; of a dinner with the Duke and Duchess of Windsor (should one curtsey to the Duchess or not?); and of a distressing burglary at the house in Smith Square, in which she lost most of her jewellery, worth over £40,000: 'I'm afraid everything is gone with the exception of my pearls and earrings. It really is the most awful blow especially Daddy's wedding present and the lovely aquamarines.'[16] Billy's cufflinks had also been stolen and young Joe's navy wings, inscribed 'to K from J'.[17] She was surprised that the robbers hadn't stolen her mink coat and short fur jacket, which she had forgotten to put away. After the burglary Kick dismissed her staff, whom she suspected might have been involved in the theft, and hired two Hungarian refugee sisters, Ilona and Elisabeth Solymossy. They were devoted to her and she to them.

The one thing she didn't talk about was the thing that most mattered to her: her intense romance with Peter.

*   *   *

It was not until the summer of 1947 that she confided in any of the Kennedys. Jack, by now a Congressman, came over to join her at Lismore. Always her closest sibling, he would be the first to know. She could trust him with her secret.

She assembled a group of illustrious guests, including Anthony Eden (Deputy Leader of Churchill's Conservative Party, now in opposition), Tony Rosslyn, Hugh Fraser, William Douglas-Home and the beautiful Pamela Churchill (née Digby), now divorced from Winston's son Randolph. Kick was pleased that all her guests mixed so well. Eden arrived laden with 'official-looking Conservative documents', but soon got into 'the Irish spirit'. Jack enjoyed meeting him and Sir Shane Leslie, the writer and cousin of Winston Churchill. They played golf and went riding. 'I really do think this is one of the loveliest spots in the world,' Kick wrote to the family. 'I have never enjoyed a month so much, & I think Jack has enjoyed it too.'[18]

Jack, with his love of history and interest in his Irish roots, planned a visit to Dunganstown in County Wexford, the home of his forefathers. He brought with him a letter of introduction from his Aunt Loretta, and he drove out to New Ross to find his origins. Pamela went with him. She recalled him looking ill, tall and scrawny and not at all like a Congressman. She remembered Jack being thrilled by meeting 'the original Kennedys'.[19] They drove in Kick's station wagon, given to her by Evelyn Waugh, on the 50-mile trip. With only Aunt Loretta's letter for reference, Jack stopped to ask for directions and was pointed to a small farmhouse. He knocked on the door and invited himself in for tea to the astonishment of his hosts. The woman of the house later recorded her meeting with the man who would become President, amazed that he just called in without prior warning and made himself at home.[20] He was deeply interested in talking about his ancestors, and was, unlike his father, proud of his Irish roots.[21]

When they returned to luxurious Lismore, Kick only asked whether the original Kennedys had a bathroom. 'No, they did not have a bathroom,' he replied, momentarily irked by her lack of interest in her Irish roots.[22]

What she talked about instead was her passion for Peter Fitzwilliam. Part of his attraction may have been that he was an embodiment of Ireland, as Billy had been an embodiment of England: the Fitzwilliam earldom belonged to the peerage of Ireland as well as to that of Great Britain and the family were deeply embedded in Irish history (albeit as occupiers), while

Peter's love of his Coolattin estate in County Wicklow matched Kick's of Lismore.

The secret was kept from Rose and sister Pat when they visited Kick in Ireland later in the year. Jack was the only family member to be told. 'I've found my Rhett Butler at last,' Kick said. Jack was slightly put out, as he had never experienced such passion himself. He told Lem that he was jealous of this. But he was happy that his dearest sister had found someone who could replace Billy.

Shortly after the Ireland trip, Jack fell ill again and was hospitalized in the London Clinic. Pamela Churchill arranged for him to see her own doctor, Sir Daniel Davis. It was Davis who finally diagnosed Addison's Disease, a condition affecting the adrenal glands. 'That American friend of yours, he hasn't got a year to live,' he told Pamela.[23] For the rest of his life, Jack was treated for Addison's, regularly injecting himself with cortisone, while keeping his condition a secret from the world.

Just weeks before Jack fell ill, Kick had visited Peter's stately home in Yorkshire. This was a sign of how serious the relationship had become. Describing Wentworth Woodhouse as 'the largest house in England', she remarked how sad it was that all the gardens had been dug up by the government for the coal that lay beneath: 'I've never seen anything so awful as the machinery is right outside one's windows and these valuable old trees have all been uprooted and it will never be the same. That part of England really is black with coal dust.'[24] For all the grandeur of the house, Wentworth Woodhouse could hardly have been in a more different setting from lovely, lost Chatsworth.

As 1947 came towards its end, Kick braced herself to tell her parents about Peter. She planned to tell them in the new year and she asked her sister-in-law Elizabeth Cavendish to accompany her for moral support. She told her father how much she was longing to see the family 'and discuss all'.

She also told him, 'Am asked every day why I don't stand for Parliament.'[25] When Rose had stayed with her in London at the end of the Irish visit, she had asked her daughter what she was doing for the church. Kick told her that she was going to Central Office once a week. Rose was placated, not realizing that the Central Office in question was the headquarters not of the Roman Catholic diocese of Westminster but of Winston Churchill's Conservative Party. Deprived of the opportunity to become a political

Duchess of Devonshire like Georgiana in the eighteenth century, she was seriously wondering about following in the footsteps of her friend Nancy Astor, Britain's first female Member of Parliament, and becoming Political Kick in her own right. Nothing would have made her brother Jack more proud, as his Washington career took flight. But such a future could hardly be reconciled with the scandal of being in a relationship with the married Lord Fitzwilliam while the Devonshires were still taking care of her (she spent Christmas 1947 with the Duke and Duchess). Once again, Kick was faced with a choice.

49

Joy She Gave
Joy She Has Found

beneath her potent personality, with which was mingled a fine unshaken integrity – there was something deeper, very beautiful and difficult to define.

Lady Anderson[1]

Evelyn Waugh was horrified when Kick told him her plan to marry Peter. 'If you want to commit adultery or fornication & can't resist, do it, but realize what you are doing, and don't give the final insult of apostasy,' he told her.[2] It was a taste of things to come. Andrew Cavendish said, with more aristocratic understatement, 'I liked Peter very much. He was so charming. But if they had married there would have been a reaction.'[3]

Kick's female friends believed that she was making a huge mistake, that she and Peter were far too different for the relationship to work out. 'You don't know him, you don't know him,' she replied, with her old stubbornness.[4] But she was terrified of facing her parents and telling them of her intentions. Early in 1948, the night before she sailed for America, she broke down over supper with the Ormsby Gores.

In New York, Kick and Elizabeth Cavendish visited Aunt Adele, who was very happy in her second marriage.[5] In New York, she confided in her old friend Charlotte McDonnell Harris. Charlotte had always been privately surprised that Kick should have married someone as seemingly tame as

Billy, but nevertheless she was shocked by Kick's passion: 'It was hysterical. It was all "I gotta do, I gotta go". Charlotte was convinced that if she couldn't marry Peter, she would elope with him.[6]

Kick and Elizabeth then went down to Palm Springs. Elizabeth, twenty-one years old and on her first trip to the United States, was amazed at the contrast between freezing New York City and balmy Florida. 'Life here is quite unbelievable,' she wrote to her mother from the Kennedys' home on North Ocean Boulevard:

> I long for you and Daddy to see it all. You really must come some-time because its like going to a new world completely and is the most perfect place in the world for a holiday. The house is heaven. Quite large and right on the sea. Its tremendously comfortable & all the bedrooms have very pretty chintzes. Its a completely tropical climate ... we have all our meals in the garden which is floodlit with hidden lighting at night & looks terribly pretty. The gentlemen all wear white dinner jackets on smart occasions & lemon yellow ones otherwise.[7]

She liked Rose Kennedy but was frightened by her – especially on the occasion of the two of them having an evening alone when Kick went to Cuba for the night with one of her many admirers.

Some time later, young Elizabeth witnessed Rose at her most terrifying when Kick announced her intention to marry a second English Protestant lord: 'Poor Kick is having rather a difficult time as she has told her parents she is getting married. Mrs K. didn't take it at all well and is threatening to write to you & Peter Fitzwilliam so look out! Don't mention to Kick that I have told you all this.' 'Getting married' was presumably Elizabeth's euphemism for having an affair. It is not clear whether at this point Kick went so far as to tell her parents that the first obstacle in the way of an actual second marriage was not the old matter of religious difference, but the fact that Peter Fitzwilliam was still married to someone else.

Kick and Elizabeth flew up to Washington DC on a DC-4 Silverliner, Kick sending a cheery postcode to the Duchess on the way, telling her that Elizabeth was looking 'very healthy & athletic' from playing tennis every afternoon in Palm Beach.[8] After a weekend with Jack in DC, she finally plucked up the courage to speak with complete candour to her parents. The family had gathered at White Sulphur Springs in West Virginia at a grand reopening of the hotel, the Greenbrier, where Joe and Rose had honeymooned. On the last night of the reunion, she confessed that Peter was a married man with a child, planning to divorce his alcoholic wife. Rose was furious, threatening to disown her, saying she would never see her beloved family again. Her allowance would be cut off. She even threatened to leave Joe if he did not support her.[9]

Kick returned to Washington, where she stayed with the Whites. Patsy thought that Kick was truly in love, indeed 'more fulfilled with Peter than in her short marriage to Billy'. Her brother John, speaking as a former boyfriend, was amazed by the force of her account of her love:

> As she talked of Fitzwilliam, the man sounded like the hero of *Out of Africa*, a professional Englishman, a charming rogue. Rarely in life do you see someone so bubbling over with love, everything that love should be, every bit of it. Poor old Billy Hartington. But again he probably would have been blown away if she had felt that way about him. Very few people could stand that love, the sheer blast of emotion.[10]

Jack supported Kick. Eunice was distraught. She blamed John White and shouted, 'You made Kathleen leave the Catholic Church. It's all your fault.'[11] Eunice had arranged for Kick to speak to Father Fulton Sheen. But Kick had been here before with Billy, and her passion for Peter was more primal than her love had been for the Marquess. She told Patsy that she didn't want to go through with the interview. 'Then don't, honey,' said Patsy. Kick phoned Eunice at two in the morning and cancelled the meeting.[12]

Kick told Patsy that she was planning a weekend in the South of France. Throughout the affair there had been snatched meetings, lunches, the odd night together, but this would be time for themselves far away from the eyes of friends, servants and gossips.

The day before she and Elizabeth left for England, Kick had lunch with Joe Jr's friend Tom Schriber. He remembered that Kick looked 'radiant' with love, 'really alive': 'She was revved up, ready to go. She had written off her mother, but not the old man.' She told Tom that she wanted her father's consent: 'He matters. But I'm getting married whether he consents or not.'[13] Her father had told Kick that he would try to find a way to make the marriage possible. He adored Kick and he wished to help as he had failed her before with Billy.

Kick's return to England was not an escape from her mother. Rose, remembering that she and Joe had been absent throughout the 'Agnes and Hartie' debacle, decided that she should go to England and reason with the headstrong daughter who had defied her before. Years before, during the war, when travel was impossible, Kick had slipped through the net. It wasn't going to happen again. This time, Rose crossed the Atlantic, knowing the full force of her powers. Kick's devoted housekeeper Ilona Solymossy listened in to the row, as Rose stormed and Kick cowered. She could hardly believe that a twenty-eight-year-old widow would allow herself to be spoken to in such a way. Kick was like a scolded child.[14] Rose was adamant that Kick was losing everything, including her family. That was the worst thought of all, that she would be disowned not just by Mother Rome but also by the real church: the Kennedy family.[15]

Kick's only resort was to appeal to her beloved father. He understood her, and he had always taken her side. Kick spoke to Joe on the telephone, begging him to meet Peter in Paris. He agreed.

Early in May 1948, she wrote a newsy letter, from where she was staying with some friends, Freddy and Sheila Birkenhead. She told of dinner parties, going to nightclubs, watching the royal family driving to Buckingham Palace in open carriages. She had been at Eastbourne with Elizabeth and Anne Cavendish and the Duchess. They were thrilled with the presents that she had brought back from America. She was as close to them as ever, even though they knew of her affair with Peter. Her old beau, Richard Wood, had visited her with his new wife. Kick had been to the Royal Ballet. She had lunched with the Irish High Commissioner. It was like a roll call of the great and the good, but there was something frenetic and dispassionate about it all. There was no mention of Peter.[16]

Peter invited Kick to fly down to Cannes on the French Riviera for a weekend. He planned to buy a racehorse as well as indulge his lover. For Kick, this was the opportunity she was waiting for: she proposed that when changing planes in Paris on the way back they would meet with her father.

Before they left, Peter took her to Wentworth Woodhouse. A woman who worked in the Post Office saw them: 'They looked so happy and care-free. Peter wanted to show her the family mausoleum. We watched them set out across the Park and I remember she was wearing an immaculate pair of beautiful white shoes. There was all that coal dust and muck around from the open-cast mining! They'd be ruined, I thought!'[17]

On the way back from Yorkshire to London, they made a stop at Milton Hall, the family's southern seat near Peterborough, home to Peter's cousin Tom. Kick joked, 'Not another big house!' 'Don't worry, Kick,' Peter said. 'We'll be living in Ireland.' He told Tom Fitzwilliam that he had Kick with him, 'May I bring her in?' 'For God's sake, do.' They stayed for dinner and Peter told Tom his plans – that they would be meeting with Joe in Paris to obtain his permission for the marriage. He joked: 'If he objects, I'll go to the Pope and offer to build him a church.'[18]

13 May 1948.

Kick packed a suitcase with beautiful clothes and jewels and a family photograph album.[19] She placed exquisite lingerie, a silk negligee and lacy garter belts alongside a vaginal douche. She was no longer the naive girl who dressed in flannel nightdresses. She was a sophisticated woman, finally in touch with her own sexuality.

For the flight she dressed in a navy suit with her trademark pearls. She carried her rosary beads. Peter laughed when he saw how much luggage she was taking for a long weekend.

'Wish me luck,' she said to her housekeeper.

'Should I cross my fingers?' Ilona asked.

'Yes, both hands.'[20]

Kick was happy and excited, but she had not forgotten Billy. Days before she left for Paris, she had spoken to Lady Anderson about her love for Billy. She had talked about her feelings of joy when she had been married. Being in love with Peter was wonderful, but he hadn't obliterated her memory of Billy and all she had lost. Lady Anderson recalled that Kick was still wistful, that in her deepest self she had not changed from the girl who in a letter to the Duchess of Devonshire the previous year had talked about her belief that she would one day be reunited with 'our beloved Billy' in heaven, where he would be waiting to greet her.[21]

Peter had chartered a private plane, a de Havilland Dove, to fly from Croydon to Nice. The pilot planned to stop for half an hour at Paris's Le Bourget airport to refuel. Peter, on a whim, and looking for fun, called some of his racing friends to meet for a quick lunch in the city.

Peter Townshend, the highly experienced pilot, consulted weather reports and saw that a thunderstorm was predicted to hit the Rhône Valley at around five o'clock. If they were to beat the storm they had to leave for Cannes as soon as possible. But Peter and Kick had failed to return to the airport from lunch. Forty minutes had turned into two and a half hours. Townshend called the air-traffic controller, telling him that he was going to be late. He was furious when the lovers finally turned up; he told them that all commercial flights had been cancelled and that it was not possible to fly. They would be flying over the Rhône at precisely the time that the storm was predicted to hit.

Peter, with his usual charm, persuaded the pilot to change his mind. There was, no doubt, a financial inducement. When they boarded, Kick was asked to sit on the back left seat, with Peter in front of her, to balance the weight. They took off into calm skies.

Passing over Valence at 10,000 feet, they entered the storm just north of the Ardèche mountains in the Cévennes. Townshend and his radio pilot lost communication, and with poor visibility, flew into the eye of the storm. Locals later testified that the storm was of exceptional strength.[22] The tiny plane was tossed about, buffeted in violent cross-currents for twenty-eight minutes. Townshend lost control of the Dove, but could see that he was about to crash into a mountain ridge and as a last-ditch effort to avoid it he yanked the controls towards him. The force of the manoeuvre broke the Dove up in mid-air. The right wing snapped off and then the engines were off. The fuselage landed on the mountainside. During the last two minutes, the pilot and co-pilot stuffed handkerchiefs into their mouths, a standard procedure for a crash landing, to avoid biting through the tongue. All four people on board would have known that they were going to crash.

A farmer called Paul Petit, looking out from his stone farmhouse high in the Cévennes mountains, had heard the noisy plane flying into the cloud, and watched in horror as it appeared out of the clouds and broke up in mid-air. He and his father climbed to the top of the mountain, where they found the fuselage, with only one wing attached, and the four bodies inside. The two pilots were crushed in the cockpit, the male passenger crumpled under his seat. The woman was still in her seat, belt fastened, the body slumped at an angle. Paul Petit called the Mairie at St Bauzile, the nearest village, and the bodies were carried down to the village in makeshift stretchers on ox-carts.[23]

Searching through the woman's handbag, the Gendarmes found a passport belonging to Lady Hartington.

Joe Kennedy was asleep in his suite at the George V hotel in Paris, when a call came through from the *Boston Globe*. His friend Joseph Timilty, who was travelling with him, took the call and broke the news. Joe was too stunned to speak to the press. First Joe Jr and then Billy and now Kick. He sat silently for half an hour and then took out a piece of paper and wrote a note to himself: 'No one who ever knew her didn't feel that life was much better that minute. And we know so little about the next world that we must think that they wanted just such a wonderful girl for themselves. We must not feel sorry for her but for ourselves.'[24]

He made arrangements to travel by train to the Ardèche to identify the body, hoping that it was a case of mistaken identity. But in his heart he knew. When he arrived, he was shown the body. The right side of her face had a long gash, and her legs, jaw and pelvis had been crushed on impact. But he said that she looked beautiful. He told the family that they had discovered her with her shoes kicked off.

One of Jack's assistants in Washington heard the news on the radio and called Eunice. She hoped, just for a single moment, that it was Debo who had been killed and not Kick. Jack was in the back room listening to a recording of the Irish musical *Finian's Rainbow*. Jack asked for confirmation, and when he heard that the body had been formally identified by his father he wept. As they had done before and would do again, when tragedy struck, the Kennedys gathered at Hyannis Port to mourn, and to take solace from each other.

Joe had been shocked when he was handed Kick's personal effects. The birth-control device was a distressing reminder that Kick had been in the sole company of a married man. The Devonshires, the Kennedys and the Fitzwilliams sprang into action.

At Wentworth, staff were dispatched to sweep Peter's bedroom, clean the sheets and remove all traces of Kick. His wife Obby was on her way from London. The staff were ordered to clear the chapel for Peter's coffin. Andrew

Cavendish ensured that the press did not report that Kick and Peter were lovers, but were merely travelling as friends.[25] It was stated that Kick had bumped into Peter at the Ritz and he had offered her a seat on his private jet.

Kick's body was taken to a Paris church while plans were being prepared. Joe had hoped that Jack would make arrangements but he was too upset about her death to do anything. The Duke and Duchess of Devonshire, who had loved her, offered to bury her in the family plot at Chatsworth. They knew about Peter, but Kick was family. The Devonshires asked the Kennedy family if they would like a Roman Catholic funeral. It was a symbol of how much they loved her. They would give her a Catholic funeral and still bury her at Chatsworth.

Joe was the only member of the Kennedy family to attend her funeral. Jack intended to, but at the last minute couldn't face it and turned back.

On 20 May a High Requiem Mass was said at Farm Street. Many friends came to pay tribute to the young woman they had loved. The chief mourners were Joe, the Duke and Duchess and Elizabeth and Andrew Cavendish. Winston Churchill sent a huge sheaf of arum lilies. The church was packed with politicians and the cream of high society. When the coffin passed Sissy Ormsby Gore she fell to her knees, put her head on the coffin and wailed.[26]

Afterwards, a special train transported Joe and 200 of Kick's friends to Chatsworth with the coffin. Joe wore a crumpled blue suit; Debo recalled that 'he was crumpled just like the suit. I never saw anything like it.'[27] It was the first funeral that she had ever attended, and she was distraught. She was exactly the same age as Kick, twenty-eight: 'not the time of life when you think about death, yet that most vital of human beings had been taken from us.'[28]

The head gardener at Chatsworth, Bert Link, lined her grave with pale purple wisteria, 'the sweet-smelling, short-lived flowers so fitting for a life cut short so tragically'.[29] The Duchess chose the words for her gravestone: 'Joy she gave Joy she has found'.

Leabharlanna Fhine Gall

EPILOGUE

An anonymous friend said to *The Times* after her death: 'No American, man or woman who has ever settled in England, was so much loved as she, and no American ever loved England more. Strangely enough, it was those in London who are most disenchanted with this day and age who perhaps derived the greatest comfort and light from her enchanting personality.'[1]

Lady Anderson, who had loved her like a daughter, wrote a beautiful tribute:

It is not always a compliment to say that a woman or man has no enemies, but the fact that everyone loved her came from no weakness in her nature, but from the sheer worth of her character ... in what lay her unusual charm? Her evident goodness, her most attractive sense of humour, her radiant blue eyes, her smile in which was reflected the beauty of her spirit? It is difficult to say, but no one could have been more richly endowed for friendship.[2]

The tributes poured in from both sides of the Atlantic. For friends of the Cavendishes, Kick's death was a reminder of her great love of Billy: 'For Kick somehow I cannot grieve, strange as it may seem,' wrote one of the Duchess's friends. 'I have always felt her life in a way ended with darling Billy and that without his help she had lost the rudder that controlled her life, and the forces of her being would always have been pulling her in different ways.'[3]

John White wrote a final 'Did You Happen to See ... Kathleen':

It is a strange, hard thing to sit at this desk, to tap at this typewriter (your old desk, your old typewriter), to tap out the cold and final word – good-by. Good-by little Kathleen. THE Wires have at last stopped rattling out the details of what happened in France, Thursday, late ... in the storm ... Kathleen. Little 'Kick' Where have you gone?[4]

In the end he never filed it. Instead, the *Washington Times-Herald* published a small tribute to their intrepid reporter: 'Everyone in this office has tried to write this piece. But the white space is more eloquent. * *Kathleen, Lady Hartington was found stretched on her back and appeared to have been asleep* * Dream, Kick.'[5]

The story concocted by the three families that it was a chance encounter that sent Kick to her death was duly reproduced. The *New York Daily News* was the first to break the news: 'Chance Invite Sends Kennedy Girl to her Death'. The paper was owned by a friend of Joe's. Kick was described as an 'old friend of both Lady and Lord Fitzwilliam'.[6] In her memoir, Rose wrote that her daughter was killed 'flying in a private plane with a few friends to Paris, where her father was waiting to meet her'.[7] Lem Billings said that for Rose 'that airplane crash was God pointing his finger at Kick and saying *no!*'[8]

Joe was broken. After the funeral, he wrote a moving letter to the Duchess in which he revealed the extent of his grief: 'I think that the only thing that helped me retain my sanity was your understanding manner in the whole sad affair.' He had sent recent photographs of Kick (the last ones he had taken of her) to be distributed among her friends: 'I can't seem to get out of my mind that there is no possibility of seeing Kick next winter and that there are no more weeks and months to be made gay by her presence.'[9]

The person most affected by her death was Jack. Of the three 'personality kids', he had been the one who suffered from ill health and had several times been close to death. Joe Jr and Kick had been the epitome of health and vitality. How could they both be dead, while he was still alive? 'Kathleen and Joe [had] everything moving in their direction. That's what made it so unfortunate. If something happens to you or somebody in your family who is miserable anyway, whose health is bad, or who has a chronic disease or something, that's one thing. But for someone who is living at the peak, then to get cut off – that's a shock.'[10] To Lem he confessed his sleepless nights thinking about his sister and all they had shared. She was the one who had always believed in him.

When he came to England, six weeks after Kick's funeral, he spoke to her housekeeper Ilona, wanting to know everything about her last days. He told Ilona that he would never speak about his sister again. Years later, Bobby did exactly the same thing. For many years, Jack couldn't bring himself to visit her grave at Chatsworth.

Ilona and her sister had been Kick's loyal staff, and after her death they were given employment at Chatsworth and set about restoring the great house at Debo's request. They were a huge success and became as devoted to Debo as they had been to Kick.

The Hungarian sisters saw Jack Kennedy once again. In June 1963 when the President of the United States made his state visit to Ireland, he diverted for an unscheduled visit 'of an extremely personal nature'. The workers on the Chatsworth estate were intrigued when a helicopter landed near Edensor, and the Commander-in-Chief got out to be met by Andrew, Duke of Devonshire. Few in the younger generation realized that His Grace was the brother-in-law of the President's late sister. John F. Kennedy was clutching a small posy of flowers. He knelt and prayed at his sister's grave.[11] Back at the White House, just four months before he was killed, he wrote to Deborah Duchess of Devonshire telling her, 'all of us felt that the arrangements that you have made for Kathleen were beautiful. The inscription "Joy she gave – joy she found" is so appropriate and moving.' The Duchess cherished his letter.[12]

The next brother down, Robert F. Kennedy, who would be assassinated just five years after his brother, had worshipped Kick and was devastated by her death. He was the first male Kennedy to marry. His eldest child, a daughter, was born in 1951, and was christened Kathleen Hartington Kennedy. The family was overjoyed, but Bobby made one stipulation: she was never to be called Kick.

ACKNOWLEDGEMENTS

I first read about Kathleen 'Kick' Kennedy when I was writing my biography of Evelyn Waugh, *Mad World: Evelyn Waugh and the Secrets of Brideshead*. I was stunned by his account of his grief at her sudden death and the remorse he felt thinking back on what he had said to her about her adulterous relationship with Peter Fitzwilliam. Waugh, a devout Catholic, felt that her death was on his hands. At the time, I had no idea who 'Kick' was and I was surprised to discover that she was the beloved sister of President John F. Kennedy and that she had married an English Protestant Lord, then died in the company of a married man, with the result that she was for many years airbrushed out of the Kennedy family history. Kick's story was utterly fascinating and tragic. She felt to me like a heroine from the novels of Henry James: this was a new-world-meets-old-world story. How she and Billy might have been part of a new political era in the aftermath of the Second World War can only be imagined, especially when her brother JFK became President.

Growing up in Birkenhead, part of a large Catholic working-class family, I remember two of my mother's prized possessions: a bust of the Pope and a bust of JFK, the very first Catholic American President. I felt that I understood what it was like for Kick to be a middle daughter among a band of boisterous Catholic siblings – especially as my mother's ancestors were Irish Kennedys. This is by far the most personal of my biographies, and the one that I have most enjoyed writing. But it could not have been done, of course, without the help and support of many people.

The best brief account of Kick's life is that in Laurence Leamer's authoritative *The Kennedy Women: The Saga of an American Family*. Amanda Smith's *Hostage to Fortune: The Letters of Joseph P. Kennedy* is a wonderful edition of Kennedy letters and an invaluable source. The only previous biography is Lynne McTaggart, *Kathleen Kennedy: The Untold Story of Jack's Favourite Sister* (1983), which contains much helpful material based on interviews, but was written long before any archival material became available.

I have been the beneficiary of the recent opening for research of the Rose Fitzgerald Kennedy Personal Papers, where many of Kick's personal papers are lodged, in the John F. Kennedy Presidential Library and Museum in the family's home town of Boston. The scale of the archive is daunting, so I would like to begin by thanking the Kennedy family and the Library staff. In particular, Reference Archivist Abigail Malangone has been tremendously helpful and supportive throughout. Connor Anderson, Laurie Austin and Jacqueline Gertner made the process of obtaining photographs the easiest I have ever experienced, and Jennifer Quan of the JFK Library Foundation is due especial thanks for arranging licensing. Above all, I am grateful to my research assistant Mitch Hanley, who was tasked with the onerous duty of photocopying over two thousand pages of archival material that enabled me to work from the comfort of my own home. Thanks to Professor David Armitage for putting me in touch with Mitch via Harvard University.

I would also like to thank his Grace the Duke of Devonshire and the Trustees of the Chatsworth Settlement for allowing me the privilege of working in the private family archive at Chatsworth. James Towe, the Archivist and Librarian, was kind and helpful. Brigadier Andrew Parker Bowles, Billy Hartington's godson, was very generous in connecting me with Chatsworth, and I benefited greatly from our conversation about Kick and the letter and presents she sent to him after Billy's death. Christopher O'Kane must be thanked in turn for introducing me to Andrew.

Many thanks to Hester Styles for checking quotations and helping with the children. Andrew Wylie remains the best of agents. This is the fifth biography I have published with HarperCollins, and once again I must thank the amazing team: Helen Ellis, Kate Tolley, Joseph Zigmond and above all my dream editor Arabella Pike. In New York, Terry Karten was once again an equally exemplary and supportive editor. My copy editor Peter James excelled himself in picking over the detail and correcting me, especially on matters aristocratic and military.

Liz Hertford, executive producer of my BBC2 documentary about Jane Austen, shares my passion for the story of Billy and Kick, and I sincerely hope that the project we are planning together will come to fruition.

I had a wonderful time on Cape Cod, footstepping in Hyannis Port, where the staff at the John F. Kennedy Hyannis Museum were charming and helpful.

Writing is a solitary occupation. My life has been greatly enriched by the friendships, new and old, that have sustained me over the three years of writing this book. Thank you to Sally Bayley, Candida Crewe, Betina Goodall and Sophie Ratcliffe, and to Matthew Catterick, Simon Curtis, Stephen Methven and Andrew Schuman. Ivo and Ottilie Schuman are two of my newest, youngest friends, and they have been extremely amusing companions.

I would like, finally, to thank my family. Thanks as ever to Tom, Ellie and Harry. They are simply remarkable children, and are very supportive of my writing. They helped me choose the pictures for *Kick*. I feel extraordinarily fortunate to be their mother. Jonathan Bate is a Prince amongst Men. To him I offer my most heartfelt thanks.

SOURCES

MANUSCRIPTS

Kennedy Family Collection, in the John F. Kennedy Presidential Library and Museum, Boston:
Box 057: Kathleen Kennedy, Scrapbooks and albums: 'Day by Day' Diary, 1935
Box 058: Kathleen Kennedy, Scrapbooks and albums: School Year Abroad, 1935–7
Box 060: Kathleen Kennedy, Scrapbooks and albums: Agenda, 1936
Box 074: 'Kick' (Kathleen Kennedy), Scrapbooks and albums: 1940
Box 076: Kathleen Kennedy, Scrapbooks and albums: 1941–3
Box 079: Kathleen Kennedy, Scrapbooks and albums: Scrapbook, 1943–4
Box 080: Kathleen Kennedy, Scrapbooks and albums: 1943–4
Box 081: Kathleen Kennedy Cavendish, Scrapbooks and albums: Wedding Photographs Album, 6 May 1944
Box 082: William Cavendish, Marquess of Hartington, and Kathleen Kennedy Hartington, Scrapbooks and albums: 'Billy and Kick' [diary and scrapbook], 1944–6

Rose Fitzgerald Kennedy Personal Papers, in the John F. Kennedy Presidential Library and Museum, Boston:
Box 002: Rose Fitzgerald Kennedy, 'Windsor Castle', April 1938; 'On the night of the Presentation', 1938
Box 003: Rose Fitzgerald Kennedy, 'Notes on my reaction at Kick marriage', 1944
Box 006: Rose Fitzgerald Kennedy, 'Raising children', 10 January 1972; 'Notes for Diary, Kathleen, Prince's Gate, trip to the Soviet Union, England', 25 January 1972; 'Kennedy family life', circa September 1975; 'Advantages of Catholic Education', undated notes; 'Advantages of Several Children While Traveling', undated notes

Box 013: Kathleen Kennedy: Diary notes; Family correspondence, 1927–43 (three folders); Newspaper clippings and correspondence on Kathleen Kennedy's death, 1948

Box 057: Kathleen Kennedy Hartington: Document list; Family correspondence etc. 1942–4; Family correspondence etc. 1945 (two folders); Family correspondence etc. 1946; Family correspondence etc. 1947–8

Box 058: Kathleen Kennedy Hartington, Family correspondence etc. 1947–8

Box 128: Kathleen Kennedy Hartington, Early writings, 1928–39; Diary, 1938–9; Scrapbook, 1938–9; Invitations, menus and letters in England, 1938–9; Correspondence with friends and family, 1941–6

Box 129: Hartington by-election, clipping, 1940s; 'Bobby's clippings on Kathleen's wedding', 1944; Clippings, 'Husband's death', 1944; Photographs and clippings, 1944

Joseph P. Kennedy Personal Papers, Series 01.2.06 ('Kathleen Kennedy Hartington, 1933–1948'), in the John F. Kennedy Presidential Library and Museum, Boston:

Box 026: Condolence mail lists; Correspondence: Extended family; Correspondence: Non-family, 1936–47; Correspondence regarding Kathleen Kennedy, 1933–45; Kathleen Kennedy's Death: Joseph P. Kennedy note, 1948; Kathleen Kennedy, 'Did You Happen to See …', newspaper articles for the *Washington Times-Herald*, 1942–3; Kathleen Kennedy: Education, 1938–40; Kathleen Kennedy Estate: Estate ledger and Taxes/estate materials (three folders); 'Impressions of the Coronation of Pope Pius XII', 1939; Miscellaneous; News clippings; Photographs; Kathleen Kennedy: Red Cross material, 1944–6; Kathleen Kennedy Scrapbooks, May 1948 (Lady Hartington)

Box 027: Scrapbooks, May 1948 (Lady Hartington); Scrapbooks: Kathleen Kennedy Personal scrapbook

John F. Kennedy Personal Papers, in the John F. Kennedy Presidential Library and Museum, Boston:

Kathleen Kennedy, Correspondence, 1942–7, and undated. Digitized at http://www.jfklibrary.org/Asset-Viewer/Archives/JFKPP-004-035.aspx

The Devonshire Collection (private family archive), Chatsworth, Derbyshire:
Letters sent to and from Kathleen Kennedy and two publications belonging to her
Letters referring to Kathleen 'Kick' Cavendish

BOOKS

Bailey, Catherine, *Black Diamonds: The Rise and Fall of an English Dynasty* (2007)
Beauchamp, Cari, *Joseph P. Kennedy's Hollywood Years* (2009)
Bzdeck, Vincent, *The Kennedy Legacy* (2009)
Collier, Peter, and David Horowitz, *The Kennedys: An American Drama* (1984)
Devonshire, Deborah, Duchess of, *Chatsworth: The House* (2002)
___, *Wait for Me! Memoirs of the Youngest Mitford Sister* (2010)
Hamilton, Nigel, *JFK: Life and Death of an American President, vol. 1: Reckless Youth* (1993)
Kennedy, John Fitzgerald, ed., *As We Remember Joe* (1945)
Kennedy, Rose Fitzgerald, *Times to Remember* (1974)
___, *Rose Kennedy's Family Album*, ed. Caroline Kennedy (2013)
Kessler, Ronald, *The Sins of the Father: Joseph P. Kennedy and the Dynasty He Founded* (1996)
Klein, Edward, *The Kennedy Curse* (2003)
Leamer, Laurence *The Kennedy Women* (1994)
Leaming, Barbara, *Jack Kennedy: The Making of a President* (2006)
McTaggart, Lynne, *Kathleen Kennedy: The Untold Story of Jack's Favourite Sister* (1983)
Nasaw, David, *The Patriarch: The Remarkable Life and Turbulent Times of Joseph P. Kennedy* (2013)
Perry, Barbara A., *Rose Kennedy: The Life and Times of a Political Matriarch* (2013)
Reeves, Thomas C., *A Question of Character: A Life of John F. Kennedy* (1991)
Riva, Maria, *Marlene Dietrich by her Daughter* (1992)
Roosevelt, James, *My Parents: A Differing View* (1976)
Sandler, Martin W., ed., *The Letters of John F. Kennedy* (2013)

Smith, Amanda, ed., *Hostage to Fortune: The Letters of Joseph P. Kennedy* (2001)

Swift, Will, *The Kennedys amidst the Gathering Storm* (2008)

NOTES

ABBREVIATIONS

BK – Bobby Kennedy
EK – Eunice Kennedy
JFK – John F. Kennedy
JK – Joe P. Kennedy Jr
JPK – Joe P. Kennedy Sr
KFC – Kennedy Family Collection
KK – Kathleen 'Kick' Kennedy/Hartington
RK – Rose Fitzgerald Kennedy

PROLOGUE: KICKING THE SURF

1. Papers of Rose Kennedy (hereafter RK), 25 Jan. 1972: 'Notes on Kathleen'. See Sources for full details of papers in the John F. Kennedy Presidential Library and Museum, Boston.
2. Vincent Bzdeck, *The Kennedy Legacy* (2009), p. 16.

CHAPTER 1: ROSE AND JOE

1. Rose Fitzgerald Kennedy, *Times to Remember* (1974), p. 141.
2. Nigel Hamilton, *JFK: Life and Death of an American President, vol. 1: Reckless Youth* (1993), p. 5.
3. David Nasaw, *The Patriarch: The Remarkable Life and Turbulent Times of Joseph P. Kennedy* (2013), p. 18.
4. Kennedy, *Times to Remember*, p. 7.
5. Laurence Leamer, *The Kennedy Women* (1994), p. 29.
6. Kennedy, *Times to Remember*, p. 13.
7. Leamer, *Kennedy Women*, p. 47.
8. Kennedy, *Times to Remember*, p. 45.
9. ibid.
10. ibid., p. 53.
11. Rose Kennedy, quoted in Nasaw, *Patriarch*, p. 20.
12. Kennedy, *Times to Remember*, p. 53.

13. Barbara A. Perry, *Rose Kennedy: The Life and Times of a Political Matriarch* (2013), p. 54.
14. ibid.
15. Nasaw, *Patriarch*, p. 38.
16. Leamer, *Kennedy Women*, p. 125.
17. *Boston Journal*, 26 July 1915, p. 4.
18. Leamer, *Kennedy Women*, p. 136.
19. Kennedy, *Times to Remember*, p. 44.
20. Leamer, *Kennedy Women*, p. 142.
21. Kennedy, *Times to Remember*, p. 70.
22. ibid.

CHAPTER 2: A BEAUTIFUL AND ENCHANTING CHILD

1. Kennedy, *Times to Remember*, p. 78.
2. Nasaw, *Patriarch*, p. 62.
3. Amanda Smith, ed., *Hostage to Fortune: The Letters of Joseph P. Kennedy* (2001), p. 9.
4. ibid., p. 37.
5. Kennedy, *Times to Remember*, p. 86.
6. Smith, *Hostage to Fortune*, p. 37.
7. 6 October 1923, quoted in ibid., p. 40.
8. ibid., p. 36.
9. ibid., p. 48.
10. Kennedy, *Times to Remember*, p. 90.
11. ibid., p. 91.
12. ibid., pp. 99–100.
13. Leamer, *Kennedy Women*, p. 145
14. Smith, *Hostage to Fortune*, p. 36.
15. Kennedy, *Times to Remember*, p. 77.
16. ibid., p. 76.
17. RK Papers, Kathleen Kennedy (hereafter KK) to RK, 19 May 1927.
18. Kennedy, *Times to Remember*, p. 111.
19. ibid., p. 75.
20. Perry, *Rose Kennedy*, p. 72.
21. Thomas C. Reeves, *A Question of Character: A Life of John F. Kennedy* (1991), p. 32.
22. John Fitzgerald Kennedy, ed., *As We Remember Joe* (1945), pp. 3–4.
23. Bzdeck, *Kennedy Legacy*, p. 30.
24. Kennedy, *Times to Remember*, p. 74.
25. ibid., p. 129
26. Quoted in Peter Collier and David Horowitz, 'The Kennedy Kick', *Vanity Fair*, July 1983, p. 49.

27. ibid., p. 130.
28. ibid., p. 131.
29. Private letter of Joe Kennedy, quoted in Peter Collier and David Horowitz, *The Kennedys: An American Drama* (1984), p. 71.
30. ibid., p. 133.
31. ibid.
32. ibid., p. 134.
33. RK Papers.
34. Smith, *Hostage to Fortune*, p. 74.
35. RK Papers, KK to Joseph P. Kennedy (hereafter JPK), 31 Jan. 1930.
36. Smith, *Hostage to Fortune*, p. 51.

CHAPTER 3: FORBIDDEN FRUIT

1. Smith, *Hostage to Fortune*, p. xvi.
2. Nasaw, *Patriarch*, p. 75.
3. Cari Beauchamp, *Joseph P. Kennedy's Hollywood Years* (2009), p. xv.
4. Nasaw, *Patriarch*, p. 98.
5. Kennedy, *Times to Remember*, p. 110.
6. Leamer, *Kennedy Women*, p. 180.
7. ibid., p. 178.
8. RK Papers, Family correspondence, 1927–43.
9. RK Papers, Family correspondence, KK to JPK, Jan. 1927.
10. Beauchamp, *Hollywood Years*, p. 122.
11. Nasaw, *Patriarch*, p. 109.
12. Kennedy, *Times to Remember*, p. 109.

CHAPTER 4: HYANNIS PORT

1. Nasaw, *Patriarch*, p. 133.
2. Perry, *Rose Kennedy*, p. 76.
3. Leamer, *Kennedy Women*, p. 185.
4. RK Papers, KK to JPK, 31 Jan. 1930.
5. *Reader's Digest*, April 1939, p. 84.
6. Kennedy, *Times to Remember*, p. 94.
7. ibid.
8. ibid., p. 468.
9. ibid., p. 122.
10. ibid., p. 389.
11. ibid., p. 111.

CHAPTER 5: BRONXVILLE

1. Kennedy, *Times to Remember*, p. 143.
2. RK Papers.
3. ibid., 17 April 1931.
4. Lynne McTaggart, *Kathleen Kennedy: The Untold Story of Jack's Favourite Sister* (1983), p. 15.
5. RK Papers, KK to RK, June 1931.
6. RK Papers, KK to RK and JPK, 26 April 1930.
7. Kennedy, *Times to Remember*, p. 178.
8. RK Papers, KK to RK, 13 Feb. 1932.
9. KK to JPK, 8 March 1932, quoted in Smith, *Hostage to Fortune*, p. 97.
10. Kennedy, *Times to Remember*, pp. 142–3.
11. RK Papers.
12. Kennedy, *Times to Remember*, p. 156.
13. ibid., p. 167.

CHAPTER 6: CONVENT GIRL

1. RK Papers, KK to RK, 17 Dec. 1933.
2. ibid., 6 Dec. 1934.
3. Kennedy, *Times to Remember*, p. 166.
4. Lem was Jack's closest aide during his presidential campaign. He had his own room in the White House, though he always refused an official position. After Bobby had been assassinated, Lem became a father figure to his children, Nasaw, *Patriarch*, p. 224.
5. Leamer, *Kennedy Women*, p. 197.
6. KK to JPK, 8 Jan. 1934, quoted in Smith, *Hostage to Fortune*, p. 123.
7. RK Papers, KK to RK, 13 Jan. 1934.
8. Martin W. Sandler, ed., *The Letters of John F. Kennedy* (2013), p. 2.
9. RK Papers, KK to RK, 13 Jan. 1934.
10. ibid.
11. McTaggart, *Kathleen Kennedy*, p. 18.
12. Papers of John F. Kennedy (hereafter JFK), Kennedy Library.
13. Leamer, *Kennedy Women*, p. 199.
14. RK Papers, KK to RK, May 1934.
15. ibid., 20 May 1934.
16. ibid., 27 May 1934.
17. Nasaw, *Patriarch*, p. 214.
18. Hamilton, *Reckless Youth*, p. 115.
19. ibid., p. 116.
20. RK Papers.
21. RK Papers, KK to RK, Sept. 1934.

CHAPTER 7: MUCKERS AND TROUBLE

1. RK Papers.
2. RK Papers, KK to RK, 6 Dec. 1934.
3. ibid.
4. RK Papers, KK to JPK, 2 Dec. 1934.
5. Leamer, *Kennedy Women*, p. 200.
6. Hamilton, *Reckless Youth*, p. 120.
7. See Smith, *Hostage to Fortune*, p. 151.
8. JPK to KK, 20 Feb. 1935, quoted in ibid., p. 151.
9. KK to JPK, 22 Feb. 1935, quoted in ibid., p. 152.
10. KK to RK and JPK, 21 Feb. 1935, quoted in ibid.
11. Kennedy, *Times to Remember*, p. 148.
12. ibid., p. 100.
13. ibid., p. 101.
14. McTaggart, *Kathleen Kennedy*, p. 13.
15. Hamilton, *Reckless Youth*, p. 115.
16. Kennedy, *Times to Remember*, p. 134.
17. ibid.
18. Leamer, *Kennedy Women*, p. 209.
19. Kennedy, *Times to Remember*, p. 134.
20. Leamer, *Kennedy Women*, p. 206.
21. McTaggart, *Kathleen Kennedy*, p. 15.
22. Leamer, *Kennedy Women*, p. 431.
23. Peter Collier and David Horowitz, *The Kennedys: An American Drama* (1984), p. 62.
24. McTaggart, *Kathleen Kennedy*, p. 10.
25. Kennedy, *Times to Remember*, p. 122.
26. ibid., p. 123.
27. McTaggart, *Kathleen Kennedy*, p. 16.
28. ibid.
29. Collier and Horowitz, *An American Drama*, pp. 45–6.
30. ibid., p. 58.
31. Hamilton, *Reckless Youth*, p. 94.
32. Collier and Horowitz, *An American Drama*, p. 71.

CHAPTER 8: MADEMOISELLE POURQUOI

1. Hamilton, *Reckless Youth*, p. 139.
2. Kennedy, *Times to Remember*, p. 186.
3. RK Papers, KK to 'Darling Mother and dad', 25 Oct. 1935.
4. ibid.
5. RK Papers, KK to 'Dearest Mother and Daddy', 31 Oct. 1935.

6. ibid.

7. RK Papers, KK to RK, 17 Feb. 1936.

8. ibid., 27 Nov. 1935.

9. ibid., 31 Oct. 1935.

10. RK Papers, KK to 'Dearest Mother', 13 Dec. 1935.

11. Leamer, *Kennedy Women*, p. 213.

12. RK Papers, KK to Eunice Kennedy (hereafter EK), 24 Nov. 1935.

13. RK Papers, KK to Bobby Kennedy (hereafter BK), Nov. 1935.

14. ibid.

15. ibid.

16. RK Papers, KK to 'Mother and Daddy Dear', 17 Nov. 1935.

17. ibid.

18. ibid.

19. ibid.

20. ibid.

21. RK Papers, KK to RK, 13 Dec. 1935.

22. RK Papers, KK to EK, 24 Nov. 1935.

23. ibid.

24. RK Papers, KK to BK, Nov. 1935.

CHAPTER 9: GSTAAD AND ITALY

1. RK Papers, KK to RK, 13 Dec. 1935.

2. RK Papers, KK to JPK, 3 Jan. 1936.

3. RK Papers, KK to BK, 23 Jan. 1936.

4. RK Papers, KK to Jean Kennedy, 23 Jan. 1936.

5. ibid.

6. RK Papers, KK to RK, 13 Dec. 1935.

7. KK to 'Dearest Mother and Daddy', 27 Nov. 1935.

8. Hamilton, *Reckless Youth*, p. 146.

9. Leamer, *Kennedy Women*, p. 215; RK Papers, JPK to KK, 20 Jan. 1936; Smith, *Hostage to Fortune*, 20 Jan. 1936, p. 170.

10. RK Papers, JPK to KK, 20 Jan. 1936.

11. RK Papers, KK to 'Dearest Mother and Daddy', 19 Jan. 1936.

12. ibid.

13. Leamer, *Kennedy Women*, p. 215, KK to 'Mother dearest', 11 Feb. 1936.

14. RK Papers, KK to 'Mother and Daddy dear', 23 Feb. 1936.

15. ibid., 27 Jan. 1936.

16. ibid., 3 Feb. 1936.

17. ibid.

18. KK to RK, 8 Feb. 1936, quoted in Smith, *Hostage to Fortune*, p. 172.

19. RK Papers, KK to EK, 2 Feb. 1936.

20. ibid.

21. RK Papers, KK to 'Dearest mother', 17 Feb. 1936.
22. ibid., to 'Mother and Daddy dear', 23 Feb. 1936.
23. ibid., 3 Feb. 1936.
24. RK Papers, KK to JFK, 'Sunday 8th', 1936.
25. ibid.
26. RK Papers, KK to 'Mother and Daddy dear', 23 Feb. 1936.
27. RK Papers, KK to 'Dearest Mother and Dad', 23 March 1936.
28. RK Papers, KK to 'Dearest Mother and Dad', 2 March 1936.
29. ibid.
30. ibid.
31. RK Papers, 26 Feb. 1936.
32. RK Papers, KK to 'Darling Mother and Dad', 29 March 1936.
33. ibid.
34. RK Papers, KK to family, 30 March 1936.
35. KK to 'Darling Mother and Dad', 29 March 1936, quoted in Leamer, *Kennedy Women*, p. 216.
36. RK Papers, KK to Misses Kennedy, postcard, 1936.
37. RK Papers, KK to Messrs Kennedy, postcard, 1936.
38. RK Papers, KK to 'Darling Mother and Dad', 29 March 1936.
39. ibid.
40. RK Papers, KK to 'Darling Mother and Dad', 2 April 1936.
41. RK Papers, KK to 'Dearest Dad', 15 April 1936.
42. ibid.
43. ibid.
44. ibid.
45. RK Papers, KK to 'Daddy Dear', 18 April 1936.
46. ibid.
47. ibid.
48. ibid.

CHAPTER 10: TRAVELS WITH MY MOTHER: RUSSIA AND ENGLAND

1. Kennedy, *Times to Remember*, p. 191.
2. ibid.
3. RK Papers, KK to RK, 26 April 1936.
4. Leamer, *Kennedy Women*, p. 217.
5. ibid.
6. Kennedy, *Times to Remember*, p. 192.
7. ibid.
8. RK Papers, RK to KK, 27 May 1936.
9. ibid., 5 June 1936.
10. KK to 'Mother dearest', 8 June 1936, quoted in Leamer, *Kennedy Women*, p. 218.

11. See McTaggart, *Kathleen Kennedy*, p. 20.
12. KK to 'Mother dearest', 8 June 1936, quoted in Leamer, *Kennedy Women*, p. 218.
13. ibid.
14. Quoted in Leamer, *Kennedy Women*, p. 206.
15. McTaggart, *Kathleen Kennedy*, p. 18.
16. ibid., pp. 18–19.
17. See ibid., p. 20.
18. Leamer, *Kennedy Women*, p. 225.
19. Smith, *Hostage to Fortune*, p. xv.
20. Kennedy Family Collection (hereafter KFC), KK to her sisters, undated.

CHAPTER 11: POLITICS AND EUROPE REVISITED

1. Nasaw, *Patriarch*, p. 252.
2. ibid., p. 253.
3. ibid., p. 111.
4. ibid., p. 255.
5. Smith, *Hostage to Fortune*, p, 193.
6. McTaggart, *Kathleen Kennedy*, p. 20; Leamer, *Kennedy Women*, p. 223.
7. Leamer, *Kennedy Women*, p. 223.
8. Hamilton, *Reckless Youth*, p. 178.
9. ibid.
10. ibid., p. 185.
11. ibid., p. 184.
12. ibid., p. 185.
13. ibid., p. 192.
14. RK Papers, KK to JPK, 18 Aug. 1937.
15. ibid., postcard, 17 Aug. 1937.
16. ibid., 18 Aug. 1937.
17. RK Papers, KK to RK, Aug. 1937.
18. Hamilton, *Reckless Youth*, p. 196.
19. ibid., p. 186.
20. ibid.
21. ibid., p. 199.

CHAPTER 12: THE AMBASSADOR

1. Edward Klein, *The Kennedy Curse* (2003), p. 100.
2. James Roosevelt, *My Parents: A Differing View* (1976), p. 208.
3. Nasaw, *Patriarch*, p. 272.
4. ibid., p. 274.
5. Kennedy, *Times to Remember*, p. 200.

CHAPTER 13: AT THE COURT OF ST JAMES'S

1. Leamer, *Kennedy Women*, p. 240; McTaggart, *Kathleen Kennedy*, p. 24.
2. Perry, *Rose Kennedy*, p. 99.
3. ibid.; Deborah Devonshire, *Wait for Me! Memoirs of the Youngest Mitford Sister* (2010), p. 204.
4. Leamer, *Kennedy Women*, p. 239.
5. ibid., p. 240.
6. McTaggart, *Kathleen Kennedy*, p. 22.
7. Bzdeck, *Kennedy Legacy*, p. 38.
8. Nasaw, *Patriarch*, p. 299.
9. ibid.
10. Kennedy, *Times to Remember*, p. 201.
11. Devonshire, *Wait for Me!*, p. 90.
12. Will Swift, *The Kennedys amidst the Gathering Storm* (2008), p. 35.
13. ibid., p. 36.
14. Joe Jr and Jack were still at Harvard but would come to England later in the summer.
15. Kennedy, *Times to Remember*, p. 203.
16. Nasaw, *Patriarch*, p. 286.
17. Cutting from KK scrapbook, 1938–9.
18. RK Papers, RK notes on Windsor Castle.
19. Barbara Leaming, *Jack Kennedy: The Making of a President* (2006), p. 32.

CHAPTER 14: 'I GET A KICK OUT OF YOU'

1. Devonshire, *Wait for Me!*, p. 90.
2. Leaming, *Making of a President*, p. 32.
3. ibid., p. 259.
4. ibid., p. 34.
5. Collier and Horowitz, *An American Drama*, p. 90.
6. Leaming, *Making of a President*, p. 36.
7. RK Papers, KK diary, 17 June 1938.
8. ibid., 18 June 1938.
9. ibid., 19 June 1938.
10. McTaggart, *Kathleen Kennedy*, p. 33.
11. ibid.

CHAPTER 15: THE DEBUTANTE

1. Leamer, *Kennedy Women*, p. 236.
2. Collier and Horowitz, *An American Drama*, p. 90.
3. Leamer, *Kennedy Women*, p. 253.

4. RK Papers, KK diary, 11 May 1938.

5. Perry, *Rose Kennedy*, p. 105.

6. McTaggart, *Kathleen Kennedy*, pp. 25–6.

7. RK Papers, KK diary, 2 June 1938.

8. Duncannon married a vivacious American heiress called Mary Munn in the year of Kick's death.

9. McTaggart, *Kathleen Kennedy*, p. 39; Leamer, *Kennedy Women*, p. 257.

10. RK Papers, KK diary, 2 June 1938.

11. McTaggart, *Kathleen Kennedy*, p. 39.

12. Devonshire, *Wait for Me!*, p. 98.

13. Swift, *Gathering Storm*, p. 54.

14. McTaggart, *Kathleen Kennedy*, p. 34.

15. McTaggart relates this story in full, ibid.

16. Leamer, *Kennedy Women*, p. 260.

17. ibid., p. 30.

18. McTaggart, *Kathleen Kennedy*, p. 33.

19. Devonshire, *Wait for Me!*, p. 90.

CHAPTER 16: LORDS A-LEAPING

1. Devonshire, *Wait for Me!*, p. 91.

2. Leaming, *Kennedy Women*, p. 36.

3. ibid., p. 260.

4. Devonshire, *Wait for Me!*, p. 91.

5. ibid.

6. RK Papers, KK diary, 14 May 1938.

7. ibid.

8. ibid.

9. ibid., 20 May 1938.

10. ibid., 23 May 1938.

11. ibid., 27 May 1938.

12. ibid., 7 June 1938.

13. ibid., 1 June 1938.

14. ibid., 22 June 1938.

15. ibid., 13 June 1938.

16. Perry, *Rose Kennedy*, p. 106.

17. Leamer, *Kennedy Women*, p. 248.

18. RK Papers, KK diary, 13 May 1938.

19. Devonshire, *Wait for Me!*, p. 95.

20. McTaggart, *Kathleen Kennedy*, p. 39.

CHAPTER 17: 'A MERRY GIRL'

1. Leamer, *Kennedy Women*, p. 30.
2. ibid.
3. Perry, *Rose Kennedy*, p. 108.
4. *The Times* press cutting, KK scrapbook.
5. McTaggart, *Kathleen Kennedy*, pp. 42–3.
6. ibid.
7. ibid., p. 42.
8. RK Papers, KK diary, 8 July 1938.
9. Hamilton, *Reckless Youth*, p. 235.
10. Devonshire, *Wait for Me!*, p. 102.
11. Smith, *Hostage to Fortune*, p. 227.
12. Leamer, *Kennedy Women*, p. 261.

CHAPTER 18: BILLY

1. RK Papers, KK diary, 18 July 1938.
2. Billy's title was Earl of Burlington until the death of his grandfather, when his father became Duke of Devonshire and he became Marquess of Hartington.
3. RK Papers, KK diary, 13 July 1938.
4. Devonshire, *Wait for Me!*, p. 99.
5. Leamer, *Kennedy Women*, p. 261.
6. RK Papers, KK diary, 25 July 1938.
7. Devonshire, *Wait for Me!*, p. 218.
8. ibid., pp. 118–19.
9. ibid., p. 118.
10. Swift, *Gathering Storm*, p. 72.
11. Devonshire, *Wait for Me!*, p. 99.

CHAPTER 19: THE RIVIERA

1. As described by Maria Riva, who met the Kennedys that summer: Maria Riva, *Marlene Dietrich by her Daughter* (1992), p. 468.
2. ibid., p. 469.
3. ibid., p. 466.
4. Kennedy, *Times to Remember*, p. 217.
5. ibid.
6. Hamilton, *Reckless Youth*, p. 236.
7. Riva, *Marlene Dietrich*, p. 467.
8. Nasaw, *Patriarch*, p. 326.
9. Riva, *Marlene Dietrich*, p. 469.
10. ibid.

11. ibid.
12. Nasaw, *Patriarch*, p. 327.
13. Riva, *Marlene Dietrich*, p. 470.
14. RK Papers, KK diary, 14 Aug. 1938.
15. ibid., 20 Aug. 1938.
16. McTaggart, *Kathleen Kennedy*, p. 35.
17. Kennedy, *Times to Remember*, p. 218.
18. ibid., pp. 218–19.
19. RK Papers, KK diary, 9 Sept. 1938.
20. ibid.

CHAPTER 20: PEACE FOR OUR TIME

1. RK Papers, KK diary, 19 Sept. 1938.
2. Swift, *Gathering Storm*, pp. 94–5.
3. RK Papers, KK diary, 19 Sept. 1938.
4. Kennedy, *Times to Remember*, p. 220.
5. Hamilton, *Reckless Youth*, p. 239.
6. Nasaw, *Patriarch*, p. 342.
7. RK Papers, KK diary, 19 Sept. 1938.
8. Swift, *Gathering Storm*, pp. 98–9.
9. Nasaw, *Patriarch*, p. 346.
10. Hamilton, *Reckless Youth*, p. 240.
11. http://www.winstonchurchill.org/resources/speeches/1930-1938-the-wilderness/the-munich-agreement.
12. RK Papers, Oct. 1938.
13. Swift, *Gathering Storm*, p. 108.
14. Nasaw, *Patriarch*, p. 343.
15. Smith, *Hostage to Fortune*, p. 289.
16. Nasaw, *Patriarch*, p. 336.

CHAPTER 21: CHATSWORTH

1. Deborah, Duchess of Devonshire, *Chatsworth: The House* (2002).
2. RK Papers, KK diary, 3 Oct. 1938.
3. ibid.
4. ibid., 23 Oct. 1938.
5. Leamer, *Kennedy Women*, p. 46.
6. Leaming, *Making of a President*, p. 46.
7. Leamer, *Kennedy Women*, p. 258.
8. Collier and Horowitz, *An American Drama*, p. 103.
9. Devonshire, *Chatsworth*, p. 94.
10. Swift, *Gathering Storm*, p. 72.

11. Collier and Horowitz, *An American Drama*, p. 103.
12. Nasaw, *Patriarch*, p. 351.
13. ibid., p. 360.
14. ibid., p. 367.
15. RK Papers, KK diary, 9 Dec. 1938.
16. Perry, *Rose Kennedy*, p. 129.
17. RK Papers, KK diary, 20 Dec. 1939.

CHAPTER 22: ST MORITZ AND ROME

1. RK Papers, KK diary, 24 Dec. 1938.
2. Swift, *Gathering Storm*, p. 126.
3. RK Papers, KK diary, 24 Dec. 1938.
4. Leamer, *Kennedy Women*, p. 270.
5. RK Papers, KK to JPK, 25 Jan. 1939.
6. Kennedy, *Times to Remember*, p. 225.
7. Perry, *Rose Kennedy*, p. 132.
8. RK Papers, KK to JPK, 3 Feb. 1939.
9. Collier and Horowitz, *An American Drama*, p. 102.
10. Leaming, *Making of a President*, p. 61.
11. RK Papers, KK diary, 10 Feb. 1939.
12. ibid., 24 Feb. 1939.
13. ibid.
14. Devonshire, *Wait for Me!*, p. 102.
15. JPK diary, 12 March 1939, quoted in Smith, *Hostage to Fortune*, p. 316.
16. ibid., p. 318.
17. ibid., p. 319.
18. RK Papers, May 1939.

CHAPTER 23: THE GATHERING STORM

1. Leamer, *Kennedy Women*, p. 274.
2. ibid., pp. 274–5.
3. Smith, *Hostage to Fortune*, p. 335.
4. Leamer, *Kennedy Women*, p. 430.
5. Leaming, *Making of a President*, p. 69.
6. ibid., p. 71.
7. RK diary, 4 May 1939, quoted in Smith, *Hostage to Fortune*, p. 332.
8. Perry, *Rose Kennedy*, p. 139.
9. Leamer, *Kennedy Women*, p. 280.
10. Perry, *Rose Kennedy*, p. 143.

CHAPTER 24: THE LAST HURRAH

1. Consuelo Vanderbilt Balsan, *The Glitter and the Gold* (2012), p. 276.
2. Leamer, *Kennedy Women*, p. 282.
3. Lady Sarah's birthday was actually in December, but her party took place in the summer. Eunice turned 18 on Monday, 10 July.
4. Smith, *Hostage to Fortune*, p. 344.
5. Leamer, *Kennedy Women*, p. 281.
6. Smith, *Hostage to Fortune*, p. 345.
7. Swift, *Gathering Storm*, p. 174.
8. McTaggart, *Kathleen Kennedy*, p. 64.
9. Leaming, *Making of a President*, p. 73.
10. Leamer, *Kennedy Women*, p. 283.
11. Although a legend has grown up that Luis was shot immediately, he was in fact executed a month later, in reprisal for an air raid. See Hugh Thomas, *The Spanish Civil War* (1961), p. 311.
12. Swift, *Gathering Storm*, p. 177.
13. ibid.; Hamilton, *Reckless Youth*, pp. 269–70.
14. Hamilton, *Reckless Youth*, p. 270.
15. Swift, *Gathering Storm*, p. 180.
16. Joe Kennedy Jr (hereafter JK) notes on Unity Mitford, Munich, 21 Aug. 1939, quoted in Smith, *Hostage to Fortune*, pp. 355–6.
17. Nasaw, *Patriarch*, p. 400.
18. JPK press release, 24 Aug. 1939, quoted in Smith, *Hostage to Fortune*, p. 360.

CHAPTER 25: 'THIS COUNTRY IS AT WAR WITH GERMANY'

1. JPK diary, 3 Sept. 1939, quoted in Smith, *Hostage to Fortune*, p. 366.
2. Quoted in Smith, *Hostage to Fortune*, p. 367.
3. ibid., p. 366.
4. Hamilton, *Reckless Youth*, p. 282.
5. Leamer, *Kennedy Women*, p. 286.
6. Smith, *Hostage to Fortune*, p. 366.
7. Leaming, *Making of a President*, p. 78.
8. Leamer, *Kennedy Women*, p. 287.
9. There is no evidence that it was published.
10. Smith, *Hostage to Fortune*, p. 371. The date, 19 September, is curious, since Kick sailed for America on 12 September. Perhaps she wrote the piece on the boat, in the hope of getting it published in New York on or soon after 19 September.
11. ibid.
12. ibid.

CHAPTER 26: THE PERSONALITY KIDS

1. Leamer, *Kennedy Women*, p. 287.
2. KK to JPK, 18 Sept. 1939, quoted in Smith, *Hostage to Fortune*, p. 381.
3. Leamer, *Kennedy Women*, p. 289.
4. McTaggart, *Kathleen Kennedy*, p. 68.
5. Leamer, *Kennedy Women*, p. 295.
6. McTaggart, *Kathleen Kennedy*, p. 69.
7. ibid., p. 70.
8. ibid., p. 71.
9. Smith, *Hostage to Fortune*, p. 392.
10. Kennedy, *Times to Remember*, p. 237.
11. Smith, *Hostage to Fortune*, p. 385.
12. Hamilton, *Reckless Youth*, p. 289.
13. ibid., p. 295.

CHAPTER 27: OPERATION ARIEL

1. Nasaw, *Patriarch*, p. 434.
2. ibid., p. 417.
3. ibid., p. 434.
4. Leamer, *Kennedy Women*, p. 300.
5. ibid., p. 78.
6. ibid., p. 301.
7. Nasaw, *Patriarch*, p. 438.
8. Kennedy, *Times to Remember*, p. 242.
9. ibid.
10. Speech to the House of Commons, 4 June 1940.
11. Nasaw, *Patriarch*, p. 450.
12. Leaming, *Making of a President*, p. 91.
13. ibid.
14. Kennedy, *Times to Remember*, p. 243.
15. ibid., p. 249.
16. ibid., p. 258.

CHAPTER 28: THE FOURTH HOSTAGE

1. Nasaw, *Patriarch*, p. 469.
2. McTaggart, *Kathleen Kennedy*, p. 75.
3. Laura Thompson, *Nancy Mitford: Life in a Cold Climate* (2003), p. 151.
4. Lara Feigel, *The Love-Charm of Bombs: Restless Lives in the Second World War* (2013), p. 87.
5. McTaggart, *Kathleen Kennedy*, p. 76.

6. ibid., p. 83.
7. Nasaw, *Patriarch*, p. 480.
8. Smith, *Hostage to Fortune*, p. 475.
9. ibid., p. 477.
10. Kennedy, *Times to Remember*, p. 253.
11. Smith, *Hostage to Fortune*, p. 489.

CHAPTER 29: BILLY AND SALLY

1. See Michael Smith, *The Debs of Bletchley Park and Other Stories* (2015).
2. McTaggart, *Kathleen Kennedy*, p. 86.
3. ibid., p. 87.
4. ibid., pp. 86–7.
5. Radio Address Announcing an Unlimited National Emergency, 27 May 1941, http://www.presidency.ucsb.edu/ws/?pid=16120.
6. McTaggart, *Kathleen Kennedy*, p. 90.
7. ibid., p. 91.
8. ibid., p. 92.
9. Smith, *Hostage to Fortune*, p. 532.

CHAPTER 30: KICK THE REPORTER

1. Quoted in *Washington Times-Herald* epitaph of Kick, undated clipping in RK Papers.
2. Leamer, *Kennedy Women*, p. 315.
3. Amanda Smith, *Newspaper Titan: The Infamous Life and Monumental Times of Cissy Patterson* (2011).
4. Leamer, *Kennedy Women*, p. 315.
5. ibid., p. 316.
6. McTaggart, *Kathleen Kennedy*, p. 95.
7. Hamilton, *Reckless Youth*, pp. 421–2.
8. Leamer, *Kennedy Women*, p. 316.
9. Hamilton, *Reckless Youth*, p. 423.
10. RK Papers, KK to JFK, 28 Jan. 1942.
11. KK to JPK, 20 Oct. 1941, quoted in Smith, *Hostage to Fortune*, p. 532.
12. ibid.
13. ibid., p. 533.
14. Leaming, *Making of a President*, p. 104.

CHAPTER 31: LOBOTOMY

1. McTaggart, *Kathleen Kennedy*, p. 97.
2. ibid., p. 96.

3. Leamer, *Kennedy Women*, p. 317.
4. ibid., p. 318.
5. Collier and Horowitz, *An American Drama*, pp. 133–4.
6. Leamer, *Kennedy Women*, p. 319.
7. ibid., p. 320.
8. Ronald Kessler, *The Sins of the Father: Joseph P. Kennedy and the Dynasty He Founded* (1996), p. 226.
9. Kennedy, *Times to Remember*, p. 263.
10. Smith, *Hostage to Fortune*, p. 516.
11. Kennedy, *Times to Remember*, p. 264.
12. Leamer, *Kennedy Women*, p. 331.
13. ibid.
14. McTaggart, *Kathleen Kennedy*, p. 100.
15. ibid.
16. ibid., p. 97.
17. ibid., p. 99.
18. ibid.
19. Collier and Horowitz, *An American Drama*, p. 142.
20. ibid.
21. Leamer, *Kennedy Women*, p. 318.
22. Collier and Horowitz, *An American Drama*, p. 143.
23. Leamer, *Kennedy Women*, p. 332.
24. McTaggart, *Kathleen Kennedy*, p. 105.
25. Smith, *Hostage to Fortune*, p. 533.

CHAPTER 32: SCANDAL

1. Ronald Kessler, *The Sins of the Father: Joseph P. Kennedy and the Dynasty He Founded* (2012), p. 237.
2. Inga quoted in Hamilton, *Reckless Youth*, p. 426.
3. Quoted in ibid., p. 427.
4. Nasaw, *Patriarch*, p. 540.
5. Leamer, *Kennedy Women*, p. 329.
6. Nasaw, *Patriarch*, p. 541.
7. Leamer, *Kennedy Women*, p. 333.
8. RK Papers, KK to JFK, n.d.
9. ibid.
10. Leaming, *Making of a President*, p. 107.
11. Smith, *Hostage to Fortune*, p. 538.
12. RK Papers, KK to Father Keller, 14 April 1942.
13. ibid.
14. McTaggart, *Kathleen Kennedy*, p. 109.
15. ibid.

16. 'Did You Happen to See ...', KK scrapbooks.

17. Smith, *Hostage to Fortune*, pp. 542–3.

18. RK Papers, KK to JFK, n.d.

19. Leaming, *Making of a President*, p. 107.

CHAPTER 33: 'DID YOU HAPPEN TO SEE ...'

1. Smith, *Hostage to Fortune*, p. 541.

2. RK Papers, KK to JPK, n.d.

3. Leamer, *Kennedy Women*, p. 339.

4. ibid., p. 114.

5. ibid.

6. ibid., p. 115.

7. ibid., p. 116.

8. ibid.

9. RK Papers, KK to JFK, 13 Feb. 1942.

10. McTaggart, *Kathleen Kennedy*, p. 117.

11. ibid.

12. Leamer, *Kennedy Women*, p. 340.

13. ibid.

14. RK Papers, KK to RK, 7 Nov. 1942.

15. RK Papers, KK to RK and JPK, 23 Nov. 1942.

16. McTaggart, *Kathleen Kennedy*, p. 119.

17. RK Papers, KK to RK and JPK, 1 Feb. [?1943].

18. RK Papers, KK to RK, 13 Feb. 1943.

CHAPTER 34: RED CROSS WORKER OF WORLD WAR II

1. List in RK Papers.

2. KK to family, 27 June 1943, quoted in Smith, *Hostage to Fortune*, p. 562.

3. ibid.

4. KFC, KK diary, 27 June 1943.

5. James H. Madison, *Slinging Doughnuts for the Boys: An American Woman in World War II* (2008), p. 25.

6. ibid., p. xii.

7. McTaggart, *Kathleen Kennedy*, p. 127.

8. KFC, KK diary, 30 May 1943.

9. ibid.

10. ibid., 31 May–7 June 1943.

11. ibid.

12. Kennedy, *Times to Remember*, p. 265.

13. McTaggart, *Kathleen Kennedy*, p. 126.

14. Hamilton, *Reckless Youth*, p. 535.

15. Leamer, *Kennedy Women*, p. 344.
16. Smith, *Hostage to Fortune*, p. 562.
17. ibid.
18. ibid.
19. 3 July 1943, quoted in ibid., p. 563.
20. RK Papers, KK diary, 1 July 1943.
21. Nasaw, *Patriarch*, pp. 551–2.
22. RK Papers, KK to 'Dearest Little Kennedys', 14 July 1943.

CHAPTER 35: COFFEE AND DOUGHNUTS

1. Kennedy, Kathleen: Correspondence, 1942–1947, in John F. Kennedy Personal Papers, JFK Library.
2. RK Papers, KK diary, 1 July 1943.
3. Leamer, *Kennedy Women*, p. 344.
4. RK Papers, KK to 'Dearest Family', 24 Aug. 1943.
5. Leamer, *Kennedy Women*, p. 344.
6. Smith, *Hostage to Fortune*, pp. 551–2.
7. JFK to KK, 3 June 1943, quoted in ibid., p. 555.
8. KK to JFK, 3 July 1943, quoted in ibid., p. 563.
9. ibid.
10. RK Papers, KK to 'Dearest Family', 23 Sept. 1943.
11. RK Papers, Earl of Rosslyn to JFK, 25 July 1943.
12. ibid.
13. ibid.
14. KK to 'Dearest little Kennedys', 15 July 1943, quoted in Smith, *Hostage to Fortune*, p. 565.
15. RK Papers, KK diary, 9 July 1943.
16. McTaggart, *Kathleen Kennedy*, p. 135.

CHAPTER 36: SISTER KICK

1. KFC Papers, KK diary, 12 July 1943.
2. KK to family, 14 July 1943, quoted in Smith, *Hostage to Fortune*, p. 565.
3. KK diary, 14 July 1943.
4. ibid., 15 July 1943.
5. ibid., 19 July 1943.
6. ibid., 21 July 1943.
7. KK to JFK, 29 July 1943, quoted in Smith, *Hostage to Fortune*, p. 566.
8. ibid.
9. ibid.
10. JFK to RK and JPK, received 10 Aug. 1943, quoted in Smith, *Hostage to Fortune*, p. 568.

11. Collier and Horowitz, *An American Drama*, p. 153.
12. Nasaw, *Patriarch*, p. 557.
13. Smith, *Hostage to Fortune*, p. 569.
14. Collier and Horowitz, *An American Drama*, p. 156.
15. RK Papers, KK to 'Dearest Family', 2 Aug. 1943.
16. Kennedy, *Times to Remember*, pp. 270–1.
17. Hamilton, *Reckless Youth*, p. 638.
18. ibid., p. 639.

CHAPTER 37: GIRL ON A BICYCLE

1. RK Papers, KK to 'Dearest Family', 23 Sept. 1943.
2. Kennedy, *Times to Remember*, p. 271.
3. RK Papers, KK to 'Dearest Family', 23 Sept. 1943.
4. ibid., 5 Oct. 1943.
5. ibid.
6. JPK Papers, JPK to Earl of Rosslyn, 17 Nov. 1943.
7. ibid., 13 Oct. 1943.
8. RK Papers, KK to 'Dearest Family', 5 Oct. 1943.
9. ibid.
10. Leamer, *Kennedy Women*, p. 347.
11. RK Papers, KK to 'Dearest Family', 5 Oct. 1943.
12. Rhona Wood Paton-Jones, quoted in Leamer, *Kennedy Women*, p. 347.
13. Nasaw, *Patriarch*, p. 553.
14. Leamer, *Kennedy Women*, p. 353.

CHAPTER 38: PARTIES AND PRAYERS

1. Kennedy, *Times to Remember*, p. 271.
2. ibid., p. 272.
3. ibid.
4. Leamer, *Kennedy Women*, pp. 356–7.
5. KFC Papers, KK diary, 16 Nov. 1943.
6. Smith, *Hostage to Fortune*, p. 572.
7. ibid., p. 573.
8. ibid.
9. Leamer, *Kennedy Women*, p. 263.
10. KFC Papers; this account is taken from a letter from Kick to an unknown friend.
11. *The Diaries of Evelyn Waugh*, ed. Michael Davie (1978), p. 320.
12. Kennedy, *Times to Remember*, p. 268.
13. ibid.
14. ibid., p. 269.

15. ibid.
16. Leamer, *Kennedy Women*, p. 356.
17. Smith, *Hostage to Fortune*, p. 576.
18. RK Papers, Marie Bruce to RK, 21 Jan. 1944.
19. JPK Papers, Rose's secretary to KK, 28 Jan. 1944.
20. Nasaw, *Patriarch*, p. 561.
21. Leaming, *Making of a President*, p. 121.

CHAPTER 39: ROSEMARY TONKS

1. Leamer, *Kennedy Women*, p. 359.
2. Hamilton, *Reckless Youth*, p. 648.
3. JPK Papers, KK to JPK, 22 Feb. 1944.
4. Leaming, *Making of a President*, p. 123.
5. ibid.
6. Smith, *Hostage to Fortune*, p. 574.
7. Leaming, *Making of a President*, p. 127.
8. McTaggart, *Kathleen Kennedy*, p. 149.
9. KK to 'Dearest Family', 22 Feb. 1944, quoted in Smith, *Hostage to Fortune*, p. 575.
10. ibid.
11. Leaming, *Making of a President*, p. 125.
12. Smith, *Hostage to Fortune*, p. 575.
13. Leaming, *Making of a President*, p. 127.
14. This by-election, said to be the most important of the war, was one of great national significance: see G. H. Bennett, 'The wartime political truce and hopes for post-war coalition: the West Derbyshire by-election, 1944', *Midland History* 17, 1992, pp. 118–35.
15. Leamer, *Kennedy Women*, p. 359.
16. Leaming, *Making of a President*, p. 128.
17. Leamer, *Kennedy Women*, p. 359.
18. Devonshire, *Wait for Me!*, p. 129.
19. KFC, KK to family, n.d.

CHAPTER 40: AGNES AND HARTIE

1. Leamer, *Kennedy Women*, p. 361.
2. Nasaw, *Patriarch*, p. 562.
3. ibid.
4. Leaming, *Making of a President*, p. 116.
5. Smith, *Hostage to Fortune*, p. 576.
6. ibid., p. 577.
7. Kennedy, *Times to Remember*, p. 273.

8. Nasaw, *Patriarch*, p. 563.
9. Smith, *Hostage to Fortune*, p. 577.
10. Evelyn Waugh, *Brideshead Revisited* (1945), p. 189.
11. KK to RK and JPK, 22 March 1944, quoted in Smith, *Hostage to Fortune*, p. 580.
12. ibid.
13. Quoted in Leamer, *Kennedy Women*, p. 357; Smith, *Hostage to Fortune*, p. 580.
14. KK to RK and JPK, 22 March 1944, quoted in Smith, *Hostage to Fortune*, p. 580.
15. JPK to KK, 3 April 1944, quoted in ibid., p. 581.
16. KK to family, 4 April 1944, quoted in ibid., p. 582.
17. Adrian Fort, *Nancy: The Story of Lady Astor* (2012), p. 313.

CHAPTER 41: TELEGRAMS AND ANGER

1. KK to 'Dearest family', 4 April 1944, quoted in Smith, *Hostage to Fortune*, p. 582.
2. KK to RK, 9 May 1944, quoted in Smith, *Hostage to Fortune*, p. 590.
3. KK to 'Dearest family', 4 April 1944, quoted in Smith, *Hostage to Fortune*, p. 582.
4. ibid.
5. Leaming, *Making of a President*, p. 130.
6. KK to 'Dearest family', 24 April 1944, quoted in Smith, *Hostage to Fortune*, p. 583.
7. Nasaw, *Patriarch*, p. 564.
8. Smith, *Hostage to Fortune*, p. 584.
9. ibid.
10. Billy Hartington to RK, 30 April 1944, quoted in ibid., pp. 584–5.
11. ibid.
12. Devonshire Collection, 10th Duke of Devonshire to his mother, 27 April 1944.
13. Devonshire Collection, King George VI to 10th Duke of Devonshire, 5 May 1944.
14. KK to RK, 9 May 1944, quoted in Smith, *Hostage to Fortune*, p. 589.
15. Quoted in ibid., p. 590.
16. JK to RK and JPK, 8 May 1944, quoted in ibid., p. 587.
17. ibid.
18. ibid., p. 588.
19. Quoted in Kennedy, *Times to Remember*, p. 274.
20. JPK Papers, Earl of Rosslyn to JPK, 6 May 1944.
21. Evelyn Waugh to his wife Laura, 12 May 1944, quoted in *The Letters of Evelyn Waugh*, ed. Mark Amory (1980), p. 184.
22. KFC, KK to RK and JPK, 3 May 1944.

23. Smith, *Hostage to Fortune*, p. 586.
24. Leamer, *Kennedy Women*, p. 367.

CHAPTER 42: 'I LOVE YOU MORE THAN ANYTHING IN THE WORLD'

1. Undated clipping in KFC Papers, probably dating from shortly after Kick's wedding.
2. Smith, *Hostage to Fortune*, p. 590.
3. Leamer, *Kennedy Women*, p. 366.
4. Smith, *Hostage to Fortune*, p. 588.
5. ibid., p. 590.
6. ibid., p. 591.
7. ibid., p. 593.
8. ibid., p. 591.
9. KFC Papers, JK to family, 6 May 1944.
10. KFC Papers, Marie Bruce and Nancy Astor to RK, 7 May 1944.
11. ibid.
12. Smith, *Hostage to Fortune*, p. 589.
13. KK to RK, 9 May 1944, quoted in ibid., p. 589.
14. ibid., p. 590.
15. ibid.
16. ibid., p. 591.
17. Hamilton, *Reckless Youth*, p. 652.
18. ibid.
19. Nasaw, *Patriarch*, p. 567.

CHAPTER 43: THE MARCHIONESS OF HARTINGTON

1. KFC, Billy and Kick diary and scrapbook.
2. Kennedy, *Times to Remember*, pp. 274–5.
3. KFC, Billy and Kick diary, 3 June 1944.
4. KK to RK and JPK, 18 May 1944, quoted in Smith, *Hostage to Fortune*, p. 592.
5. ibid., p. 593.
6. KFC, Billy Hartington to KK, undated, 1944.
7. KFC, Billy and Kick diary.
8. KFC, Thomas Mair to KK, undated, 1944.
9. Smith, *Hostage to Fortune*, p. 591.
10. McTaggart, *Kathleen Kennedy*, p. 167.
11. Smith, *Hostage to Fortune*, p. 595. The naming never happened.
12. Leamer, *Kennedy Women*, p. 369.
13. McTaggart, *Kathleen Kennedy*, p. 165.
14. KK to 'Dearest Family', 23 May 1944, quoted in Smith, *Hostage to Fortune*, p. 595.

CHAPTER 44: OPERATION APHRODITE

1. KFC, Billy and Kick diary.
2. ibid.
3. ibid.
4. ibid.
5. ibid.
6. ibid.
7. KFC, Billy and Kick diary.
8. ibid (unidentified newspapers).
9. Smith, *Hostage to Fortune*, p. 595.
10. Nasaw, *Patriarch*, p. 568.
11. KFC, KK to Billy Hartington, undated, 1944.
12. Clippings were kept in KK scrapbook.
13. RK to KK, 30 June 1944, quoted in Smith, *Hostage to Fortune*, p. 595.
14. JK to RK and JPK, 26 July 1944, quoted in Smith, *Hostage to Fortune*, p. 598.
15. ibid., p. 589.
16. Smith, *Hostage to Fortune*, p. 598.
17. ibid.
18. 'Operation Aphrodite' was the US Army Air Force codename, 'Operation Anvil' that of the US Navy. The USAAF had overall command of the mission, in which Joe and his colleague served as the first Navy flight crew.
19. Hamilton, *Reckless Youth*, p. 659.
20. ibid.
21. Quoted in Collier and Horowitz, *American Drama*, p. 137.
22. McTaggart, *Kathleen Kennedy*, pp. 170–2.
23. Nasaw, *Patriarch*, p. 571.
24. Kennedy, *Times to Remember*, p. 277.
25. Nasaw, *Patriarch*, p. 571.
26. ibid.
27. Leaming, *Making of a President*, p. 136.
28. KFC, Billy and Kick diary.
29. McTaggart, *Kathleen Kennedy*, p. 175.
30. Hamilton, *Reckless Youth*, pp. 662–3.
31. Leamer, *Kennedy Women*, p. 374.
32. Kennedy, *Times to Remember*, p. 282.
33. Smith, *Hostage to Fortune*, p. 600.

CHAPTER 45: BILLY THE HERO

1. Frank William Clarke to his sister Vera, http://www.bbc.co.uk/history/ww2peopleswar/stories/79/a4801079.shtml.
2. ibid.

3. Devonshire Collection, Billy Hartington to KK, 4 Sept. 1944.
4. Quoted by Kick in letter to 'Dearest Family', 23 Sept. 1944, quoted in Smith, *Hostage to Fortune*, p. 604.
5. The following account is based primarily on 'War Diary: 5th Battalion Coldstream Guards, Jan–Dec 1944', Public Record Office, Kew, WO 171/1252, transcribed at http://ww2talk.com/forums/topic/33691-war-diary-5th-battalion-coldstream-guards-jan-dec-1944/, unseen by previous Kennedy biographers.
6. ibid.
7. Smith, *Hostage to Fortune*, p. 606.
8. Leamer, *Kennedy Women*, p. 376.
9. McTaggart, *Kathleen Kennedy*, p. 181.
10. ibid., pp. 181–2.
11. KFC, Billy Hartington to KK, 4 Sept. 1944.
12. Devonshire Collection, 'Moucher' to KK, 24 Aug. 1944.
13. Captain Charles Waterhouse, personal tribute in *The Times*, 20 Sept. 1944.
14. Smith, *Hostage to Fortune*, p. 606.
15. Waterhouse letter to *The Times*.
16. 'War Diary: 5th Battalion Coldstream Guards'.
17. Account given by Frans Mangelschots to the Belgian historian Henriëtte Claessens (a.k.a. Hauten), 20 Dec. 1989, in Hamilton, *Reckless Youth*, p. 862n, but unnoticed by other Kennedy biographers.
18. ibid.
19. ibid.

CHAPTER 46: 'LIFE IS SO CRUEL'

1. Leamer, *Kennedy Women*, p. 378.
2. ibid., p. 379.
3. ibid.
4. McTaggart, *Kathleen Kennedy*, p. 187.
5. Smith, *Hostage to Fortune*, p. 600.
6. ibid., p. 601.
7. Leaming, *Making of a President*, p. 138.
8. Nasaw, *Patriarch*, p. 573.
9. KK to RK, 20 Sept. 1944, quoted in Smith, *Hostage to Fortune*, p. 601.
10. KFC, Billy and Kick diary.
11. This does not seem to have been previously noticed.
12. KK round-robin letter to family, 23 Sept. 1944, quoted in Smith, *Hostage to Fortune*, p. 603.
13. ibid.
14. 23 Sept. 1944, quoted in ibid., p. 603.
15. 23 Sept. 1944, quoted in ibid., p. 602.

16. ibid., p. 602.
17. Devonshire, *Wait for Me!*, p. 130.
18. Newspaper clipping in Kick's papers, *Evening Standard*, 19 April 1945.
19. Quoted by KK, in letter to 'Dearest Family', 23 Sept. 1944, in Smith, *Hostage to Fortune*, p. 604.
20. Devonshire, *Wait for Me!*, p. 130.
21. Smith, *Hostage to Fortune*, p. 604.
22. Devonshire Collection, KK to Duchess of Devonshire ('My dearest Dutch'), 8 Nov. 1944.
23. Devonshire, *Wait for Me!*, pp. 219–20.
24. Smith, *Hostage to Fortune*, p. 602.
25. ibid., pp. 602–3.
26. ibid., p. 602.
27. Nasaw, *Patriarch*, p. 574.
28. ibid., p. 577.
29. ibid.
30. JFK Papers, KK to 'Dearest Jackie', 31 Oct. 1944.
31. Leamer, *Kennedy Women*, p. 380.
32. ibid.
33. RK Papers, on Convent paper (undated), to RK.
34. RK Papers, KK to 'Dearest family', 24 Jan. 1945.
35. ibid., 6 Feb. 1945.
36. RK Papers.
37. RK Papers, undated letter to parents.
38. Catherine Bailey, *Black Diamonds: The Rise and Fall of an English Dynasty* (2007), p. 415.
39. Smith, *Hostage to Fortune*, p. 604.

CHAPTER 47: THE WIDOW HARTINGTON

1. KK to 'Dearest family', 12 May 1945, quoted in Smith, *Hostage to Fortune*, p. 619.
2. KK to RK and JPK, 12 May 1945, quoted in Smith, *Hostage to Fortune*, pp. 618–19.
3. ibid., p. 619.
4. JK to KK, 1 May 1945, quoted in ibid., p. 615.
5. KFC, Duchess of Devonshire to RK, 15 May 1945.
6. RK Papers, KK to 'Dearest Family', 24 March 1945.
7. Private communication from Brigadier Andrew Parker Bowles.
8. JFK Papers, KK to 'Dearest family', 19 Dec. 1944.
9. ibid., 10 March 1945.
10. ibid.
11. KFC Papers, undated letter.

12. ibid.
13. Hamilton, *Reckless Youth*, p. 706.
14. ibid.
15. ibid.
16. Leaming, *Making of a President*, p. 152.
17. ibid., p. 153.
18. RK Papers, KK and JFK to family, 15 July 1945.
19. Hamilton, *Reckless Youth*, pp. 712–13.
20. RK Papers, KK to family, Aug. 1945.
21. KFC Papers, Adele Cavendish to Joe Kennedy, summer 1945.
22. RK Papers, KK to family, Aug. 1945.
23. RK Papers, KK to 'Dearest family', 18 Aug. 1945.
24. ibid., 2 Sept. 1945.
25. RK Papers, KK to 'Dearest Mother and Father', 24 Aug. 1945.
26. Smith, *Hostage to Fortune*, p. 619.
27. Leamer, *Kennedy Women*, p. 381.
28. McTaggart, *Kathleen Kennedy*, p. 198.
29. RK Papers, KK to family, 10 Sept. 1945.
30. Devonshire Collection, KK to Duchess of Devonshire, 5 Nov. 1945.
31. Nasaw, *Patriarch*, p. 620.
32. RK Papers, KK to 'Dearest family', 4 May 1946.
33. Collier and Horowitz, *An American Drama*, p. 199.
34. Leamer, *Kennedy Women*, p. 399.
35. ibid., p. 400.
36. Devonshire Collection, KK to Dowager Duchess of Devonshire, 13 May 1945.
37. Devonshire Collection, KK to Duchess of Devonshire, 19 March 1945.
38. ibid., 5 March 1946.

CHAPTER 48: POLITICS OR PASSION?

1. KFC Papers.
2. KK to JFK, 13 July 1946, quoted in Smith, *Hostage to Fortune*, p. 627.
3. Leaming, *Making of a President*, p. 157.
4. ibid., p. 163.
5. Bailey, *Black Diamonds*, p. 406.
6. Paula Byrne, *Mad World: Evelyn Waugh and the Secrets of Brideshead* (2009), p. 273.
7. Bailey, *Black Diamonds*, p. 202.
8. ibid., pp. 327–8.
9. ibid., p. 407.
10. ibid., pp. 408–9.
11. Leamer, *Kennedy Women*, p. 402.

12. Collier and Horowitz, *An American Drama*, p. 200.

13. Devonshire, *Wait for Me!*, p. 171.

14. ibid., p. 174.

15. Leamer, *Kennedy Women*, p. 399.

16. KK to family, 27 Oct. 1946, quoted in Smith, *Hostage to Fortune*, p. 631.

17. McTaggart, *Kathleen Kennedy*, p. 214.

18. KFC Papers, KK to 'Dearest Daddy', 18 Sept. 1947.

19. Collier and Horowitz, *An American Drama*, p. 201.

20. http://www.munster-express.ie/opinion/to-be-honest-with-you/ tea-with-jfk-and-why-dunganstown-matters/.

21. As he revealed publicly in his famous speech when he revisited Ireland shortly before his assassination: 'When my great-grandfather left here to become a cooper in East Boston, he carried nothing with him except two things: a strong religious faith and a strong desire for liberty. I am glad to say that all his great-grandchildren have valued that inheritance.'

22. Leamer, *Kennedy Women*, p. 399.

23. Leaming, *Making of a President*, p. 165.

24. RK Papers, KK to family, 3 Aug. 1947.

25. KFC Papers, KK to 'Dearest Daddy', 10 Dec. 1947.

CHAPTER 49: JOY SHE GAVE JOY SHE HAS FOUND

1. KFC Papers, letter to RK.

2. *The Letters of Evelyn Waugh*, ed. Mark Amory (1980), p. 382.

3. Leamer, *Kennedy Women*, p. 402.

4. McTaggart, *Kathleen Kennedy*, p. 217.

5. Devonshire Collection, Elizabeth Cavendish to 'Darling Mummy', 1948.

6. Leamer, *Kennedy Women*, p. 405.

7. Devonshire Collection, Elizabeth Cavendish to 'Darling Mummy', 1948.

8. Devonshire Collection, KK to 'Darling Dutch', postcard, 9 April 1948.

9. Leamer, *Kennedy Women*, p. 405.

10. ibid., p. 406.

11. ibid.

12. ibid.

13. Collier and Horowitz, *An American Drama*, p. 204.

14. Leamer, *Kennedy Women*, p. 407.

15. This was Lem's view: Hamilton, *Reckless Youth*, p. 716.

16. KFC Papers, KK to family, May 1948.

17. Bailey, *Black Diamonds*, p. 418.

18. ibid., p. 419.

19. McTaggart, *Kathleen Kennedy*, p. 231.

20. ibid.

21. Devonshire Collection, KK to Duchess of Devonshire, 7 April 1947.

22. This account is much indebted to McTaggart, *Kathleen Kennedy*, pp. 232–6, which is based on the official investigation, 'Final Report into the Accident, 27 October 1948', Bureau d'Enquêtes et d'Analyses, France.
23. Bailey, *Black Diamonds*, p. 425.
24. Smith, *Hostage to Fortune*, p. 636.
25. Leaming, *Making of a President*, p. 106.
26. ibid., p. 167.
27. Nasaw, *Patriarch*, p. 622.
28. Devonshire, *Wait for Me!*, p. 220.
29. ibid., p. 221.

EPILOGUE

1. Leamer, *Kennedy Women*, p. 410.
2. KFC Papers, letter to RK.
3. Devonshire Collection, condolence letter to 'Moucher' from unidentified correspondent, 14 May 1948.
4. KFC.
5. RK Papers, *Washington Times-Herald*, 17 May 1948.
6. Bailey, *Black Diamonds*, p. 427.
7. Kennedy, *Times to Remember*, p. 306.
8. Collier and Horowitz, *An American Drama*, p. 208.
9. JFK to Duchess of Devonshire, 1 Sept. 1948, quoted in Smith, *Hostage to Fortune*, p. 637.
10. Collier and Horowitz, *An American Drama*, p. 208.
11. Leaming, *Making of a President*, pp. 1–2.
12. Devonshire Collection, JFK to Duchess of Devonshire, 12 July 1963.

PICTURE CREDITS

Page 1 (top): © JFK Library Foundation; page 2 (top): © JFK Library Foundation; page 2 (bottom): © Royal Atelier; page 3 (top): © JFK Library Foundation; page 4 (top and bottom): photographs by Richard Sears; page 5 (top): © JFK Library Foundation; page 5 (bottom): © Sport and General Press Agency; page 6 (top): © JFK Library Foundation; page 6 (bottom): © Robert Stevens; page 7 (top): © Corbis; page 8 (bottom): photograph by Felici; page 13 (top) © JFK Library Foundation; page 14 (top): Shutterstock (Creative Commons licence); page 15 (top): Shutterstock (Creative Commons licence)

The author has made every effort to trace copyright holders of images reproduced in this book, but will be glad to rectify any omissions in future editions.

INDEX

Abercorn, James Hamilton, 3rd Duke 108
Ace of Clubs ball 7
Airlie, David Ogilvy, 12th Earl 81, 91
Airlie, Mabel Ogilvy, Dowager Duchess 109
Alcázar, fort of 132
Allied Relief Fund 150
Alsop, Joe 71
Amagiri (Japanese destroyer) 194
Ambrose, Benjamin Baruch (bandleader) 87, 92–3, 131, 142
Ambrose, Margaret 78
American Red Cross (ARC) 181–3, 186, 189, 191, 193, 197, 200, 227, 234, 241, 259, 265
Anderson, Lady Ava 259, 280, 285
Anderson, Sir John 259
Antibes 104–5
Arvad, Inga
  friendship with Kick 158–9, 160, 163, 172–3, 208
  affair with Jack Kennedy 160, 164–5, 170, 171–2
  gossip concerning Hitler and the Olympic Games 170–1
  leaves Washington for New York 177
  marries quickly after Jack's rejection 178
  interviews Jack on his courage and heroic survival 196
Ascot 93
Asquith, Raymond 122, 256
Associated Press 121–2
Astaire, Fred 100, 193, 264, 272
Astor, Jakie 92, 101, 109, 264
Astor, Nancy, Viscountess
  affectionate relationship with Kick 12, 188, 192, 197–8, 205, 269
  invites Kick to Cliveden 79
  character and description 81, 192
  gives dinners and dances in London 81, 92, 96, 128

sees and hears of Kick's charm and personality 82, 102
  correspondence with Kick 83, 142, 172
  heckles Churchill 112
  prepares Cliveden as a military hospital 129, 192
  attends Kick and Billy's wedding 227
  sends telegram to Rose concerning Kick's wedding 228
  as first female Member of Parliament 275
Astor, Lady Violet 92
Astor, Waldorf, 2nd Viscount 79, 81, 197–8

Bader, Douglas 184
Balado, nr Kinross 110
Baring, Maurice 259
Beaverbrook, Max Aitken, 1st Baron 183, 186, 230, 257
Belvoir Castle, Leicestershire 108
Beneš, Edvard 110
Bennett, Constance 22
Benning, Osla 149, 154
Berlin, Irving 201–2
Bernadette, Mother 44
Bess of Hardwick *see* Cavendish, Bess of Hardwick
Bessborough, Roberte, Countess 91
Bessborough, Vere Ponsonby, 9th Earl 87, 91
Biddle, A. J. 'Tony' Drexel Jr 191–2
Biddle, Margaret Thompson Schulze 192, 228
Billings, Kirk LeMoyne 'Lem'
  lifelong friendship with Jack 31, 34, 45, 122
  nicknames 31
  character and description 32
  visits Kick at Noroton 33
  as member of The Muckers Club 37, 38
  comment on the Kennedy family 40